Baby-Safe Houseplants
& Cut Flowers

A Guide to Keeping Children and Plants Safely Under the Same Roof

John I. Alber and Delores M. Alber

Principal Illustrator: Dolores R. Santoliquido
Additional Illustrations: Daniel Allen

genus books
highland, illinois

The authors and the publisher have made all reasonable efforts to assure the accuracy and completeness of the information contained in this book. However, parents retain ultimate responsibility for insuring the health and safety of their children and the authors and publisher therefore assume no such responsibility.

Table of Contents

Acknowledgements

The authors gratefully acknowledge the library staffs of the Missouri Botanical Garden, the New York Botanical Garden and the St. Louis College of Pharmacy for their assistance in locating botanical and toxicological literature, as well as the efforts of librarian-sleuth Kim Cassin in tracking down rare and out-of-print sources. The authors also wish to acknowledge the skillful editing of Elizabeth C. Carver and the further assistance of Dr. Susan Nelson, Vicki L. Little, Sally Greenwood, Jeanne E. Miller (of Perfectly Safe, Inc.), La Leche League leader Peg Winter and the many others who reviewed and commented on the manuscripts for this book. We also thank Dolores R. Santoliquido for her talented and relentless efforts to locate accurate botanical sources and render them for this book and Jeanna Pashia for her creative assistance in designing an appealing and intelligible presentation for the information in this book.

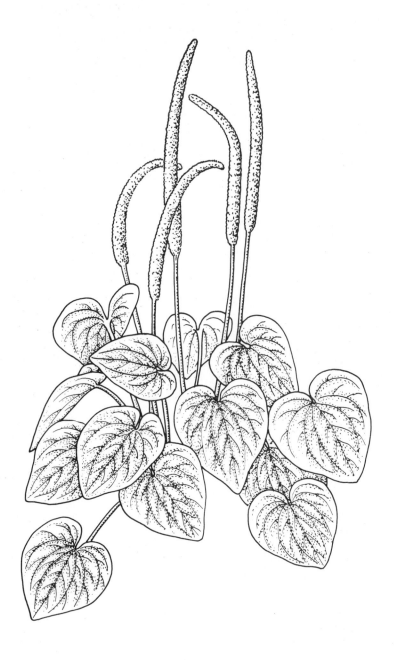

Peperomia caperata

Introduction

Imagine this scene:

You walk into your living room to find your child chewing on the leaves and berries of a houseplant. Horror-stricken, you run to your child and pull him away from the plant. In response to your initial scream and to being yanked forcibly from his feet, your child starts sobbing hysterically. Barely in control yourself, you gather up your child and rush him to the emergency room of a local hospital.

There, after a seeming eternity of waiting in a cold, fluorescent-lit waiting room, a young resident quizzes you on what has happened. He asks the name of the plant your child ate, but you can't remember what the man called it at the store where you bought it. The resident asks whether, by any chance, you know the botanical name of the plant. Of course you don't. You are asked how much of the plant your child ate. But in your haste you didn't notice. In exasperation at receiving so little information, the doctor asks to see the plant. But you haven't brought it with you.

Because they have so little information, the hospital staff gives your child the most conservative treatment possible. You wait in the waiting room as his stomach is pumped and he is fed activated charcoal. You are told he must be kept in the hospital overnight for observation. So you sit by his hospital bed through the night, worrying all the while that he might be permanently affected by plant poisons...

Something about being a parent activates the imagination, so most parents have no trouble imagining the scene just set. For tens of thousands of parents and children each year, however, that scene is very real. According to the American Association of Poison Control Centers, each year nearly 100,000 accidental plant ingestions, most of them involving young children and houseplants, are reported. In 1988, for instance, more than 92,000 accidental plant exposures were reported to poison control centers. Almost 80,000 involved children under the age of six.

Inevitably, some of these plant ingestions result in serious poisonings and, occasionally, even death. Almost all of these accidental poisonings are preventable. But too many parents just don't know that some plants are *very* dangerous.

Fortunately, most plant ingestions result in no injury to the children involved, principally because the plants ingested are harmless. But each year thousands of parents and children go through needless uncertainty and trauma following a plant ingestion—trauma much like that described in the scene above—because they do not know whether the plants they keep are poisonous or safe.

These parents and their children are victims of an information gap that has existed for decades. It is often difficult, or even impossible, to obtain reliable, accessible information on the poisonous properties of common houseplants and cut flowers. Some poisonous plant guides have been published over the years. But none have focused on interior plants. Ironically, indoor plants are the very plants young children are most likely to encounter.

The scarcity of information on the toxic (or nontoxic) properties of houseplants leads many cautious parents to eradicate plants from their lives for the duration of their child-rearing years. These parents force themselves and their children to live in sterile surroundings devoid of the rich and enlivening effect of plants, against the possibility that their children might one day ingest a toxic plant.

Plant poisonings are preventable by the exercise of only a little common sense and judgement. And it is not necessary to eliminate houseplants from a home to prevent poisonings. With a little information and, again, some common sense and judgement, parents can keep their homes lush with safe and beautiful plants.

This Guide was written to fill the information void surrounding indoor plants and to provide parents and others all the information necessary to eliminate the risk of plant poisoning *without* eliminating plants. It does so in the following ways:

■ **This Guide identifies truly dangerous plants—those that present a serious threat of harm to children.**

Many such plants exist and some are common houseplants. There are houseplants, for instance, so toxic that even one well-chewed fallen leaf presents a serious, and possibly deadly, risk to children. The common Oleander, which is often kept indoors, contains compounds that can dangerously alter the function of the heart. Leaves, stems, even vase water from this plant can be dangerous in minute quantities.[1] And some common houseplants have juices so caustic that they can cause the throat and airways of children who have eaten the plants to swell shut. Dieffenbachia, an extremely common houseplant, contains such juices. Because of these poisonous properties, Dieffenbachia has been used to torture slaves and in inhuman experiments on concentration camp victims.[2] Many other similarly dangerous houseplants are discussed in this Guide. The first step in reducing the risk of plant poisoning is to identify such dangerous plants and eliminate them as possible risks, either by removing them from the household or displaying them appropriately.

■ **This Guide lists many attractive plants that present little or no risk to small children under normal circumstances.**

Experience, and in some cases empirical scientific testing, has shown that certain ornamental plants and flowers pose little or no risk if accidentally ingested in small quantities. Many such plants are listed and discussed in this Guide. In addition, the Guide includes a separate chapter to aid in finding the most attractive low-risk plants for a particular setting. Tall plants, short plants, hanging and trailing plants, plants preferring sunny locations and plants suitable for low light are all listed by category.

■ **This Guide provides a simple, five-step strategy for greatly reducing or eliminating the risk of poisoning from household plants.**

In addition to listing and discussing many poisonous and non-poisonous houseplants, this Guide provides parents and others caring for young children with a conscious strategy to minimize the risk of harm to children from houseplants. With it, parents and others can learn to identify truly deadly plants and deal appropriately with them.

---

[1] See the entry in this Guide on *Nerium oleander* for more information.
[2] See the entry in this Guide on *Dieffenbachia* species for more information.

Those caring for young children can also learn to select and display other houseplants so as to pose the least risk to children. Finally, this guide helps prepare for the possibility that—despite all their precautions—a child is exposed to a plant that may be poisonous. In the scene set above, there were many things that could have been done to ease the trauma of the episode and to make the job of the health professionals involved less difficult. This book helps prepare for such emergencies.

How to Use This Book

In order to make best use of this book, it's a good idea to read the chapter entitled: "Five Important Steps to Eliminate Risks of Plant Poisoning" first. Follow the suggestions in that chapter and you will have done a great deal to reduce, or even eliminate, the risks to your child from houseplant poisoning. It's also good to pay special attention to the section in that chapter entitled "What to do if your child eats a nonfood plant." You may want to make some notes and keep them handy—just in case.

If you are buying plants for a household with a new baby, the chapter entitled "Buyer's Guide To Selecting Safe Houseplants" will help. This chapter lists appropriate low-risk plants for all interior settings. Included are many small, trailing, medium and tall plants, as well as plants suited to either sunny or low-light settings. For more information on how particular toxins work, consult the chapter entitled "A Primer on Plant Poisons." That chapter discusses how poisons work and describes the principal plant toxins listed in this Guide.

Finally, for questions about particular plants and flowers, consult the plant listings in the back of this book. Houseplants and cut flowers are listed in alphabetical order according to their botanical names. To identify a plant by botanical name, follow the procedures outlined in the section entitled "How to identify your plants." Cross references to common names are provided in the index. Beware, however, of using only the common name to obtain information on a plant. The same common names are sometimes used for different species.

Each plant listing in this Guide provides the following information:

- the common names most frequently used in the United States and Canada;
- the principal toxins active in the plant, if any;
- the plant parts likely to contain toxins;
- a description of the plant;

- a discussion of the effect of ingestion or other exposure to the plant;
- a recommendation of how (or whether) to display the plant in households with children; and
- specific page references to publications listed in the bibliography. Many of the sources can be obtained through local libraries. Some, however, are available only through university or botanical garden libraries.

Five Important Steps to Eliminate Risks of Plant Poisoning

Prevention is the best antidote for plant poisonings in the home. Fortunately, preventing plant poisonings is a simple matter. We have reduced prevention to a simple, five-step strategy, which anyone can implement. Those five important steps are:

(1)   Identify your plants

(2)   Learn which plants are poisonous, and which are not

(3)   Display plants safely

(4)   Teach your children never to eat nonfood plants

(5)   Be prepared for emergencies

Following these five steps will effectively eliminate almost all risks from plants in your home.

1. *Identify your plants*

Here's a fundamental point: if you can't identify the plants in your home, you can't tell which plants are dangerous and which are not.

Here's another fundamental point: if you don't know the names of the plants in your home, you should throw them out. Keeping plants without knowing their names could prove dangerous, or even deadly, to your child.

Now, one last fundamental point, and we've been saving this one to soften the blow: when we say you have to know the names of your plants, we mean the *botanical names*, those funny-sounding Latin names, not the common names.

Fortunately, identifying most common houseplants—even down to the botanical names—is easy. And you don't have to memorize anything or even learn to pronounce the botanical names of your plants. All you have to do is find the botanical names for your plants, write them down (preferably on plant tags attached to your plants) and keep them on hand for future reference.

Before we describe how to go about identifying your plants, we thought it useful to provide an example of *why* identifying plants accurately is so important. So, once again, imagine this scene:

Sheila, your friend from Florida with the green thumb, drops by just after your new baby has come home from the hospital. She has in tow a potted plant—a gift in celebration of the new arrival. Sheila stays to chat for a while and then departs. As she is leaving, you ask her for the name of the plant. The response: "Oh, you know me. I never know the names of these things. But let's see...Coral something. I think it's called Coral something. Coral Berry maybe. Or Coral Plant maybe...Coral something. Listen, why don't you just call it a Sheila plant and leave it at that."

A year passes, and both child and plant have grown. One day, you walk into the living room and find your child near the plant. On closer examination, you see that a branch is broken off the plant and your child has a small amount of plant material in her mouth. You cannot tell how much of the plant she has eaten.

In a panic, you rush your child off to the local emergency room. The emergency room physician asks what plant your child ingested. You think back and remember Sheila's struggle with the name. "Coral something," you say. "I think it's called Coral something or other."

After consulting by telephone with the regional poison control center (something you should have done first), the young physician returns to the emergency room and, with a sense of urgency, explains that nearly 30 species of plant are known as "Coral" something. Among common houseplants, there are three "Coral Berry" plants, one of which is toxic and will cause gastric upset. There is also a houseplant sometimes called "Coral Plant" which is extremely toxic, so much so that even a small quantity of plant material can be deadly.

The physician immediately begins a drastic treatment regimen on the assumption that your child has eaten *Jatropha multifida*, known as Coral Plant. Because the plant can be deadly and because it acts quickly, the hospital cannot afford to delay even a few minutes while someone attempts to obtain more information. As a result, your child's stomach is pumped, she is given activated charcoal and I.V. solutions are started. Her physicians monitor her closely, waiting for the toxins, or the treatment, to take effect.

While your child is being treated, a police squad car is dispatched to your home to retrieve a sample of the plant. The officer takes the plant to a local nursery for a solid identification. He learns that the plant is *Aechmea fulgens*, a common Bromeliad sometimes called Coral Berry. It is harmless.

This imaginary episode highlights two points. First, it is extremely important that you identify any plants in your home *before* your child has a chance to taste test them. Second, in most cases, knowing part or even all of the common name of a plant is not enough. You must make complete identification of the plants in your home, and that means identifying them according to their botanical name.

It is not enough to know the common names of your plants. Most plants, including houseplants, acquire their common names by accident. The names may be descriptive. *Jatropha multifida*, for instance, almost certainly takes the name "Coral Plant" from the coral-colored flowers it produces. Common names are also often the product of whim and fancy. We found, for instance, that almost any plant with caustic or unattractive properties has at some time been called "Mother-in-law Plant." One thing about common names which is certain, however, is that they are a terrible way of identifying plants. We have just seen that at least three separate plants are known as Coral Berry. This is not an isolated instance; it often happens that one common name is used on several different plants.

It is also extremely common for one plant to have many different common names, sometimes as many as a dozen. For instance, one popular houseplant, *Monstera deliciosa*, is known in many parts of the United States as the Monstera. It is also known as: Breadfruit Vine, Ceriman, Ceriman de Mejico, Cut Leaf Philodendron, Fruit Salad Plant, Hurricane Plant, Mexican Breadfruit, Piñanona,

Casiman, Shingle Plant, Split Leaf Philodendron, Swiss Cheese Plant, Window Plant, and Window Leaf. There are probably other names as well in the various regions where the Monstera occurs naturally. The listed names are merely the most common. Which name is used may depend on the region, the preference of the user or accident.

All of this variety in common names is perhaps tolerable for the average adult. Many households acquire plants by routes that separate plant from name anyway. So the fact that a plant is known by thirty names doesn't matter much. A few serious plant lovers may make the effort to learn botanical names. But the rest of us tend to identify the plant as "that cute plant Sheila got from her mother."

When a baby enters the picture, however, it's not enough to know that the plant came from Sheila. Most parents also want to be sure that what Sheila's mother cultivates is not also the same plant that Brazilian natives use to tip their poison arrows.[3]

The only way to be certain of the identity of a plant is to use its botanical name. This is because, by international agreement among scientists, *only one botanical name is assigned to each plant species.*

Understanding botanical names

Most laypersons are completely thrown by botanical names. It's the Latin we think; botanical names are always in Latin (actually, fake Latin, as we will explain). Eyes naturally glaze over when they encounter anything in a dead language. But these funny-sounding names written in a dead language are the only sure way to identify a plant, because scientists take care to use each name only once.

Here is how botanical names work:

Scientists classify every living thing on this earth according to what they call kingdom, phylum, class, order, family, genus and species. These categories of classification start at a very general level—the two kingdoms, for instance, are plant and animal—and move to the highly specific—individual species and subspecies.

By convention, plants are referred to by a "binomial" or botanical name consisting of genus and species. A genus (referred to in the plural as genera) may comprise a single species or several hundred species. A species is distinguishable from other species in the same genus by species-specific characteristics.

As an example, the Heart Leaf Philodendron—probably the most popular houseplant in North America—is known by the binomial *Philodendron scandens*. It is thus in the *Philodendron* genus and is known by the species name

---

3   For an example of a plant used as an arrow poison, see *Ceropegia woodii*.

scandens. Philodendrons are in the Araceae (Arum) family, along with such other common houseplants as Arum, Colocasia and Alocasia. However, the family name is not included in the binomial.

Botanical names are constructed using Latin rules of grammar. These are used because Latin has widely-known rules of grammar that are easily adaptable to names in most western languages. Species names are chosen by the first scientist to identify a new plant species.

One of the privileges of being the first to identify a plant is that you can choose absolutely *any* species name you want, as long as you make it an adjective using Latin rules of grammar. Sometimes the species name chosen is merely descriptive. The term *"alba,"* for instance, means "white" and is a common species name in many genera. But some species names are much more fanciful than mere descriptions.

The genus name is a Latin singular noun or made-up word spelled as though it were a noun. Often genus names are taken from real or mythical persons. Sometimes they are the ancient Latin or Greek common names for plants. Not infrequently, however, genus names are simply made up.

By convention, genus and species are italicized in printed plant descriptions and the first letter of the genus name is always capitalized. We abide by that convention in this book.

A plant species may be further classified according to subspecies or variety. Formal subspecies and varietal names are chosen according to the same rules as species names and are also usually italicized. Often they are preceded by an abbreviation such as "subsp." or "var." to indicate their relationship to the species. Species, subspecies or varieties may also be further classified according to cultivar. A cultivar name is not Latinized, is often set out in single quotes and is sometimes preceded by the abbreviation "cv."

Binomial names are also sometimes accompanied by non-italicized abbreviations of the name of the scientist who first classified a plant by its current name. For instance, English Ivy is often referred to as *Hedera helix* L. *Hedera* is the genus name, *helix* is the species name and "L." is a reference to the Swedish botanist Carolus Linnaeus (1707–1778), who first classified English Ivy by the name *Hedera helix.*

We have omitted reference to the classifier's name in our plant entries. However, the "References" section accompanying each entry includes a page reference to *Hortus Third,* by L. H. Bailey and E. Z. Bailey. *Hortus Third* is a standard botanical reference book. Its entries include a great deal of descriptive and historical information about each plant species, including the name of the first classifier of the species.

Hybrids, which result from the interbreeding of separate species and, occasionally, species from separate genera, have a special designation. A multiplication sign (X) is used in the botanical name to indicate that the genus or species is the result of a hybrid cross. In some genera, so much hybridization has taken place that the exact lineage of the hybrid has been lost. It is the practice to give such plants the species name *"hybridum"* to indicate the fact that it is an undifferentiated hybrid.

From time-to-time, botanical names are changed, for various reasons. A variety may be elevated into a new species. A new genus may be created or a genus eliminated. For instance, Azaleas and Rhododendrons used to be classified in separate genera. They are now (over a storm of protest from some quarters) both classified in the *Rhododendron* genus. In this book, we will refer to a former name only if plants are still sold using that name. In many cases, prior names are available under a current species entry in *Hortus Third*.

All of this sounds horribly formal, scientific and dry. That's because it *is* formal, scientific and dry. But a valuable byproduct of the formality of botanical naming science is that, when you identify a plant by its botanical name, you can be sure that there is one and only one plant by that name. It's worth putting up with a little dry science to protect children from harmful plants.

How to identify your plants

How do you learn the botanical names of plants? One way is to buy from vendors who supply you with the complete plant name at the time you purchase a plant. Unfortunately, not all vendors take care to display the botanical names of the plants they sell. If you want a plant and you don't see the complete name displayed, ask for it. Most responsible plant retailers either have the botanical name at hand or have a reference work such as *Exotica, Tropica,* the *Manual of Cultivated Plants* or *Hortus Third* that will help identify the plant on the spot (complete bibliographic information on these works can be found in the Bibliography).

If all of this is unavailing, tell the plant retailer why you want the complete botanical name and encourage future display of such names, not only for parents trying to select safe houseplants, but for plant lovers as well.

However, plant retailers can't always identify the plants they sell. Also, many people obtain plants from other than retail sources. As we have seen, the plant Sheila brings over doesn't come complete with botanical name. You may therefore have certain plants that you will have to identify yourself.

The safest and best way to identify plants is to take the plant or a cutting to an experienced and reputable nursery, plant store or florist dealing in plants. Most experienced plant retailers can recognize plants on sight and will either know the botanical name of the plant or have an easy way to find it.

It is not always practical to take your plants out for identification, however. Fortunately, it is relatively easy to identify most common houseplants and cut flowers. All of the entries in this Guide include brief descriptions and many include drawings that may help narrow down the identity of your plants. If you know the common name of a plant, use the index in this Guide to determine if a plant is listed and then compare your plant with the drawing or the description in each entry.

Using the entries in this Guide is only a first step, however. Locate color photographs of your plants to confirm your preliminary identification. There are many fine houseplant and flower guides available in bookstores and libraries that include high-quality color photographs. Several of these guides are listed in the Bibliography.

In some cases you need only to identify the genus of the plant to have enough information with which to make a decision. Any *Dieffenbachia* species, for instance, is likely to be intensely irritating. Because all such species should be kept away from children, it is not necessary to decide which species you have. Likewise, all species in the *Philodendron* genus contain caustic compounds and it is unnecessary to identify the particular species or variety before deciding that the plant must be kept away from children.

Whatever identification method is used, you must take care to confirm the identification carefully before deciding that a plant is safe to display in your home. *If there is any doubt about the identity of a plant, always assume that it is highly toxic and act accordingly.*

Once you have identified a plant, record its botanical name someplace. One sensible way to do this is to obtain plant tags from a local nursery and tag each plant. Using an indelible marker, you can record any necessary information on the tag. For reasons that are obvious to anyone who has ever had a two-year-old, plant tags that attach to the plant are better than plant stakes that are designed to be stuck in the soil. Anything that may be unstuck *will* be unstuck. And it is not beyond a two-year-old to mix and match plants and plant stakes.

2.   *Learn which plants are poisonous, and which are not*

Once you have identified your plants by botanical name, next classify the plant according to its relative toxicity so that you can decide how (or whether) the plant should be displayed.

Each plant entry in this Guide provides the necessary information. In the event you have a plant that is not listed in this Guide, then you will have to locate another source of information. A number of books on poisonous plants are listed in the Bibliography. Probably the best of those is the *AMA Handbook of Poisonous and Injurious Plants* by Kenneth F. Lampe and Mary Ann McCann. It was written for physicians and is therefore somewhat technical. But it is still useful to laypersons, especially for wild and landscape plants.

Another source of information on the poisonous properties of plants is the regional poison control center for your area of the country. The telephone numbers for regional poison control centers are listed in the Appendix to this

Guide. Most regional poison control centers subscribe to computerized databases containing information on poisons, including poisonous plants. The foremost of such databases is probably *Poisindex,* which is compiled by Micromedix, Inc. Your regional poison control center can check *Poisindex,* or another source, and will gladly provide the information to you.

Regional poison control centers are rich sources of information. They were originally established to aid in the emergency treatment of accidental poisonings, drug overdoses and other ingestions of toxic substances. However, over the last two decades, their role has evolved into an information resource for the treatment *and prevention* of poisonings. As many as 90% of the calls to a poison control center are from persons seeking information on toxic substances and poisoning prevention. Poison control centers welcome such calls, so do not hesitate to take your questions to your nearest regional poison control center.

In addition to considering the poisonous properties of the plants you have, you need to consider the presence and properties of substances applied to the plants. The two categories of substances most likely to be applied are floral preservatives and insecticides.

Floral preservatives

Florists sometimes use floral preservatives to extend the length of time over which cut flowers and greenery are attractive and to preserve dried floral arrangements. The simplest of these is citric acid, added to vase water for roses and other cut flowers (there is no reason to believe citric acid presents much of a risk to children).

However, florists sometimes use more potent preservatives as well. It is best to ask your florist what preservatives are used on cut flowers and greenery before displaying such plants where children can reach them. If you have not asked, or if the flowers and greenery you buy have been exposed to a preservative the composition of which you do not know, then assume that preservatives are present and that they are harmful. If you learn the name of the preservative used, but have no information on its toxicity, consult a regional poison control center. It will have access to the ingredients in the preservative and will be able to assess its toxicity.

Organophosphates and other dangerous insecticides

Organophosphate pesticides were an outgrowth of nerve gas research done in Germany in the 1930s. Like their nerve gas predecessors, organophosphate pesticides are extremely potent, even in small quantities. If ingested, such pesticides can cause serious systemic poisoning or even death. Of the 3,000 or so pesticide-related hospitalizations each year, about 80 percent involve organophosphates. Other pesticides are in use as well, such as carbamate-based pesticides. Most of these are less toxic than organophosphates. Nonetheless, they too can cause serious harm if ingested.

Organophosphate and other pesticides are in regular use by commercial growers and nurseries for the control of insect pests. It is unusual for such pesticides to be applied immediately prior to sale, since they sometimes make the plant less vigorous and hence less attractive for a short time. But it is still a good idea to wash all new plants purchased from a commercial source. A thorough washing will not only remove most pesticide residues, it will clear the minute stomata (pores) in plant leaves of dust and debris that can impair plant vitality.

Many plant care books recommend the use of Malathion, Diazanon or other organophosphate pesticides for the control of spider mites, aphids, mealy bugs and other pests. However, we believe the use of such insecticides is inappropriate inside the home. It results in dangerous pesticide residue on leaves and stems as well as the infiltration of pesticide vapor into the air. Use of such pesticides may nullify all of your effort to identify your plants and display them safely. Such pesticides may be as dangerous as the most dangerous indoor plants.

It is not necessary to use organophosphates or any other similarly dangerous pesticides to maintain healthy plants. Adherence to good cultural practices such as regular fertilization, careful watering, careful attention to plant location and regular washing of leaves will almost always prevent any insect infestation.

Where an insect infestation does occur, parents can use non-ionic insecticidal soaps such as Safer Insecticidal Soap by Safer, Inc. These are irritating or fatal to most insects and do not leave dangerous residues. We recommend them highly as safer substitutes for dangerous insecticides. Safer Insecticidal Soap is widely available in garden centers and plant stores.

3. Display plants safely

Once you have learned the relative toxicity of your plants, you should then decide how best to display them. To help decide how to display your plants, each entry in this Guide contains a recommendation of how to display the listed plant. Generally, the plants fall into one of three categories:

(a) Plants that should not be displayed in households with children;

(b) Plants that should be displayed out of the reach of children; and

(c) Plants that are suitable for display in households with children.

Category (a) is reserved for those very few plants that present a risk so significant that they should never be kept in homes with children. *Nerium oleander* is an example of such a plant. Even if that plant is displayed on a high shelf out of reach of young children, its leaves may still fall within reach. These leaves are so toxic that even one may pose a risk of serious poisoning or death in a young child. That, in our opinion, is a risk not worth taking.

Category (b) encompasses a wide range of plants that, in our opinion, may safely be displayed in households with children, provided care is taken to keep them out of reach (such as putting them on a high shelf). Included are many plants such as *Philodendron* that contain calcium oxalate raphides. Those raphides are tiny sharp crystals that are intensely irritating to mucous tissue. Plants containing calcium oxalate raphides cause immediate pain when ingested and, if enough is ingested, can pose a risk of serious injury or death as a result of swelling of throat tissues, resulting in the closure of airways.

Even though *Philodendron* species contain calcium oxalate crystals, we believe they can safely be put out of the reach of children. The small amounts of plant material that may fall do not usually present a serious health risk.

Many other plants are put into category (b) because there is simply not enough information on or experience with these plants to justify declaring them safe to display without restriction in households with children. We sometimes have reason to believe such plants are in fact harmless, but are unwilling to recommend unrestricted display because of the absence of information.

Category (c) is reserved for those plants which wide experience and/or empirical testing have shown to be harmless if touched or ingested. Most palms and most ferns fall into this category. Humans have lived with palms and ferns for hundreds of years and plant ingestions of palms and ferns are common. Yet little or no indication exists that they cause local tissue irritation or systemic poisoning.

Some plants have been the subject of laboratory testing, both to isolate the toxic compounds in the plants and to determine the effects of ingesting portions of the plant. Usually testing alone is not a sufficient basis to justify assignment of a plant to category (c). In most cases the test results are also corroborated by experience or at least by an absence of any reports of toxic effects where such plants are widely available.

A category (c) plant may be further classified as one that is "probably suitable" for unrestricted display or one that "is suitable" for such display. The latter classification is reserved for those few plants with which there is longstanding experience showing the plant to be non-toxic <u>and</u> on which laboratory testing has been done confirming the harmless nature of the plant.

The fact that a plant has been assigned to category (c) is not a license to abandon common sense. Infants, especially, can come to harm in a number of ways in the presence of plants, even nontoxic plants. For instance, *any* plant displayed within an infant's reach can cause problems if the infant grabs the plant. Plant material may become lodged in the infant's throat, causing suffocation. Even plants as innocuous as Sweet Bay, the flavoring herb, have resulted in such suffocations.

Infants may also pull plants over on themselves or pull plants off shelves or hangers. Special care should be taken to keep plants away from cribs. More than one serious accident has resulted when an infant pulled a plant into a crib.

As a general rule, *never* leave an infant unsupervised in the presence of any plant, no matter how innocuous you think the plant is. The possibilities of harm befalling an unsupervised infant are simply too varied and many to take such a risk.

4. Teach your children never to eat nonfood plants

Some parents may be tempted to think that by stocking their house with low risk plants, they can forget about the rest of plant safety. Even if you have been extremely careful to select only the safest plants for your household, however, it is still important to teach your children that they should *never* eat a nonfood plant. This is true for a number of reasons.

First, the fact that a plant has been identified as safe can never preclude the possibility that a particular child will be allergic to the plant or will otherwise react adversely to it. Even food plants can cause adverse reactions in some people. For instance, common food plants such as strawberries, onions and cabbage cause certain children, and even some adults, to react adversely. Those reactions may, from time to time, be quite severe. The same is true of otherwise innocuous houseplants; they, too, can cause adverse reactions from time to time.

Another reason to instruct children never to eat a nonfood plant is that you are helping children form attitudes about plants that will carry over to the time when they will be unsupervised and outdoors. There are many more toxic plants in nature than there are among cultivated plants. Every year, many poisonings and almost always some deaths involve wild plants. Children who may encounter alluring but deadly *Amanita* mushrooms fifty feet from their back door must learn *never* to eat a nonfood plant, no matter how familiar it may appear.

Finally, despite great care, you can never be quite sure that you have done everything right. You can never preclude the possibility that a plant has been misidentified, or that your plants have been treated with a pesticide, and you can never be sure that you will be able to supervise your child every moment. Children who have been trained to avoid eating all nonfood plants are the last and best assurance that an error will not lead to a trip to the emergency room.

We leave to each parent the choice of how to train children to avoid nonfood plants. We only observe that, with our own children, we started early, were always gentle but also always firm in conveying that plant safety was a very serious matter. We can confirm that children, even very young ones, can be made to understand that they should never put anything in their mouths that they do not know to be food.

5. *Be prepared for emergencies*

There are two parts to being prepared for plant poisoning emergencies. First, be sure you have on hand everything you will need in the event your child consumes a poisonous plant. Second, learn what to if your child does eats a poisonous plant—or any plant for that matter.

What to keep on hand

All parents should keep on hand first aid supplies and information necessary in an emergency. For plant poisoning, the two most important first-aid supplies are:

- Syrup of ipecac; and
- Activated charcoal

Syrup of ipecac is a nearly universal remedy for serious plant poisoning. It is extracted from the rootstock of the tropical shrub *Cephaelis ipecacuanha*. The extract contains an emetic alkaloid that causes vomiting and, hence, expulsion of plant material from the stomach. Ipecac usually takes about 15 minutes to produce vomiting. It is effective if administered soon after a plant has been eaten, before plant material has been digested or otherwise has passed out of the stomach into the intestines.

Some plants, certain species in the *Euphorbia* genus, for instance, have extremely caustic latex which causes damage to mouth and throat tissues when swallowed. Where caustic latex has been swallowed, use of syrup of ipecac to induce vomiting may cause still more damage by exposing already damaged tissue to the caustic latex once again. Therefore, always consult with your poison control center before using syrup of ipecac.

Activated charcoal is administered because it can absorb a wide range of toxins and render them ineffective. Unlike syrup of ipecac, activated charcoal is also sometimes effective after toxic plant material has passed beyond the stomach into the intestines. Hence, it is an indispensable part of any home first-aid kit.

Both syrup of ipecac and activated charcoal are available at any well-stocked pharmacy. No prescription is needed. They are also available in a Poison First Aid Kit sold by Perfectly Safe, 7245 Whipple Avenue N.W., North Canton, Ohio 44720. Perfectly Safe is a company specializing in child safety products.

In addition to keeping first-aid supplies on hand, it is important to know or have quick access to emergency telephone numbers. Keep the numbers of family physicians, local hospitals and the regional poison control center by the telephone. Regional poison control center telephone numbers are included in the Appendix to this Guide.

What to do if your child eats a nonfood plant.

If you've taken the steps outlined above to reduce the risk of plant poisoning, you shouldn't have much to worry about. But it's not a perfect world, and things sometimes go wrong. So, take a few minutes to read this section. Should your child ever eat a plant, refer back to this section for help.

Here's a quick overview of what to do if your child eats a nonfood plant—even a plant you think is harmless.

- Keep calm, keep your child calm.

- Examine your child.

- Quickly learn how much material your child has eaten.

- Quickly identify the plant.

- Call your poison control center, and follow their directions.

- If directed to a hospital, take the plant along.

Keep calm, keep your child calm

The first rule is to stay composed. As soon as you suspect that your child has eaten a plant, take a moment to collect yourself and assess the situation. Even the most deadly plants take time to act. The few moments you spend now to gather information can be far more valuable than any action taken in haste.

By keeping calm yourself, you also help to keep your child calm. This is no time for hysteria or to punish your child. Any action that excites your child imposes additional stress, both physically and emotionally. That stress can accelerate or worsen the effect of any poisonous materials your child has consumed. That stress can also make a healthy child sick. We suspect that many reported reactions to plants are actually the result of stress imposed on children by excited parents. Stay calm and avoid making your child sick or sicker.

Examine your child

As soon as you realize that your child has encountered a potentially dangerous plant—or even a plant you consider harmless—become alert for adverse reactions. When you call the poison control center, the health professionals there may ask whether your child has any unusual symptoms. It will help them if you have been paying attention to such things.

First, remove any plant material from your child's mouth and save it. Then look for obvious injury. Some plants can damage skin or mucous tissues mechanically. Others have a strong irritant effect. Look for cuts, redness, blistering or other signs of irritation on your child's hands and eyes and in your child's mouth and throat. Remain alert for any unusual behavior or symptoms.

If your child has eaten a plant that contains calcium oxalate raphides, such as *Dieffenbachia, Philodendron, Colocasia* or other members of the Arum family, be especially alert for redness and swelling in the mouth and throat. Serious irritation of the throat tissues in a child can cause swelling that threatens to close off airways. This occurs very rarely, but because blockage of breathing airways can cause suffocation, it pays to watch for signs of throat irritation very closely.

As a safety precaution, any time a child eats a plant with irritating properties that can cause swelling, the child should be examined by a physician.

Even plants generally regarded as harmless can cause allergic reactions in susceptible children. Be alert for common signs of such reactions: blotchy or red skin, swelling, difficulty breathing, nausea and diarrhea. Allergic reactions are quite rare. Just the same, remain alert for unusual behavior or symptoms.

A final word on this step: As soon as you start eyeing your child closely, he *will* begin acting strangely. You won't be able to conceal your concern from your child, and he will naturally react to that concern. So don't worry too much when your child acts a little odd. You would too.

Quickly learn how much material your child has eaten

If your child can speak, ask how much material he has eaten. Ask your child to show you where he got the plant material. Be sure to ask what parts of the plant were eaten: leaves, flowers, berries or other fruits, seeds, stems, roots or bulbs.

Once you have obtained this information, verify it. Look at your plants for missing or disturbed parts. Then, look around to see whether your child discarded any of the parts he pulled off the plant. Do not assume that your child has eaten just one plant. Your child may have sampled more than one. Ask whether that is so, and then check other plants in the room or area.

If your child cannot speak, your job is more difficult, but perhaps even more important. Ask your child to show you what he ate. If that fails, try to retrace your child's steps since you last saw him or her (with luck, only a few moments). Examine plants in the area for damage. Try to determine what parts are missing. Examine the plant material you found in your child's mouth, and try to match it with a plant in the area where you suspect your child ate the plant.

Spend a few minutes trying to track down just what your child ate. If you cannot quickly find the plant your child ate, however, then it is probably best to make a note of all the plants in the area and consult your local poison control center for guidance.

Quickly identify the plant

Before a physician or poison control center can help your child, they must have at least some information about the plant your child consumed. The more information you can provide, the better. The ideal is to be able to provide both the common name and the botanical name of the plant. If you have not already labelled your plants as we suggest, then look for labels that may remain in the pot from the plant vendor.

Alternatively, consult any plant reference books you have on hand. If you attempt a plant identification yourself, tell the poison control center what you have done so that they are aware of the possibility of error.

Don't waste too much time on this, however. If you cannot quickly identify the plant, take it or a portion of it over to the telephone so that it will be handy for reference when you call your regional poison control center.

If someone else is in your home with you, consider having that person take a portion of the ingested plant to a local nursery, plant center or florist for identification while you call the poison control center or go to a hospital emergency room.

Call your poison control center

Any time your child eats a nonfood plant, it is best to call the poison control center for guidance. Even if you strongly believe the plant consumed is innocuous, call. Your poison control center can advise you of symptoms to watch for, can confirm your views on the safety of the plant consumed and can provide other guidance and reassurance.

Don't worry that you will be diverting them from other, more serious, emergencies. Answering parents' questions and providing non-emergency help and guidance are some of the most important functions of a poison control center. They will gladly help you with any problem or concern.

In many cases, your poison control center will simply tell you that a plant is thought to be harmless and to remain alert for unusual reactions. And that will be the end of it. In some cases, you will be asked, as a precaution, to take your child to an emergency room or physician. Follow the poison control center's advice promptly and completely. They know what they are doing.

A list of regional poison control centers and their telephone numbers is provided in the Appendix. Other local poison control services may be available. Consult your telephone directory yellow pages under "Poison Control" to identify local services.

If directed to a hospital, take the plant along

If you are directed to a hospital or physician, *take the plant along with you to confirm the identity of the plant.* If the plant is large, cut off a significant portion of it and take that along. If the plant has flowers, seeds, fruits or exposed bulbs, take those along as well. No matter how confident you are of the identity of the plant your child ingested, take the plant along.

A Primer on Plant Poisons

This chapter describes at least a dozen different ways to die. It tells you how the basic plant toxins do their damage, and in some instances, how they do not. But this chapter is optional reading, for those with an interest in plant poisons. If you have no such interest skip this chapter and read on. The plant listings which follow will still make sense.

What does poisonous mean?

Before discussing plant poisons, we ought to agree on terms. The word "poison" is a good place to start, in part because it is so often misunderstood. "Poison" is often taken by laypersons to mean a deadly substance—if you eat it, you die.

Most dictionaries, however, refer to a poison as a substance that has *any* adverse health effect. Webster's New Universal Unabridged Dictionary defines "poison" as follows:

> "a substance, usually a drug, causing illness or death when
> eaten, drunk or absorbed in relatively small quantities."

This meaning is usually the one adopted by scientists and physicians studying the effects of plant ingestions,[4] and is how the word is used here.

---

[4]   For instance, Ara Der Marderosian, a noted scientist working in the field of poisonous plants, defines a poisonous plant as one which "when introduced into or on an organism in any manner may chemically produce an injurious or deadly effect." A. Der Marderosian. 1966. "Poisonous Plants in and Around the Home," 30 *American Journal of Pharmaceutical Education,* 115.

By this definition, the effects of "poisonous" plants can range from mild irritation to the skin to certain death. Poison ivy is poisonous in that if you touch it (or eat it, or stand in its smoke or touch an animal that has been exposed to it) you may itch. Ricin, the principal toxin in the Castor Bean is poisonous in that if you eat even a minute quantity, you will almost certainly die. The fact that a plant has been determined to be poisonous, then, really tells us little more than that the plant may cause some unpleasant effect on humans.

The term "toxin" as used here refers to a poison that may be found in a plant. However, a "poisonous" plant is different from a plant that contains toxins. Many plants contain toxins, but not all of those plants will make you ill if you eat them. To understand why this is so, it helps to know why toxic compounds are present in certain plants and how they operate.

Active and inactive toxins

All plants have metabolisms, just as all humans have metabolisms. Like humans, plants consume food, process it chemically to release vital nutrients, and use those nutrients for growth and movement.

In plant metabolism, as in any metabolism, not all of the substances taken up as food will be completely consumed in growth and movement. No metabolic process is ever complete or completely balanced. As a result, secondary compounds remain at the end of the metabolic cycle. These are the waste products of a plant's metabolism.

The human body very efficiently eliminates the waste of the human metabolism (in ways which we won't go into here). When our bodies fail to eliminate that waste, we are poisoned by it and may even die.

Plants, like humans, must eliminate metabolic waste, because their waste products, too, are toxic. To dispose of toxic waste compounds, many plants concentrate those compounds in metabolically inactive areas such as bark or the tough outer cells of roots and leaves. In this way, plants protect themselves from their own toxins.

Plants containing such waste toxins frequently have an advantage over plants without such toxic compounds, because such compounds are toxic to plant-eating insects. These toxins thus serve as an effective defense against insect attack. Unfortunately, some of these same metabolic waste products are also toxic to mammals and other vertebrates.

Human ingestion of a plant containing toxic compounds will often cause an adverse reaction. However, the presence of toxic compounds in a plant does not always mean that ingestion of that plant will cause harm. This may be true for many reasons.

Sometimes the plant itself has a characteristic that prevents the compound from acting on the individual eating it. For instance, apple seeds, peach pits and cherry pits all contain cyanide compounds that can prove deadly to humans. But in each plant, the seed or pit is covered with a hard shell that prevents digestion of the cyanide compounds. As a result, the cyanide usually passes through the digestive tract without causing harm. Apples, peaches and cherries have thus locked up their toxic compounds so effectively that these compounds may usually be regarded as inactive and not harmful.

It is only when human stupidity or extraordinary circumstances intervene that toxic compounds locked away in such a manner are released. Thus, the only reported fatality from apple-seed poisoning resulted when a person ate more than a *cup* of well-chewed apple seeds. Chewing the apple seeds crushed the outer seed coat and released toxic cyanide compounds. Likewise, there are regular poisonings when misguided herbalists brew concoctions made from pulverized peach or cherry pits.

Sometimes, the digestive system itself furnishes a defense against plant toxic waste products. There are many toxins which will cause harm when injected into the bloodstream, but will not cause harm when eaten. The acids and enzymes in the digestive system neutralize such toxins. Some of the most potent toxins, however, are unaffected by the digestive process. For instance, ricin, which is produced by the Castor Bean, is unaffected by digestive acids and enzymes.

Finally, often toxins are simply not present in sufficient concentration to cause harm. For instance, it is well known that calcium oxalate raphides present in plants can cause intense irritation of the skin and mucous tissues. Yet some plants that definitely contain such raphides are staple foods. *Colocasia esculenta,* known as Taro, is a tuberous plant that clearly contains calcium oxalate raphides. It is a staple food in South America. Other species in the Colocasia genus, however, contain more of such raphides and are considered poisonous.

In this Guide only what are referred to as "active" toxins are discussed. These are toxins that have an adverse health effect on persons who come in contact with or eat the plant containing such toxins. Toxins present in too small a quantity to have an effect, or toxins otherwise not active, are not discussed.

The main groups of toxins

Many toxins have been identified in plants. Professor J. M. Kingsbury, a long-recognized authority on plant poisonings, reports that over 750 separate toxic compounds in over 1,000 species of plants have been identified.[5] Most of these toxins fall into two chemical categories: alkaloids and glycosides. But there are other toxins as well. Following are descriptions of the principal cate-

---

[5]   Kingsbury, J. M. 1979. "The Problem of Poisonous Plants." Contained in A. D. Kinghorn. 1979. *Toxic Plants.* Columbia University Press, New York.

gories of toxins which are found in houseplants and cut flowers. Within each category are examples.

Alkaloids. Alkaloids are nitrogen-containing compounds, so named because of their chemical resemblance to alkalis. Some authorities estimate that as many as ten per cent of plant species contain alkaloids. Most alkaloids act with great power on human systems, sometimes for the good, as in the case of quinine, but frequently with unpleasant or deadly results. Most often alkaloids act on the nervous system, but some affect the liver or other internal organs as well. Alkaloids are almost always unpleasant or bitter-tasting and are usually not soluble in water. Hence, they do not usually become dissolved in vase water. Alkaloids are usually distributed throughout the entire plant.

Among the many deadly alkaloids found in common plants are:

> *Nicotine.* Nicotine is found in common tobacco (*Nicotiana tabacum*) and a few other *Nicotiana species,* some of which are cultivated indoors. Its deadly properties make nicotine an effective insecticide. When ingested it can cause vasomotor collapse—the body loses the ability to regulate the size of blood vessels. In addition, nicotine can cause a curare-like failure of the muscles of respiration.

> *Taxine.* Taxine is found in the *Taxus* genus—common yew. It acts on heart function and respiration. The heartbeat may become irregular or slow, and may fail. Respiration may be disrupted or fail. Ingestion can quickly lead to coma and death.

> *Gelsemine.* Gelsemine, which is found in Yellow Jessamine, depresses and paralyzes the motor nerve endings. Muscular weakness may occur, manifesting itself in a falling jaw or other such loss of control. Strychnine-like contractions or spasms may occur. In severe poisonings, convulsions and respiratory arrest may result.

> *Atropine.* Atropine is extracted from belladonna for medicinal use. It is also found in other members of the nightshade family. On ingestion, atropine may cause difficulty in swallowing or speaking, rapid heart beat, dilation of pupils and, in severe cases, dangerously high body temperature and delirium.

Glycosides. Glycosides are a group of compounds containing one or more sugars. The sugar and one or more other substances are released when the glycoside is hydrolyzed by exposure to dilute acids or enzymes, as happens when the glycoside is eaten. Glycosides are even more prevalent in the plant kingdom than alkaloids. Many glycosides, however, are nontoxic. Glycosides are generally water-soluble. Hence, they may dissolve in vase water or in cooking water.

Among the toxic glycosides are:

Cardioactive glycosides. These affect the action of the heart in various ways. Digitalis, which is found in Foxglove (*Digitalis purpurea*), strengthens the force of contractions of the heart muscle and slows it. For centuries, digitalis has been used therapeutically in small doses to strengthen a weak heart and slow rapid heartbeat. In larger doses, it can dangerously depress heart function, resulting in death. Other "digitoxins," so-called because of their similarity to digitalis, are found in *Nerium oleander* and members of the lily family.

Cyanogenic glycosides. Cyanogenic glycosides give off hydrocyanic acid or other cyanide compounds when acted upon by acids and enzymes in the digestive tract. Hydrogen cyanide is the substance used by state governments to execute prisoners in the gas chamber. It is highly toxic. When it is produced by cyanogenic glycosides, it interferes with oxygen uptake by the blood, leading to the blue skin color characteristic of cyanide poisoning. Symptoms can range from abdominal pain and vomiting to convulsions, coma and death. Cyanogenic glycosides are found in the pits of various species of the *Prunus* genus, such as apricot, cherry, and peach, in the seeds of the apple, and in various other commonly cultivated plants, such as Hydrangea.

Saponins. These glycosidal compounds foam like soap when mixed well with water and shaken. Saponins are not readily absorbed by the bloodstream in the healthy digestive tract. However, when saponins are present along with other substances, such as calcium oxalate crystals, which irritate or injure the digestive tract, they can attack the lining of the digestive tract and cause irritation, pain, vomiting and diarrhea. The concentration of saponins in a plant varies with plant part, season and stage of growth.

Irritant oils. A number of glycosidal oils have irritating properties. In some cases, these properties are beneficial. The oils present in many members of the Mustard family account for the "spicy" taste of mustard, horseradish and radishes. In high concentrations, however, these oils can prove very irritating to the digestive tract. They also can upset the digestion of young children in any concentration. Another intensely irritating oil is protoanemonin. It accounts, at least in part, for the intensely irritating properties of various *Anemone* species and for the mildly irritating properties of many members of the Buttercup family.

Oxalates. Oxalates are a class of compounds containing or related to oxalic acid. Oxalic acid was so-named because it was first discovered in the wood sorrel (Oxalidaceae) family. Oxalic acid and many oxalate salts are soluble and may concentrate in the kidneys or elsewhere to cause systemic poisoning. But more common are insoluble crystalline calcium oxalate and raphides of calcium oxalate. These compounds are found in *Philodendron, Dieffenbachia* and other species and can prove extremely irritating to skin and mucous tissue. Exposure to calcium oxalate raphides can cause swelling, inflammation, blistering and digestive tract irritation. In severe poisonings, swelling of throat tissues may result in closure of airways, leading to suffocation.

Photosensitizers. A number of diverse chemical compounds cause the body to generate certain pigments. These enter the bloodstream and make the skin sensitive to sunlight. In an affected individual usually the first sign of poisoning is a reddening of the skin. Other symptoms may follow, ranging from swelling and itching of the skin to sloughing off of skin in severe cases. Liver damage may also result.

Phytotoxins or Toxalbumins. Phytotoxins (which are also called toxalbumins) are protein molecules of extremely high toxicity produced by a few plants. Among phytotoxins are some of the most deadly plant toxins known, such as ricin (from the castor bean, *Ricinus communis*), and abrin (from the precatory bean, *Abrus precatorius*). Both ricin and abrin are believed to inhibit function of the intestine. Ingestion of even one well-chewed seed of these plants can prove fatal, despite hospitalization and intensive care. Most phytotoxins are destroyed by heat.

Resins or Resinoids. Resins or resinoids encompass a wide range of chemically diverse substances that have the common characteristic of being resinous and semisolid at room temperature. These substances include poisons of considerable virulence, such as the andromedotoxin found in *Rhododendron* and *Kalmia* (laurel) species. Those resinoids cause gastric irritation, vomiting and diarrhea, headache, muscular weakness, heartbeat irregularities, decreasing blood pressure, convulsions, coma and, in severe intoxications, death. Some other resins and resinoids are equally or even more potent.

Terpenoids. Terpenoids are any of a large class of compounds derived from isoprene, a hydrocarbon found in some plants. Included in the class of terpenoids are terpenes, which are often subclassified into mono-, bi-, tri- and diterpenes. Many terpenoids give a characteristic odor or flavor to a plant oil. Lemon oil, for instance, gets its flavor in part from the terpene limonene. Likewise, turpentine's strong smell is attributable to a terpene. Terpenoids can have a strong irritant effect on skin and, if ingested, can cause nausea, vomiting, diarrhea or other gastric upset.

Buyer's Guide to Selecting Safe Houseplants

If you're just now buying plants for a home with children, we have compiled some lists to help you make your selections. First, we have categorized selected low-risk plants by height or growth habit. To achieve the best decorative effect, it's a good idea to use a mix of plants of different heights and textures. To help you achieve that pleasing mixture of heights, we have grouped selected plants into the following groups (1) Tall plants—those that usually grow taller than five feet, (2) Medium height plants—those that usually reach from one to five feet tall, (3) Small plants—those that do not usually exceed one foot in height, and (4) Hanging basket plants—plants that have a trailing growth habit or other features that make them appropriate for hanging baskets.

Another important selection criterion is the amount of light required by the plants you want. A plant that requires several hours of direct sunlight each day will not do well in a dim corner. But there are a few low risk plants that will do well in low light settings. We have grouped selected low-risk plants into the following groups to help you be sure that the plants you select are right for their setting: (1) Plants requiring direct sunlight, (2) Plants that do well in bright indirect light, (3) Plants that do well in medium indirect light and (4) Plants that will grow in low-light settings such as artificially-lighted office or home interiors.

Finally, to help you add color and variety to your home, we have selected a number of flowering or otherwise colorful plants and some plants that grow in unusual forms or are otherwise novel and interesting.

Before buying any plant, be sure that you look it up in the plant listings in this book so that you understand the risks it presents, if any.

Tall plants—those reaching five feet or more in height

Araucaria excelsa
(Norfolk Island Pine)

Bambusa glaucescens
(Bamboo, Oriental Bamboo)

Beaucarnea recurvata
(Ponytail Palm, Elephant-foot Tree,
Mexican Bottle Plant, Bottle Palm)
This plant is often sold in smaller sizes
as well.

Chamaedorea elegans
(Parlor Palm, Neanthe bella)

Chamaerops humilis
(European Fan Palm)

Chrysalidocarpus lutescens
(Areca Palm, Butterfly Palm, Cane
Palm, Golden Butterfly Palm, Golden
Feather Palm, Madagascar Palm)

Cibotium species
(Tree Fern, Hawaiian Tree Fern, Mexican
Tree Fern)

Dizygotheca elegantissima
(False Aralia)

Fatsia japonica
(Fatsia, Japanese Fatsia)

Ficus benjamina
(Fig, Weeping Fig, Java Fig, Benjamin Tree,
Small-Leaved Rubber Plant)

Ficus elastica
(Rubber Plant, India Rubber Tree, Assam
Rubber Plant)

Hibiscus rosa-sinensis
(Hibiscus, Chinese Hibiscus, Hawaiian
Hibiscus, Rose-of-China, China Rose,
Blacking Plant)

Howea species
(Sentry Palm, Howea Palm)

Laurus nobilis
(Laurel, Sweet Bay)

Olea europaea
(Olive)

Phoenix roebelenii
(Pygmy Date Palm, Miniature Date Palm,
Roebelin Palm)

Phyllostachys aurea
(Bamboo, Yellow Bamboo)

Plants of medium height—those between five feet and one foot tall

Aechmea fasciata
(Urn Plant)

Aspidistra elatior
(Aspidistra, Barroom Plant, Cast Iron
Plant)

Asplenium nidus
(Bird's Nest Fern, Nest Fern)

Billbergia species
(Billbergia)

Bromelia species
(Heart-of-Flame, Volcano Plant)

Coleus species
(Coleus)

Cordyline terminalis
(Ti Plant, Ti Log, Good Luck Plant, Hawaiian Good Luck Plant, Tree-of-Kings)

Crassula argentea
(Jade Plant, Jade Tree, Baby Jade, Dollar
Plant, Cauliflower Ears, Chinese Rubber
Plant, Dwarf Rubber Plant, Japanese Rub-
ber Plant)

Cyrtomium falcatum
(Holly Fern, Japanese Holly Fern, Fish Tail
Fern)

Gasteria species
(Gasteria)

Guzmania lingulata
(Guzmania)

Hypoestes phyllostachya
(Polka-Dot Plant, Pink Polka-Dot Plant, Measles Plant, Flamingo Plant, Freckle Face)

Mimosa pudica
(Sensitive Plant, Touch-Me-Not, Action Plant, Humble Plant, Shame Plant, Live-and-Die Plant)

Pandanus veitchii
(Screw Pine)

Pleomele reflexa (Dracaena reflexa)
(Pleomele)

Pteris cretica
(Cretan Brake, Brake Fern, Table Fern, Dish Fern)

Rhapis excelsa
(Lady Palm, Slender Lady Palm, Broad-leaved Lady Palm, Bamboo Palm, Fern Rhapis, Miniature Fan Palm)

Rumohra adiantiformis
(Leatherleaf Fern)

Vriesea species
(Vriesea, Bromeliad, Flaming Sword, Vase Plant)

Yucca species
(Yucca)

Small plants—those under one foot in height

Aphelandra squarrosa
(Zebra Plant, Saffron Spike)

Cryptanthus species
(Earth Stars)

Echeveria species
(Echeveria, Hen-and-Chicks, Hen-and-Chickens)

Fittonia verschaffeltii
(Mosaic Plant, Silver Net Plant, Nerve Plant, Silver Fittonia, White-Leaf Fittonia, Silver Nerve, Silver Threads)

Gynura aurantiaca
(Purple Passion, Velvet Plant, Purple Velvet Plant, Royal Velvet Plant)

Lithops species
(Lithops, Living Stones, Stoneface, Flowering Stones, Mimicry Plant)

Neoregelia species
(Neoregelia, Blushing Bromeliad)

Nidularium species
(Nidularium)

Peperomia caperata
(Emerald Ripple Peperomia)

Peperomia argyreia
(Watermelon Peperomia)

Platycerium bifurcatum
(Staghorn Fern, Elk's Horn Fern, Antelope Ears)

Saintpaulia ionantha
(African Violet)

Schlumbergera species
(Christmas Cactus, Thanksgiving Cactus)

Sempervivum tectorum
(Hen-and-Chickens, Common Houseleek, Roof Houseleek, Old-Man-and-Woman)

Tillandsia cyanea
(Tillandsia)

Plants suitable for hanging baskets

Adiantum raddianum
(Maidenhair Fern, Delta Maidenhair Fern)

Asparagus densiflorus cv. 'Sprengeri'
(Asparagus Fern, Sprengeri Fern, Emerald Fern, Emerald Feather)

Chlorophytum comosum
(Spider Plant, Spider Ivy, Ribbon Plant, Walking Anthericum)

Cissus rhombifolia
(Grape Ivy)

Columnea hirta
(Goldfish Plant)

Davallia species
(Davallia, Rabbit's Foot Fern, Squirrel's Foot Fern, Deer's Foot Fern)

Nephrolepis exaltata
(Boston Fern, Sword Fern)

Pellaea rotundifolia
(Button Fern, Pellaea)

Pellionia daveauana
(Trailing Watermelon Begonia)

Peperomia obtusifolia
(Pepper Face, Baby Rubber Plant)

Plectranthus species
(Swedish Ivy, Swedish Begonia, Prostrate Coleus, Spur Flower)

Schlumbergera species
(Christmas Cactus, Thanksgiving Cactus)

Sedum morganianum
(Burro's Tail, Donkey's Tail, Sedum)

Tolmiea menziesii
(Piggyback Plant, Youth-on-Age, Thousand Mothers)

Tradescantia fluminensis
(Wandering Jew, Variegated Wandering Jew)

Zebrina pendula
(Wandering Jew (Red and Green))

Plants that do well in direct sunlight

Ananas comosus
(Pineapple)

Asparagus densiflorus cv. 'Sprengeri'
(Asparagus Fern, Sprengeri Fern, Emerald Fern, Emerald Feather)

Chamaerops humilis
(European Fan Palm)

Crassula argentea
(Jade Plant, Jade Tree, Baby Jade, Dollar Plant, Cauliflower Ears, Chinese Rubber Plant, Dwarf Rubber Plant, Japanese Rubber Plant)

Echeveria species
(Echeveria, Hen-and-Chicks, Hen-and-Chickens)

Hibiscus rosa-sinensis
(Hibiscus, Chinese Hibiscus, Hawaiian Hibiscus, Rose-of-China, China Rose, Blacking Plant)

Hoya carnosa
(Wax Plant, Honey Plant)

Hypoestes phyllostachya
(Polka-Dot Plant, Pink Polka-Dot Plant, Measles Plant, Flamingo Plant, Freckle Face)

Lithops species
(Lithops, Living Stones, Stoneface, Flowering Stones, Mimicry Plant)

Mimosa pudica
(Sensitive Plant, Touch-Me-Not, Action Plant, Humble Plant, Shame Plant, Live-and-Die Plant)

Olea europaea
(Olive)

Pandanus veitchii
(Screw Pine)

Phoenix roebelenii
(Pygmy Date Palm, Miniature Date Palm, Roebelin Palm)

Phyllostachys aurea
(Bamboo, Yellow Bamboo)

Pittosporum tobira
(Pittosporum, Japanese Pittosporum)

Platycerium bifurcatum
(Staghorn Fern, Elk's Horn Fern, Antelope Ears)

Plectranthus species
(Swedish Ivy, Swedish Begonia, Prostrate Coleus, Spur Flower)

Sedum morganianum
(Burro's Tail, Donkey's Tail, Sedum)

Sempervivum tectorum
(Hen-and-Chickens, Common Houseleek, Roof Houseleek, Old-Man-and-Woman)

Tradescantia fluminensis
(Wandering Jew, Variegated Wandering Jew)

Vriesea species
(Vriesea, Bromeliad, Flaming Sword, Vase Plant)

Yucca species
(Yucca)

Zebrina pendula
(Wandering Jew (Red and Green))

Plants that do well in bright indirect light

Aechmea fasciata
(Urn Plant)

Aechmea fulgens 'Discolor'
(Coral Berry)

Aphelandra squarrosa
(Zebra Plant, Saffron Spike)

Bambusa glaucescens
(Bamboo, Oriental Bamboo)

Billbergia species
(Billbergia)

Bromelia species
(Heart-of-Flame, Volcano Plant)

Chlorophytum comosum
(Spider Plant, Spider Ivy, Ribbon Plant, Walking Anthericum)

Chrysalidocarpus lutescens
(Areca Palm, Butterfly Palm, Cane Palm, Golden Butterfly Palm, Golden Feather Palm, Madagascar Palm)

Cibotium species
(Tree Fern, Hawaiian Tree Fern, Mexican Tree Fern)

Cissus rhombifolia
(Grape Ivy)

Coleus species
(Coleus)

Columnea hirta
(Goldfish Plant)

Cordyline terminalis
(Ti Plant, Ti Log, Good Luck Plant, Hawaiian Good Luck Plant, Tree-of-Kings)

Cryptanthus species
(Earth Stars)

Dizygotheca elegantissima
(False Aralia)

Fatsia japonica
(Fatsia, Japanese Fatsia)

Ficus benjamina
(Fig, Weeping Fig, Java Fig, Benjamin Tree, Small-Leaved Rubber Plant)

Ficus elastica
(Rubber Plant, India Rubber Tree, Assam Rubber Plant)

Fittonia verschaffeltii
(Mosaic Plant, Silver Net Plant, Nerve Plant, Silver Fittonia, White-Leaf Fittonia, Silver Nerve, Silver Threads)

Gasteria species
(Gasteria)

Guzmania lingulata
(Guzmania)

Gynura aurantiaca
(Purple Passion, Velvet Plant, Purple Velvet
Plant, Royal Velvet Plant)

Howea species
(Sentry Palm, Howea Palm)

Neoregelia species
(Neoregelia, Blushing Bromeliad)

Nephrolepis exaltata
(Boston Fern, Sword Fern)

Nidularium species
(Nidularium)

Pellaea rotundifolia
(Button Fern, Pellaea)

Pellionia daveauana
(Trailing Watermelon Begonia)

Peperomia caperata
(Emerald Ripple Peperomia)

Polypodium aureum
(Rabbit's-Foot Fern, Hare's-Foot Fern,
Golden Polypodium)

Pteris cretica
(Cretan Brake, Brake Fern, Table Fern,
Dish Fern)

Rhapis excelsa
(Lady Palm, Slender Lady Palm,
Broadleaved Lady Palm, Bamboo Palm,
Fern Rhapis, Miniature Fan Palm)

Rumobra adiantiformis
(Leatherleaf Fern)

Saintpaulia ionantha
(African Violet)

Tillandsia cyanea
(Tillandsia)

Tolmiea menziesii
(Piggyback Plant, Youth-on-Age,
Thousand Mothers)

Plants that do well in low light conditions

Aspidistra elatior
(Aspidistra, Barroom Plant, Cast Iron
Plant)

Asplenium nidus
(Bird's Nest Fern, Nest Fern)

Pleomele reflexa (Dracaena reflexa)
(Pleomele)

Plants that provide color

Aechmea fasciata
(Urn Plant)

Aechmea fulgens 'Discolor'
(Coral Berry)

Aphelandra squarrosa
(Zebra Plant, Saffron Spike)

Billbergia species
(Billbergia)

Bromelia species
(Heart-of-Flame, Volcano Plant)

Hypoestes phyllostachya
(Polka-Dot Plant, Pink Polka-Dot Plant,
Measles Plant, Flamingo Plant, Freckle
Face)

Neoregelia species
(Neoregelia, Blushing Bromeliad)

Nidularium species
(Nidularium)

Pellionia daveauana
(Trailing Watermelon Begonia)

Platycerium bifurcatum
(Staghorn Fern, Elk's Horn Fern, Antelope
Ears)

Saintpaulia ionantha
(African Violet)

Schlumbergera species
(Christmas Cactus, Thanksgiving Cactus)

Tillandsia cyanea
(Tillandsia)

Vriesea species
(Vriesea, Bromeliad, Flaming Sword,
Vase Plant)

Plants that are novel or of unusual form

Ananas comosus
(Pineapple)

Beaucarnea recurvata
(Ponytail Palm, Elephant-foot Tree, Mexican Bottle Plant, Bottle Palm)

Echeveria species
(Echeveria, Hen-and-Chicks, Hen-and-Chickens)

Lithops species
(Lithops, Living Stones, Stoneface, Flowering Stones, Mimicry Plant)

Mimosa pudica
(Sensitive Plant, Touch-Me-Not, Action Plant, Humble Plant, Shame Plant, Live-and-Die Plant)

Platycerium bifurcatum
(Staghorn Fern, Elk's Horn Fern, Antelope Ears)

Sedum morganianum
(Burro's Tail, Donkey's Tail, Sedum)

Sempervivum tectorum
(Hen-and-Chickens, Common Houseleek, Roof Houseleek, Old-Man-and-Woman)

Nicotiana alata

Plant Listings

Acacia dealbata

Common Name(s)   Acacia, Mimosa, Silver Wattle
Family   Leguminosae (Pea or Pulse)
Active Toxins   See text
Toxic Plant Parts   See text

Acacia dealbata is a woody shrub native to Australia. It has silver-green leaves that resemble those of a locust tree, but it is known principally for its highly-scented yellow flowers. These are spherical tufts that grow in close clusters and are often used by florists in cut flower arrangements. This is the species most often sold as 'Mimosa' by florists, although at least a half-dozen other plant species are also called Mimosa. *Acacia dealbata* is also used in the production of gum arabic. Reported ingestions of any *Acacia* species by humans are rare. However, range animals grazing on *Acacia berlandieri* have been reported to lose muscular control after consuming large quantities over an extended period. Some species of *Acacia* are reported to cause skin rashes on those coming in contact with the plant. The lack of reliable information on this species of *Acacia* requires treating it with caution.

Acacia dealbata

Recommendation   Instruct children never to eat this or any nonfood plant. Display this plant out of the reach of small children.

References   Bailey and Bailey, 4-6; Micromedix, Inc. 1989 *Poisindex* reference 3205873; Mitchell and Rook, 379-381. See Bibliography for complete references.

Acalypha species

Common Name(s)   Acalypha, Chenille Plant, Red-hot Cattail, Red Cattail, Foxtail, Phillipine Medusa, Jacob's Coat, Copperleaf, Fire Dragon, Beafsteak Plant, Match-Me-If-You-Can

Acalypha wilkesiana

Family Euphorbiaceae (Spurge)
Active Toxins Diterpenes
Toxic Plant Parts Latex
Plants in the *Acalypha* genus are fast-growing bushy shrubs from the subtropics. Two species are common indoors: *Acalypha hispida* and *Acalypha wilkesiana.* *Acalypha hispida,* called Chenille Plant, Red-hot Cattail, Red Cattail, Foxtail or Phillipine Medusa, is cultivated for its showy, fluffy red or pink flower spikes that dangle from the leaf axil. These flower spikes range from eight to 20 inches long. It grows to a height of about 30 inches and has bright green leaves that are hairy underneath and that may reach 10 inches in length. *Acalypha wilkesiana,* called Jacob's Coat, Copperleaf, Fire Dragon, Beafsteak Plant or Match-Me-If-You-Can, has red ovate leaves that reach five inches in length and that are colorfully marbled in crimson, copper or purple. Flower spikes are reddish and may reach eight inches in length. Like many other members of the Spurge family, these plants contain a caustic and acrid latex—the milky liquid beneath the skin of the plant. If ingested, it can cause nausea, vomiting and gastrointestinal upset. If it touches the skin of an adult or a child, it can cause acute skin rashes.
Recommendation Instruct children never to eat this or any nonfood plant. Display these plants out of the reach of small children.
References Bailey and Bailey, 8; Micromedix, Inc. 1989 *Poisindex* references 2318734, 2329989, 3296459; Mitchell and Rook, 261; Souder, 15-29. See Bibliography for complete references.

Aconitum napellus

Common name(s) Aconite, Friar's Cap, Soldier's Cap, Turk's Cap, Helmet Flower, Monkshood, Wolfsbane, Bear's Foot
Family Ranunculaceae (Crowfoot)
Active Toxins Alkaloids, including aconitine
Toxic Plant Parts Entire plant, including possibly vase water.
Aconitum napellus, although commonly an outdoor perennial, is also cultivated for use as a cut flower by florists. Its violet, helmet-shaped flowers reach about three fourths of an inch across and are carried in clusters along a stalk that reaches one foot or so in length. Aconitine, an alkaloid present in Aconite, disrupts heart nerve impulses at low doses and inhibits them at higher doses. It is used in medical research to disrupt the normal heartbeat so that the effects of other drugs may be studied. On ingestion, immediate symptoms are tingling and burning in the mouth, throat and face, followed by numbness and constriction in the throat.

Aconitum napellus

Speech may be impaired. Nausea, vomiting, vision disturbances and cardiac rhythm disturbances may follow. Fatalities have been reported as a result of these cardiac disturbances in cases where large doses were ingested, with death occurring a few hours after ingestion. Pharmaceutical workers handling large quantities of this plant have experienced severe skin rashes.

Recommendation Instruct children never to eat this or any nonfood plant. Display this plant completely out of the reach of small children. If you cannot keep this plant out of reach, do not keep it in households with children.

References Bailey and Bailey, 20-21; Fiddes, 779-780; French, 140-142; Hardin and Arena, 52-53; Lampe and McCann, 20-21; Levy and Primack, 118-120; Mitchell and Rook, 573-574; Stephens, 5. Woodward, 22-23; 53. See Bibliography for complete references.

Acorus gramineus

Common Name(s) Japanese Sweet Flag, Grassy-Leaved Sweet Flag

Family Araceae (Arum)

Active Toxins Volatile oils, possibly other toxic - compounds

Toxic Plant Parts Entire plant

Acorus gramineus

Two species of *Acorus* are cultivated commercially: *Acorus calamus* and *Acorus gramineus*. *Acorus calamus* is grown for its volatile oils, which are aromatic and have been used medicinally for centuries. *Acorus calamus* is also used as an insecticide in some locales. But only *Acorus gramineus* is commonly grown as a houseplant. It is a grasslike plant with small, stiff tufts of Iris-like leaves. Two cultivars of this species are usually sold in nurseries and plant stores. *Acorus gramineus* 'Variegatus' reaches a height of eight to 12 inches and has attractive leaves marked with lengthwise white and green stripes. *Acorus gramineus* 'Pusillus' is shorter, reaching only four inches in height, and has solid green leaves. Information about *Acorus gramineus* is scarce. It does contain volatile oils much like those in *Acorus calamus,* which have been reported to cause skin irritation. Because this plant is a member of the Arum family, in which toxic calcium oxalates are common, and because information is scarce, caution is advised.

Recommendation Instruct children never to eat this or any nonfood plant. As a precaution, display this plant out of the reach of small children.

References Bailey and Bailey, 22; Mitchell and Rook, 108; Rost and Bos, 350-361. See Bibliography for complete references.

Adiantum species

Common Name(s) Maidenhair Fern, Delta Maidenhair Fern, Southern Maidenhair Fern, Venus's Hair, Dudder Grass
Family Polypodiaceae (Common Ferns)
Active Toxins See text
Toxic Plant Parts See text

Adiantum species number about 200. Their attractive, many-leaved fronds and preference for shade make them well-suited as pot plants. *Adiantum raddianum,* which is sometimes sold as *Adiantum cuneatum,* is popular with florists for use as greenery in flower arrangements, because it retains its fresh appearance long after being cut. It is sometimes called Delta Maidenhair Fern. This plant has delta-shaped or triangular leaves with fan-like pinnules on dark leaf stalks. Its leaves are delicate and light green and may reach from seven to 12 inches in length, depending on the cultivar (of which there are many). *Adiantum capillus-veneris,* sometimes called Southern Maidenhair Fern, Venus's Hair or Dudder Grass, is similar to the Delta Maidenhair, except that the leaves are narrowly triangular and may reach 18 inches in length. No evidence exists that any *Adiantum* species is toxic.

Recommendation Instruct children never to eat this or any nonfood plant. This plant is probably suitable for display in households with children.

References Bailey and Bailey, 26-27; Micromedix Inc. 1989 *Poisindex* reference 2319641. See Bibliography for complete references.

Aechmea species

Common Name(s) Urn Plant, Coral Berry
Family Bromeliaceae (Bromelia or Pineapple)
Active Toxins See text
Toxic Plant Parts See text

The *Aechmea* genus has over 160 species of herbaceous plants. All of these are epiphytic, meaning they grow on other plants without drawing nourishment from them. Two of the most common species for indoor cultivation are *Aechmea fasciata* and *Aechmea fulgens*. *Aechmea fasciata* is one of the most common Bromeliads. It has broad, thick leaves mottled with grey and green stripes and striking pink bracts with blue flowers emerging from the center of the plant. Because its leaves seem to form a vase-like container, this plant is sometimes called Urn Plant, although that name is also used often with other Bromeliads. *Aechmea fulgens* 'Discolor' is a

Aechmea fasciata

striking variety of the Bromeliad *Aechmea fulgens,* which has broad, two-colored leaves; they are green on top and purple underneath. *Aechmea fulgens* is also available in an all-green variety, *Aechmea fulgens - * 'Fulgens'. Both varieties produce a purple flower and, after the flower dies, reddish berries. These berries give rise to the common name of this plant, Coral Berry. Note that *Rivina humilis* and *Ardisia crenata* are also called Coral Berry. The Bromeliad family as a whole exhibits low toxicity. As a result, many poison control centers treat the entire family as non-toxic. No evidence exists that these plants are toxic. Some Bromeliads have coarse or spiny leaves or bracts. These may pierce or scratch the skin.

Recommendation Instruct children never to eat this or any nonfood plant. Evaluate each Bromeliad plant for its potential to scratch or injure the skin. This may vary within a species or as a plant ages. Plants which do not pose undue risk of injury to children's skin are suitable for display in households with children.

References Bailey and Bailey, 28-29; Micromedix, Inc. 1989 *Poisindex* reference 2330275. See Bibliography for complete references.

Agapanthus africanus

Common Name(s) Agapanthus, African Lily, Lily-of-the-Nile

Family Amaryllidaceae (Amaryllis)

Active Toxins See text

Toxic Plant Parts Sap

Agapanthus africanus is native to the Cape of Good Hope in South Africa. It is a large, summer-flowering plant that is usually kept in large pots or tubs. *Agapanthus africanus* produces showy, deep blue clusters of small one to two inch flowers on long, up to 36 inch stems. These flowers rise above long lance-shaped leaves that may reach 18 inches in length. The tuberous roots of this species are so vigorous that they can sometimes burst clay pots. Florists use the striking blue flowers of this and *Agapanthus orientalis* (also called Lily-of-the-Nile) in cut flower arrangements. The thick, sticky sap of *Agapanthus* contains an unknown acrid irritant that can cause skin rashes and may cause damage to the eyes, mouth and throat on contact.

Recommendation Instruct children never to eat this or any nonfood plant. Display this plant out of the reach of small children. The size of the potted plant may make moving it to a high shelf difficult.

References Bailey and Bailey, 34; Micromedix, Inc. 1989 *Poisindex* references 3734567 and 3734575; Mitchell and Rook, 438. See Bibliography for complete references.

Agapanthus africanus

Agave victoriae-reginae

Agave species

Common Name(s) Agave, Century Plant, Maguey, American Aloe, Dwarf Century Plant

Family Agavaceae (Agave)

Active Toxins Saponins and raphides of calcium oxalate

Toxic Plant Parts Sap

There are more than three hundred species of these striking plants, which are native to arid regions of the western hemisphere. They all have stiff, heavy leaves that are long, narrow, pointed and arranged in a rosette. Most species have leaves with toothed margins or spiny edges or tips. The smaller species of *Agave* are common as houseplants. Among those regularly cultivated indoors are *Agave americana* (Century Plant, Maguey, American Aloe), *Agave desmettiana* (Dwarf Century Plant), *Agave picta, Agave pumila* and *Agave victoriae-reginae*. The spines on the edges of the leaves may keep all but the most inquisitive children away from these plants. The sap of many *Agave* species has been reported to contain irritant saponins and raphides of calcium oxalate. If ingested, these can cause nausea, vomiting and irritation of the digestive tract. The sap of some species has also been reported to be intensely irritating to the skin and can cause severe skin rashes on contact.

Recommendation Instruct children never to eat this or any nonfood plant. Display this plant out of the reach of small children.

References Bailey and Bailey, 36-39; Hardin and Arena, 12; Lampe and McCann, 197; Mitchell and Rook, 50. See Bibliography for complete references.

Aglaonema commutatum

Aglaonema commutatum

Common Name(s) Chinese Evergreen

Family Araceae (Arum)

Active Toxins Raphides of calcium oxalate

Toxic Plant Parts Entire plant

This broad-leaf is famous for its tolerance of abuse. Its tapering oblong leaves are carried on a thin cane and are dark green marked with white or cream blotches. Creamy calla lily-like flowers bloom in summer, followed by yellow berries. The plant's pleasing foliage and tolerance for low light make it a favorite of commercial interior plant designers. Like other members of the Arum family, this plant is reported to contain calcium oxalate raphides. There are not many reports regarding this plant, but in general, if plants containing calcium oxalate raphides are ingested, pain, swelling and intense irritation of the mouth, lips and throat can result. Calcium oxalate raphides can also irritate the digestive tract, causing abdominal pain, nausea, vomiting and diarrhea. Ingestion of a significant amount may cause swelling of the throat and dangerous obstruction of the airways. However, because of the immediate discomfort caused by eating plants containing calcium oxalate raphides, it is unlikely a child will consume enough to cause such a severe reaction.

Recommendation   Instruct children never to eat this, or any, nonfood plant. Display this plant out of the reach of small children.

References   Bailey and Bailey, 39-40; Micromedix, Inc. 1989 *Poisindex* reference 2508484; Mitchell and Rook, 109. See Bibliography for complete references.

Allium giganteum

Common Name(s)   Allium
Family   Amaryllidaceae (Amaryllis)
Active Toxins   Sulfides and disulfides
Toxic Plant Parts   Bulbs, flowers and stems

Included in the *Allium* genus is the common cooking onion. *Allium giganteum* is an outdoor perennial, also sometimes cultivated for use as a cut flower. It grows from large onion-like bulbs. Flowers are small and clustered around a globe-shaped umbel. The effect is like that of a globe-shaped pincushion. Flowers are carried on a very long stalk that may reach four feet in height outdoors. As with common onions, *Allium giganteum* contains sulfides and disulfides that can irritate the skin and eyes and cause digestive upset. Ingestion may cause stomach irritation, nausea and vomiting, especially in very young children.

Recommendation   Instruct children never to eat this or any nonfood plant. Display Allium cut flowers out of the reach of infants and toddlers.

References   Bailey and Bailey, 47-50; Lampe and McCann, 28-29; Mitchell and Rook, 55-56; Van Etten, 103-142. See Bibliography for complete references.

Alocasia species

Common Name(s)   Alocasia
Family   Araceae (Arum)
Active Toxins   Raphides of calcium oxalate
Toxic Plant Parts   Entire plant

Sixty to seventy species of *Alocasia* are found in nature. A half dozen species are regularly cultivated in greenhouses and as houseplants. In general, most have large, exotic heart or shield-shaped leaves, pointed at the tips. *Alocasia sanderana* is one *Alocasia* species commonly kept indoors and is perhaps typical of several others. It has narrowly triangular leaves that may reach 16 inches in length and seven inches in width. Leaves are a dark,

Alocasia sanderana

almost metallic green with a bright luster and, like many other *Alocasia* species, have lateral veins in a contrasting, lighter silver-green. The *Alocasia* genus has been the subject of hybridization efforts and many striking forms have resulted. For instance, *Alocasia x amazonica,* which is derived from *Alocasia sanderana,* has leaves much like its parent, except that they may reach up to two feet in length. Like other members of the Araceae (Arum) family such as Arum, Colocasia, and Philodendron, the plants in the *Alocasia* genus contain calcium oxalate raphides. Eating these plants can cause pain, swelling and intense irritation of the mouth, lips and throat. It can also irritate the digestive tract, causing abdominal pain, nausea, vomiting and diarrhea. Ingestion of a significant amount may lead to swelling of the tongue, back of the mouth and throat. Such swelling can lead to dangerous obstruction of airways. However, because of the immediate discomfort caused by eating this plant, it is unlikely a child will consume enough to cause such a severe reaction.

Recommendation Instruct children never to eat this or any nonfood plant. Alocasia should be kept out of the reach of small children.

References Bailey and Bailey, 56-57; Hardin and Arena, 48-51; Lampe and McCann, 29-30; Mitchell and Rook, 109; Plowman, 97-122; Sakai and Hanson, 739-748. See Bibliography for complete references.

Aloe species

Common Name(s) Aloe, Barbados Aloe, Medicinal Aloe, Unguentine Cactus, Torch Plant, Lace Aloe, Tiger Aloe, Partridge-Breast, Pheasant's Wings
Family Liliaceae (Lily)
Active Toxins Barbaloin, a glycoside
Toxic Plant Parts Latex

Over 250 species of *Aloe* exist in nature. Some are cultivated as houseplants, others for the medicinal properties of their latex (latex is the thick liquid found beneath the skin of the plant). *Aloe barbadensis* (commonly called Barbados Aloe, Medicinal Aloe or Unguentine Cactus) is a principal source of latex for medicinal use, but it is also perhaps the most common *Aloe* species kept as a houseplant. It is frequently sold as *Aloe vera. Aloe barbadensis* is a stemless plant with long, narrow lance-shaped leaves that may reach 18 inches in length indoors. Its leaves are thick, fleshy, hairless and have margins armed with fine whitish or reddish teeth. *Aloe aristata* (Torch Plant or Lace Aloe) is also common as a houseplant. It reaches only four inches or so in height. Its many leaves are armed with soft white teeth and are banded with transverse bands of raised white tubercles. It produces a reddish-yellow

Aloe variegata

torch-like flower carried above the leaves. *Aloe variegata* (Tiger Aloe, Partridge-Breast, Pheasant's Wings) is also common. Its leaves reach four to six inches in length and are triangular and lance-shaped. They are banded with irregular transverse white spots, hence the common name Tiger Aloe. The thick gel in the latex of some species of *Aloe* is used as a skin moistener. Glycosides in the latex of other species are used in purgatives to induce evacuation of the bowels. Because Aloe is advertised as an ingredient in a number of commercial products, from shampoos to skin creams, we tend to think of Aloe as harmless. In fact, some species have a strong irritant effect on the large intestines and can cause purging of the bowels. Dangerous dehydration is a possible result of such purging in infants. Aloe may also cause kidney inflammation in high doses. The latex of some species of *Aloe* has been reported to cause irritation on contact with the skin.

Recommendation Instruct children never to eat this or any nonfood plant. *Aloe* should be displayed out of the reach of small children.

References Bailey and Bailey, 57-59; Jasperson-Schib, 424-433; Lampe and McCann, 30-31; Mitchell and Rook, 438-439. See Bibliography for complete references.

Alstroemeria species

Common Name(s) Alstroemeria, Peruvian Lily, Lily-of-the-Incas
Family Amaryllidaceae (Amaryllis)
Active Toxins Tulipalin
Toxic Plant Parts Possibly entire plant

Alstroemeria pelegrina

Well-known for its showy flowers, Alstroemeria, especially *Alstroemeria pelegrina,* is extremely popular with florists as a cut flower. The flowers of *Alstroemeria pelegrina* are lily-like and lilac-colored, with darker reddish purple spots. Leaves are lance-shaped and may reach two inches in length. Some *Alstroemeria* species are also grown outdoors in pots and sometimes brought indoors. *Alstroemeria* species contain a substance called tulipalin, which is also found in Tulips. This substance is an allergen that can cause skin rashes in individuals who have become sensitized by previous exposure. This substance may also cause nausea and vomiting if taken in quantity.

Recommendation Instruct children never to eat this or any nonfood plant. Display this plant out of the reach of small children.

References Bailey and Bailey, 62; Micromedix, Inc. 1989 *Poisindex* references 3663808, 3794777, 3794785 and 3794793; Mitchell and Rook, 447; see also Froline and Pfander. See Bibliography for complete references.

Ananas comosus

Ananas comosus

Common Name(s) Pineapple
Family Bromeliaceae (Bromelia or Pineapple)
Active Toxins See text
Toxic Plant Parts See text

Ananas comosus is the common food pineapple. It is often grown as a novelty houseplant. It reaches about three feet in height and has spiny green leaves that may reach two feet or more in length. When the plant is about three years old, if conditions have been right, a flower stalk will develop, and then a small pineapple. Pineapple fruit is edible by adults. But it contains small concentrations of proteolytic enzymes and, possibly, calcium oxalate crystals that can irritate the digestive tract of a small child and can cause skin rashes. The variety named Mauitius appears to be the most potent of the Pineapples. The fruit of all Pineapples has sharp spears on its outer surface that can piece the skin.

Recommendation This plant is probably suitable for display in households with children. If fruit develops, the plant should be set out of reach, because the spines on Pineapple fruit can cause injury.

References Bailey and Bailey, 72; Mitchell and Rook, 142. See Bibliography for complete references:

Anemone coronaria

Anemone coronaria

Common Name(s) Anemone, Poppy Anemone, Pasque Flower, Wind Flower
Family Ranunculaceae (Crowfood)
Active Toxins Protoanemonin
Toxic Plant Parts Entire plant and, possibly, vase water

Many species of *Anemone* are cultivated as perennial outdoor landscape plants. *Anemone coronaria* is cultivated commercially for use as a potted plant and cut flower. It grows from tuberous rootstocks called rhizomes and develops solitary flowers that may reach two to three inches across. These are elliptic and poppy-like and come in red, blue and white. Protoanemonin, which is found in all parts of the plant, causes inflammation, blistering and, possibly, ulceration of the skin and mucous membranes. Eating any part of this plant can lead to severe gastric irritation, vomiting and diarrhea (possibly with blood).

Recommendation Instruct children never to eat this or any nonfood plant. Display this plant out of the reach of small children.

References Bailey and Bailey, 74-75; Lampe and McCann, 30-32; Hardin and Arena, 57; Mitchell and Rook, 575-577; Stephens, 151; Woodward, 58. See Bibliography for complete references.

Anthemis tinctoria

Common Name(s) Golden Marguerite Daisy
Family Compositae (Composite)
Active Toxins See Text
Toxic Plant Parts See Text

Anthemis tinctoria is a bushy perennial that is used outdoors as a border plant. Florists use the cut flowers as filler in mass arrangements. Called the Golden Marguerite Daisy, it is a biennial or perennial that produces a large daisy-like flower with bright golden or yellow rays. Little information is available on this plant. Chamomile, which is often used for tea by herbalists, is in the *Anthemis* genus. But some species of *Anthemis* are reported to cause allergy-like skin rashes and have been associated with livestock poisonings. It is best to exercise caution with this plant.

Recommendation Instruct children never to eat this or any nonfood plant. Display this plant out of the reach of small children.

References Bailey Bailey, 82-83; Hardin and Arena, 12; Kingsbury (1964), 393; Lampe and McCann, 198; Mitchell and Rook, 186-187. See Bibliography for complete references.

Anthurium scherzeranum

Common Name(s) Anthurium, Flamingo Flower, Flamingo Lily, Tail Flower, Oilcloth Flower
Family Araceae (Arum)
Active Toxins Raphides of calcium oxalate
Toxic Plant Parts Leaves and stems

There are about 500 species of *Anthurium*. *Anthurium scherzeranum* is cultivated both as a houseplant and as a commercial cut flower. The spathe of this species forms a striking, bright red or pink showy shield three to five inches long. A tail- or spike-like flower grows in the center of this shield. This and other *Anthurium* species are popular in modern flower arrangements. Like other

Anthurium scherzeranum

members of the Araceae (Arum) family such as *Alocasia, Colocasia,* and *Philodendron,* the plants in the *Anthurium* genus contain calcium oxalate raphides. If eaten, they can cause pain, swelling and intense irritation of the mouth, lips and throat. They can also irritate the digestive tract, causing abdominal pain, nausea, vomiting and diarrhea. Ingestion of a significant amount may lead to swelling of the tongue, back of the mouth and throat. Such swelling can cause dangerous obstruction of airways. However, because of the immediate discomfort caused by eating these plants, it is unlikely a child will consume enough to cause such a severe reaction. During the 1970s, the toxicity of *Anthurium andraeanum* was tested by administering emulsions equal to up to three percent of body weight to mice. There was no indication of toxicity. Despite these test results, it is wise to treat all *Anthurium* species with caution.

Recommendation Instruct children never to eat this or any nonfood plant. *Anthurium* should be displayed out of the reach of small children.

References Bailey and Baily, 84-86; Der Marderosian and Roia, in Kinghorn at 108, 110; Hardin and Arena, 51; Lampe and McCann, 32-33; Levy and Primack, 68; Mitchell and Rook, 110; Plowman, 97-122. See Bibliography for complete references.

Aphelandra squarrosa

Aphelandra squarrosa

Common Name(s) Zebra Plant, Saffron Spike
Family Acanthaceae (Acanthus)
Active Toxins See Text
Toxic Plant Parts See Text

This Brazilian native, although known for its flowering habit, also displays spectacular foliage. Most Zebra Plants flower in yellow or saffron four-sided, bracted spikes. Leaves are bright emerald green, strikingly veined in white. Zebra Plant grows to at least 12 inches and may reach three feet in height. Most poison control centers report Zebra Plant as harmless. Given the absence of any evidence of toxicity from reported ingestions, this view appears correct.

Recommendation Instruct children never to eat this or any nonfood plant. This plant is probably suitable for display in households with children.

References Bailey and Bailey, 87; Micromedix, Inc. 1989 *Poisindex* references 2330085, 3626889. See Bibliography for complete references.

Araucaria heterophylla

Araucaria heterophylla

Common Name(s) Norfolk Island Pine, Australian Pine, House Pine
Family Araucariaceae (Araucaria)
Active Toxins See text
Toxic Plant Parts See text

Araucaria heterophylla is often sold as *Araucaria excelsa*. Both are known as Norfolk Island Pine. This plant takes its name from Norfolk Island, off the coast of Australia, where it is native, and from its strong resemblance to plants from the *Pinus* genus. It has flattened awl-shaped leaves that resemble pine needles. In addition, it has a thick sap much like pine resin. Outdoors in its native habitat, this plant may reach 200 feet in height. Indoors, it is generally kept to six feet or under. The needle-like leaves of this plant present some small risk of mechanical injury to the skin. Otherwise, it is a good choice as a floor or low-level houseplant. It is generally treated as nontoxic by poison control centers, a view confirmed by the absence of any evidence of toxicity.

Recommendation Instruct children never to eat this or any nonfood plant. This plant is probably suitable for display in households with children.

References Bailey and Bailey, 98; Micromedix, Inc. 1989 *Poisindex* references 2318701, and 2330093. See Bibliography for complete references.

Ardisia crenata

Common Name(s) Coral Berry (see also *Rivina humilis* and *Aechmea fulgens* 'Discolor', also called Coral Berry), Spice Berry
Family Myrsinaceae (Myrsine)
Active Toxins See text
Toxic Plant Parts See text

Ardisia crenata

Ardisia crenata, which is sometimes called *Ardisia crenulata,* is a woody evergreen shrub that grows outdoors in warm climates. The foliage is waxy and shiny and itself an attraction, but the plant is known for its bright red, holly-like berries. The plant takes a tree-like form, and attains considerable maturity before it will produce the fragrant white or pink blossoms that precede the berries. There are no reported toxic ingestions of this plant. However, not enough experience has been accumulated with this plant to consider it harmless. Note that *Rivina humilis,* a plant which is definitely toxic, and *Aechmea fulgens discolor* are also called Coral Berry.

Recommendation Instruct children never to eat this or any nonfood plant. Because not much is known about the toxicity of this plant, display it out of the reach of small children.

References Bailey and Bailey, 101; Micromedix, Inc. 1989 *Poisindex* references 2318701, and 2419136. See Bibliography for complete references.

Arum species

Common Name(s) *Arum,* Italian Arum, Cuckoo-Pint, Lords-and-Ladies, Adam-and-Eve, Black Calla, Solomon's Lily
Family Araceae (Arum)
Active Toxins Raphides of calcium oxalate
Toxic Plant Parts Entire plant.

There are about a dozen species in the *Arum* genus. Several are sometimes cultivated as houseplants. They grow from underground tubers and frequently carry a flower-like spathe. The most commonly cultivated are *Arum italicum,* known as Italian Arum, *Arum maculatum,* known as Cuckoo-Pint, Lords-and-Ladies and

Adam-and-Eve and *Arum palaestinum* known as Black Calla or Solomon's Lily. *Arum italicum* is a highly variable species. Generally, it has leaves that are oblong to triangular that may reach 12 inches in length and that grow on long petioles or stalks. These leaves have a pale yellow midrib and conspicuous yellow veins. *Arum maculatum* is similar to *Arum italicum* except that the leaf blades may reach only eight inches in length and they are dark-spotted with a dark green midrib. *Arum palaestinum* has oval leaf blades up to eight inches long that are carried on long petioles. Leaves are very veiny and flecked with red. The spathe of this plant is dark purple on one side, hence the name Black Calla. Like other members of the Araceae (Arum) family such as *Alocasia, Colocasia,* and *Philodendron,* the plants in the *Arum* genus contain calcium oxalate raphides. If eaten by a child, these plants can cause pain, swelling and intense irritation of the mouth, lips and throat. They can also irritate the digestive tract, causing abdominal pain, nausea, vomiting and diarrhea. Ingestion of a significant amount may lead to swelling of the tongue, back of the mouth and throat. Such swelling can cause dangerous obstruction of airways. However, because of the immediate discomfort caused by eating this plant, it is unlikely a child will consume enough to cause such a severe reaction.

Recommendation   Instruct children never to eat this or any nonfood plant. Plants in the *Arum* genus should be kept out of the reach of small children.

References   Bailey and Bailey, 113-114; Hardin and Arena, 48-51; Lampe and McCann, 35-36; Mitchell and Rook, 112; Plowman, 97-122; Woodward, 62. See Bibliography for complete references.

Asparagus densiflorus cv. 'Sprengeri'

Common Name(s)   Asparagus Fern, Sprengeri Fern, Emerald Fern, Emerald Feather
Family   Liliaceae (Lily)
Active Toxins   See text
Toxic Plant Parts   See text

Asparagus densiflorus cv. 'Sprengeri' (also sold as *Asparagus sprengeri* and *Asparagus setaceus*) and the other cultivars of this species are closely related to edible asparagus. They are not, despite their common names, members of the fern family. These plants have thread-like drooping stems that can reach three feet or more in length. The somewhat spiny stems are covered with flattened needle-like cladophylls (flattened pseudo-leaves), usually three to a node. The plant produces insignificant flowers and red berries. It grows to a height of three feet or so. Most often, it is grown in brightly-lit locations in hanging baskets. Its bright green, lacy

Asparagus densiflorus cv. 'Sprengeri'

foliage trails over the edge of such containers. Asparagus Fern is also used by florists as greenery in cut flower arrangements. Edible Asparagus has been shown to cause skin rashes among workers repeatedly exposed to the plant for long periods. Despite reported ingestions, however, no evidence exists that the species listed here cause either rashes or any toxic reaction.

Recommendation Instruct children never to eat this or any nonfood plant. This plant is probably suitable for display in households with children.

References Bailey and Bailey, 118; Lampe and McCann, 3, 5; Micromedix, Inc. 1989 *Poisindex* reference 3557076; Mitchell and Rook, 439. See Bibliography for complete references.

Aspidistra elatior

Common Name(s) Aspidistra, Barroom Plant, Cast Iron Plant
Family Liliaceae (Lily)
Active Toxins See text
Toxic Plant Parts See text

Aspidistra elatior has been a favorite for generations, in large part because of its tolerance of abuse. As the common names "Cast Iron Plant" and "Barroom Plant" suggest, the plant can tolerate low light, infrequent watering and little fertilizer, as well as cigar smoke and an occasional beer. It is used as a houseplant and in commercial interior plantscapes. Its attractive shiny dark green leaves, which can reach two feet in length (when well cared for), are sometimes cut and used as greenery in flower arrangements. These leaves sprout from a half-buried rootstock and are long and lance-shaped. Insignificant purple flowers appear in late summer at ground level. Many poison control centers treat Aspidistra as harmless, a view that seems warranted by the absence of any evidence of toxicity.

Aspidistra elatior

Recommendation Instruct children never to eat this or any nonfood plant. This plant is probably suitable for display in households with children.

References Bailey and Bailey, 120; Micromedix, Inc. 1989 *Poisindex* reference 2337312. See Bibliography for complete references.

Asplenium nidus

Common Name(s) Bird's Nest Fern; Nest Fern
Family Polypodiaceae (Common Fern)
Active Toxins See text
Toxic Plant Parts See text

Asplenium nidus, native from India to Queensland and Japan has fairly wide fronds that rise in rosettes. These fronds are "entire," meaning they are not divided into

Asplenium nidus

many small leaflets as are most household ferns. Each leaf, which is slightly wavy with a strong central vein, may reach three feet in length. On the lower side of each mature leaf are rounded formations called sori, which contain dust-like yellow spores. This plant's durability and tolerance of abuse are its principal attractions, since it lacks the lacy charm of some other ferns. Many poison control centers treat Bird's Nest Fern as harmless, a view that seems warranted by the absence of any evidence of toxicity.

Recommendation   Instruct children never to eat this or any nonfood plant. This plant is probably suitable for display in households with children.

References   Bailey and Bailey, 120-121; Micromedix, Inc. 1989 *Poisindex* reference 2318718. See Bibliography for complete references.

Aster novi-belgii

Common Name(s)   Aster

Family   Compositae (Composite)

Active Toxins   None known, but the plant absorbs selenium

Toxic Plant Parts   See text

Asters are mostly summer or autumn-flowering perennials used in the outdoor border. There may be as many as 500 species in the wild. Among cultivated Asters, *Aster novi-belgii* is one frequently used indoors and is cultivated commercially for use by florists. This species grows from a thickened underground stem called a rhizome and produces long-stemmed (2 to three feet) flowers. Flower heads are one inch across and have bright blue or blue-violet rays emanating from them. Asters have been shown to absorb the mineral selenium. Range animals forced by scarce forage to graze on Asters have shown evidence of selenium poisoning, although there are no accounts of such poisoning in humans. Selenium poisoning usually results only when selenium is taken in large doses or is a regular part of the diet. It should not occur from the accidental ingestion of an Aster grown in selenium-rich soils. Apart from their tendency to absorb selenium, no evidence exists that Asters are harmful if ingested. Patch tests conducted with Asters have shown that they rarely cause allergic reactions.

Recommendation   Instruct children never to eat this or any nonfood plant. Asters are probably suitable for display in households with children.

References   Bailey and Bailey, 121-123; Kingsbury (1964), 44-50, 393; Mitchell and Rook, 191. See Bibliography for complete references.

Aucuba japonica 'Variegata'

Common Name(s)   Gold-Dust Tree, Japanese Aucuba, Japanese Laurel, Spotted Laurel
Family   Cornaceae (Dogwood)
Active Toxins   See text
Toxic Plant Parts   Fruits, possibly other parts of plant

Aucuba japonica 'Variegata' is an evergreen shrub from Asia. Its shiny, opposite, ovate or elliptical leaves are covered with golden-yellow spots. It produces small red flowers in summer, followed by very bright red, persistent berries. The leaves, stalks and seeds of *Aucuba japonica* contain aucubin, a substance reported to have antimicrobial and other medicinal properties. *Aucuba japonica* has been used for thousands of years in oriental medicine. Extracts from its leaves are used by oriental herbalists to treat liver ailments, among other maladies. There are no reports of toxic reaction on ingestion of *Aucuba japonica* in this country. However, there are reports from Europe that the berries of *Aucuba japonica* are poisonous. Caution is warranted.

Aucuba japonica 'Variegata'

Recommendation   Instruct children never to eat this or any nonfood plant. Display this plant out of the reach of small children.

References   Bailey and Bailey, 129-130; Davini et al., 2420-2422; Leveau, Durand and Paris, 199-204; Micromedix, Inc. 1989 *Poisindex* reference 2336893; Yang, et al., 429-441. See Bibliography for complete references.

Bambusa glaucescens

Common Name(s)   Bamboo, Oriental Bamboo
Family   Gramineae (Grass)
Active Toxins   See text
Toxic Plant Parts   See text

Bambusa glaucescens, which is often called *Bambusa nana* by purveyors of houseplants, is a small (up to 10 feet) bamboo. It is planted outdoors in tropical climates. Further north, it is kept in tubs or pots. Its canes first grow green and, with age, turn yellow. Outdoors, these canes may reach well over one inch in diameter. Indoors they are usually half that size. Leaves of this plant are long and lance-shaped or, in some cultivars, vaguely fernlike. Species of the *Bambusa* genus are known to have edible shoots, although this species is not sold or recommended for food use. It is probably harmless if ingested.

Recommendation   Instruct children never to eat this or any nonfood plant. This plant is probably suitable for display in households with children.

References   Bailey and Bailey, 135-136. See Bibliography for complete references.

Beaucarnea recurvata

Beaucarnea recurvata

Common Name(s) Ponytail Palm, Elephant-foot Tree, Mexican Bottle Plant, Bottle Palm
Family Liliaceae (Lily)
Active Toxins See text
Toxic Plant Parts See text

Beaucarnea recurvata is a desert-dwelling member of the lily family. It is known—and named—for the swollen base in which it can store up to a year's supply of water. Old plants can attain the height of 30 feet outdoors. The leaves of this plant are borne in a terminal rosette at the trunk end. Leaves are rough, slightly leathery, blue-green or grayish and are quite narrow. Leaves may reach up to three feet in length. Clusters of small white flowers are sometimes produced indoors. Because of its odd shape, this plant is most popular as an indoor curiosity. Its ability to store water also makes it somewhat forgiving of the neglectful owner, which may account for its popularity as well. No evidence exists of toxicity in this plant.

Recommendation Instruct children never to eat this or any nonfood plant. This plant is probably suitable for display in households with children.

References Bailey and Bailey, 142; Micromedix Inc. 1989 *Poisindex* reference 2336950. See Bibliography for complete references.

Begonia species

Common Name(s) Begonia
Family Begoniaceae (Begonia)
Active Toxins Alkaloids suspected in some species
Toxic Plant Parts Leaves in some species, perhaps other parts

Over 1,000 species of *Begonia* exist in nature and, by some estimates, there are over 10,000 recorded *Begonia* hybrids and cultivars. Many of these (far too many to list here) make attractive flowering and foliage pot plants. Few *Begonia* species, hybrids and cultivars have been tested for toxicity, and reported ingestions involve only a few species and hybrids. Nonetheless, many poison control center pamphlets report all *Begonia* species to be nontoxic. These pamphlets do not take proper account of the fact that some *Begonia* species have been documented as toxic. For instance, *Begonia* hyb. C.P. Raffill, *Begonia gracilis, Begonia rex* and *Begonia sutherlandii* have been reported as having some toxicity. During testing in the 1970s, *Begonia* hyb. C.P. Raffill caused high mortality among rats injected with large doses, probably as a result of alkaloids. *Begonia sutherlandii* has also been reported to contain oxalic acid. There are also many reports of the leaves of various *Begonia* species being edible, however. Many common potted begonias probably are relatively harmless, but the difficulty is in telling which of the many choices available are indeed nontoxic. Because some *Begonia* species are probably toxic and the qualities of the rest are uncertain, a prudent approach to all Begonias is warranted.

Recommendation Instruct children never to eat this or any nonfood plant. As a precaution, display *Begonia* species out of the reach of small children.

References Bailey and Bailey, 142-154; Der Marderosian and Roia, in Kinghorn at 110-111; Mitchell and Rook, 130-131. See Bibliography for complete references.

Billbergia species

Billbergia
'Theodore L. Mead'

Common Name(s) Billbergia, Vase Plant, Friendship Plant, Queen's Tears

Family Bromeliaceae (Bromelia or Pineapple)

Active Toxins See text

Toxic Plant Parts See text

Billbergia number about 50 species and many more hybrids. They are grown as ornamentals outdoors in warm areas and as greenhouse plants or houseplants elsewhere. As a whole, they are sometimes referred to as "Vase Plants." Primarily, *Billbergia* species are grown for their exceptional flowers. Flowers are borne in clusters on tall, occasionally drooping, spikes well above the foliage. The bracts surrounding the true flowers are themselves colorful, and sometimes contrast with the colors of the flowers. Like some other Bromeliads, the leaves of *Billbergia* are distinctive in that they form a cup-like rosette that can sometimes hold water. *Billbergia nutans* (Friendship Plant, Queen's Tears) is one of the most common species used indoors, and is often used in hybridization. Also grown as houseplants are *Billbergia zebrina, Billbergia windii, Billbergia iridifolia* and many others. *Billbergia nutans* is regarded as harmless. Other species of *Billbergia* are only infrequently involved in reports of ingestion, so there is little information. However, the Bromeliad family as a whole exhibits low toxicity. As a result, many poison control centers treat the entire family as non-toxic. What evidence there is suggests that all *Billbergia* species are probably harmless. Note that many Bromeliads have coarse or spiny leaves or bracts, which may pierce or scratch the skin.

Recommendation Instruct children never to eat this or any nonfood plant. Evaluate each Bromeliad plant for its potential to scratch or injure the skin. This may vary within a species or as a plant ages. Plants which do not

pose undue risk of injury to children's skin are suitable for display in households with children.
References Bailey and Bailey, 163-164; Micromedix, Inc. 1989 *Poisindex* reference 2330142. See Bibliography for complete references.

Bougainvillea glabra

Bougainvillea glabra

Common Name(s) Bougainvillea, Four-O'Clock
Family Nyctaginaceae (Four-O'Clock)
Active Toxins See text
Toxic Plant Parts See text
Bougainvilleas are woody vines or shrubs grown for their dense flowers and the colorful three-part bracts surrounding the flowers. They are the only representative of the Four O'Clock family regularly grown indoors. As a house plant, *Bougainvillea glabra* grows to a height of eight feet or more (though florists often sell the plant grown to a height of less than two feet). The sharply-spined woody branches bear deciduous ovate leaves, but neither these, nor the plant's small, creamy white flowers are the principal attraction of this plant. The real attraction of this plant is the striking color provided by the bright purple or violet papery bracts that surround the flowers. These appear in spring and last for several months. Many poison control center publications correctly list this plant as nontoxic. However, the spines on the plant are sharp enough to injure to the skin.
Recommendation Instruct children never to eat this or any nonfood plant. Because Bougainvilleas have sharp spines, they should be displayed out of the reach of small children. Alternatively, the spines may be pruned off.
References Bailey and Bailey, 174; Micromedix, Inc. 1989 *Poisindex* reference 2330291. See Bibliography for complete references.

Brassaia actinophylla

Common Name(s) Schefflera, Australian Umbrella Tree, Queensland Umbrella Tree, Queen's Umbrella Tree, Australian Ivy Palm, Octopus Tree, Starleaf, Umbrella Tree
Family Araliaceae (Ginseng)
Active Toxins Oxalic acid, saponins, possibly other toxins
Toxic Plant Parts Entire plant
Brassaia actinophylla (sometimes sold as *Schefflera actinophylla)* is the only member of the *Brassaia* genus to be grown indoors regularly. Native to Australia and Java, it is a fast-growing, sturdy shrub that may reach as much as six feet in height. Schefflera is grown strictly

for its foliage. Leaves are palmately divided into long, oval, leathery leaflets growing from a central point. These bright green leaflets number from three to five in young plants, and may number as many as 15 on the leaves of adult plants. The plant usually grows from one stem, which becomes woody and tree-like with age. In its 1988 annual report, the American Association of Poison Control Centers National Data Collection System reported that there were 1,835 exposures to *Brassaia* or *Schefflera* species during the reporting period. Schefflera is often listed as nontoxic in poison control center pamphlets based on the low incidence of reported problems. But chemical analysis and laboratory testing of Schefflera in the mid-1980s showed that the plant was indeed toxic. Rats and mice fed or injected with extract from Schefflera became ill and died. Chemical analysis revealed that the plant contains significant amounts of saponins and oxalic acid, as well as other toxins. There are also reports of poisoning (involving vomiting, loss of coordination, and other symptoms) among household pets eating the plant, and reports that the plant can cause skin rashes. Clearly, this plant should not be treated as nontoxic.

Brassaia actinophylla

Recommendation   Instruct children never to eat this or any nonfood plant. Display this plant out of the reach of small children.

References   Bailey and Bailey, 177; Micromedix, Inc. 1989 *Poisindex* reference 2318883; Mitchell and Rook, 124; Quam, Schermeister and Tanner, 15-17; Stowe, Fangman and Trampel, 74. See Bibliography for complete references.

Brodiaea elegans

Common Name(s)   Brodiaea, Harvest Brodiaea
Family   Amaryllidaceae (Amaryllis)
Active Toxins   See text
Toxic Plant Parts   See text

About 10 species of *Brodiaea* are cultivated. Most species are used outdoors in borders and a few are grown outdoors in pots. *Brodiaea elegans* is cultivated commercially for use as a cut flower by florists. Flowers of this species are borne in clusters on a long leafless stalk. These flowers reach about one and one half inches in length and are pinkish purple to purple. There are few reports of ingestion of these plants. What evidence there is does not suggest that *Brodiaea* species are toxic, but insufficient evidence exists upon which to base a judgment. Because other members of the Amaryllis family have shown toxicity, caution is therefore warranted.

Recommendation Instruct children never to eat this or any nonfood plant. As a precaution, this plant should be displayed out of the reach of small children.
References Bailey and Bailey, 181-182; Micromedix, Inc. 1989 *Poisindex* references 2904153, 3398157, 3770933. See Bibliography for complete references.

Bromelia species

Common Name(s) Heart-of-Flame, Volcano Plant
Family Bromeliaceae (Bromelia or Pineapple)
Active Toxins See text
Toxic Plant Parts See text
About 48 species of this Brazilian Bromeliad are present in nature. A few are grown indoors and, of those, the most common probably is *Bromelia balansae* (sometimes called *Bromelia serra*). This is a large Bromeliad, with leaves that can reach four feet or longer. As with most Bromeliads, the leaves are arranged in a rosette, forming a cup at the base of the rosette. *Bromelia balansae* produces maroon or violet flowers, adjoined by vivid scarlet bracts that give rise to the common names of this plant. The Bromeliad family as a whole exhibits low toxicity. As a result, many poison control centers treat the entire family as non-toxic. No evidence exists that *Bromelia* species are toxic, and in fact some *Bromelia* species are reported to be edible. Note that many Bromeliads have coarse or spiny leaves or bracts, which may pierce or scratch the skin.
Recommendation Instruct children never to eat this or any nonfood plant. Evaluate each Bromeliad plant for its potential to scratch or injure the skin. This may vary within a species or as a plant ages. Plants which do not pose undue risk of injury to children's skin are suitable for display in households with children.
References Bailey and Bailey, 182; Micromedix, Inc. 1989 *Poisindex* reference 2336968. See Bibliography for complete references.

Buxus species

Common Name(s) Boxwood, Common Boxwood, Little-leaved Boxwood, Korean Boxwood
Family Buxaceae (Box)
Active Toxins Buxene, an alkaloid
Toxic Plant Parts Leaves, twigs, possibly entire plant
Boxwoods have long enjoyed an excellent reputation as an outdoor evergreen hedge or shrub. In the last twenty years or so, however, Boxwoods have increasingly been used as houseplants. Most common of the Boxwoods used indoors are *Buxus microphylla* (Little-leaved Boxwood or Korean Boxwood) and *Buxus sempervirens*

Buxus sempervirens

(Common Boxwood). *Buxus microphylla* is a compact shrub that may reach two to three feet in height. It has distinctly four-sided branches and oval to lance-shaped lustrous green leaves that may reach one inch in length. *Buxus sempervirens* has a similar form, but grows taller and has larger leaves. These two species have been reported as toxic, causing abdominal pain, nausea, vomiting and diarrhea. Deaths have been reported in livestock grazing on Boxwood, with the lethal dose being estimated at .15 per cent of body weight. Buxus has also been reported to cause skin rashes.

Recommendation   Instruct children never to eat this or any nonfood plant. Display this plant out of the reach of small children.

References   Bailey and Bailey, 192; Hardin and Arena, 77-78; Kingsbury (1964), 181. See Bibliography for complete references.

Caladium species

Common Name(s)   Caladium, Angel Wings, Elephant's Ears, Mother-in-Law Plant
Family   Araceae (Arum)
Active Toxins   Raphides of Calcium Oxalate
Toxic Plant Parts   Entire Plant

Caladium x *hortulanum*

Caladium is a deciduous plant known for its showy, veined leaves. Caladium grows from an underground tuber to a height of about 16 inches. Its large ovate, wing or arrow-shaped leaves may reach 14 inches in length and are available in many colors, including pink, red, green and white. Caladium is cultivated outdoors (as an annual in colder climates) and is a popular houseplant. Like other members of the Araceae (Arum) family such as *Alocasia, Colocasia* and *Philodendron,* the plants in the *Caladium* genus contain calcium oxalate raphides. Ingestion of these plants can cause pain, swelling and irritation of the mouth, lips and throat. They can irritate the digestive tract, causing abdominal pain, nausea, vomiting and diarrhea. Ingestion of a significant amount may lead to swelling of the tongue, back of the mouth and throat. Such swelling can cause dangerous obstruction of airways. However, because of the immediate discomfort caused by eating this plant, it is unlikely a child will consume enough to cause such a severe reaction.

Recommendation   Instruct children never to eat this or any nonfood plant. Caladium should be kept out of the reach of small children.

References   Bailey and Bailey, 197; Hardin and Arena, 51, 58; Lampe and McCann, 42-43; Mitchell and Rook, 112; Plowman, 97-122. See Bibliography for complete references.

Calathea species

Common Name(s)   Calathea, Peacock Plant, Zebra Plant

Family   Marantaceae (Maranta or Arrowroot)

Active Toxins   See text

Toxic Plant Parts   See text

Calathea zebrina

Plants of the *Calathea* genus, which are often mistaken for species of the closely related *Maranta* (Prayer Plant) genus, are known for their beautiful variegated leaves. Over 100 species of *Calathea* exist in nature. More than a dozen are available commercially, with perhaps thirty more species available from specialty growers. Among the most popular species for use indoors are *Calathea makoyana* (Peacock Plant), *Calathea picturata, Calathea roseopicta, Calathea vittata* and *Calathea zebrina* (Zebra Plant). Of these, *Calathea zebrina* is perhaps the most popular and is typical of the genus. It grows to three feet in height in nature and perhaps half that indoors. Leaves, which are elliptic and may reach one foot in length indoors, are emerald green with dark-green transverse marks that create a zebra-like effect. Leaf undersides are purple. Note that two other house-plants are also called Zebra Plant: *Aphelandra squarrosa* and *Cryptanthus zonatus* 'Zebrinus'. Many regional poison control center publications list Prayer Plant, which is botanically very close to *Calathea,* as nontoxic. Those references are apparently based on the relatively low incidence of serious symptoms reported in connection with ingestion of *Maranta leuconeura*. However, when scientists studied the toxicity of *Maranta leuconeura* in the mid-1970s by administering large doses to rats, the rats died. Although it is extremely unlikely that children could consume as much as the rats were administered, the test results suggest the presence of an active toxin. It is best to assume that this toxin is also present in all *Calathea* species.

Recommendation   Instruct children never to eat this or any nonfood plant. As a precaution, this plant should be displayed out of the reach of small children.

References   Bailey and Bailey, 198-199; Micromedix, Inc. 1989 *Poisindex* reference 2330150. See Bibliography for complete references.

Calendula officinalis

Common Name(s)   Marigold, Pot Marigold

Family   Compositae (Composite)

Active Toxins   See text

Toxic Plant Parts   See text

Known as Marigolds, *Calendula* species are widely cultivated in the garden and as border plants for their summer-long blooming habit. *Calendula officinalis* is cultivated commercially for use as a cut flower and is also grown indoors in pots. This plant produces the one and one half to four inch golden or yellow to bright orange flowers known to all. Extracts of *Calendula officinalis* have been used medicinally by homeopaths for years to treat lesions of the skin and have sometimes been used as a drug to promote menstrual flow. Marigolds are known to contain saponins, but they are also regularly used for herbal teas, and also as garnishes in certain oriental dishes. This suggests that the saponins present in *Calendula officinalis* are not of sufficient concentration to cause digestive upset as saponins sometimes do. There is evidence to suggest that persons with botanical allergies will react to Marigolds as well. Other than apparently allergic reactions, however, there are no reports of toxic reactions to Marigolds. It seems likely that ingestions of small quantities of Marigolds are relatively harmless.

Recommendation   Instruct children never to eat this or any nonfood plant. This plant is probably suitable for display in households with children.

References   Bailey and Bailey, 200; Micromedix, Inc. 1989 *Poisindex* reference 2139279; Mitchell and Rook, 193; Nutrition and the M.D., 4. See Bibliography for complete references.

Camellia japonica

Common Name(s)   Camellia
Family   Theaceae (Tea)
Active Toxins   See text
Toxic Plant Parts   See text

The *Camellia* genus is the source of commercial tea leaves and tea oils. *Camellia japonica* produces flowers of unique form and color and is therefore extremely popular, both as a landscape plant and as a potted indoor plant. More than 2000 cultivars have been derived from *Camellia japonica,* and a substantial following has developed for this plant. Several horticultural societies are devoted solely to Camellia culture. Camellias are regularly sold blooming in pots by florists and nurseries. However, their culture is such that they will not usually bloom again in the average house. Many poison control center publications treat Camellias as harmless. The fact that the *Camellia* genus is the source of palatable teas and the absence of any evidence of toxicity in this genus strongly suggests that the plant is indeed harmless if ingested.

Camellia japonica

Recommendation Instruct children never to eat this or any nonfood plant. This plant is probably suitable for display in households with children.

References Bailey and Bailey, 208-210; Micromedix, Inc. 1989 *Poisindex* reference 2337320; Mitchell and Rook, 671. See Bibliography for complete references.

Capsicum annuum

Common Name(s) Christmas Pepper, Pepper Plant, Red Pepper
Family Solanaceae (Nightshade)
Active Toxins Capsaicin
Toxic Plant Parts Fruit and seeds

Capsicum annuum is a bushy, shrub-like annual with bright green foliage, star-like white flowers and, after the flowers, peppers of various shapes and colors. Three varieties of this plant (classified as *Capsicum annuum* var. *annuum*) are edible: the bell pepper, sweet pepper and green pepper. But the Pepper Plants usually sold as ornamentals by nurseries and florists are not edible. Their fruit and seeds contain high concentrations of capsaicin, a material that irritates mucous tissue. If eaten, the peppers and seeds will cause a very painful burning sensation in the mouth and throat. If juice from the pepper comes in contact with the eyes, painful inflammation may result. Handling the peppers may irritate and redden the skin. Indeed, workers harvesting some varieties of *Capsicum annuum* peppers that are used as very hot seasonings in Chinese cooking are subject to an affliction called "Hunan hand," after the style of cooking which originated in the Hunan province of China and which features hot peppers. In its 1988 annual report, the American Association of Poison Control Centers National Data Collection System reported that there were 1,783 exposures to *Capsicum* species during the reporting period.

Recommendation Instruct children never to eat this or any nonfood plant. Display this plant out of the reach of small children.

References Bailey and Bailey, 219; Lampe and McCann, 48-49; Litovitz, et al., 525; Micromedix, Inc. 1989 *Poisindex* reference 2903949; Mitchell and Rook, 648. See Bibliography for complete references.

Capsicum annuum

Carissa grandiflora

Common Name(s) Natal Plum, Amatungulu
Family Apocynaceae (Dogbane)
Active Toxins Possibly cardiac glycosides
Toxic Plant Parts Entire plant

Carissa grandiflora is a dense Old World shrub with leathery, shiny ovate leaves. The plant produces occasional white flowers and an ovoid plum-like fruit that may reach up to two inches in length. *Carissa grandiflora* has broad, branched spines up to one and one half inches in length. This species is used as a landscape plant and can reach 18 feet. Dwarf cultivars, however, are also grown indoors and are sometimes trained as bonsai subjects. There are reports that *Carissa* species contain cardiac glycosides that, if ingested, may disrupt heart function. This and the spines common on this species call for caution.

Carissa grandiflora

Recommendation Instruct children never to eat this or any nonfood plant. Display this plant out of the reach of small children.

References Bailey and Bailey, 222-223; Zaki et al., 113-126. See Bibliography for complete references.

Caryota mitis

Common Name(s) Fishtail Palm
Family Palmaceae (Palm)
Active Toxins Raphides of calcium oxalate
Toxic Plant Parts Fruit pulp

Caryota mitis, the Fishtail Palm, has a thick trunk, many spreading branches and a slow growth habit. These characteristics and the ease with which it grows make the plant popular in commercial interior plantscapes. It is sometimes kept as a houseplant. This palm has compound bipinnate leaves, each consisting of a stalk with a secondary axil to which are attached fishtail-shaped leaves. These leaves are deeply divided with fringed borders. The leaves grow long and wide from a short stem. After many years, this plant may reach eight feet in height indoors. *Caryota mitis,* and its close relative, *Caryota urens* (Wine Palm) are among the few members of the palm family shown to be toxic. The fruit pulp contains raphides of calcium oxalate that may cause burning and swelling in the mouth and throat and may irritate the skin. It is uncommon for the Fishtail Palm to produce this fruit indoors.

Caryota mitis

Recommendation Instruct children never to eat this, or any, nonfood plant. If fruit is present, this plant should be kept out of the reach of young children.

References Bailey and Bailey, 227; Hardin and Arena, 154, and sources cited therein; Lampe and McCann, 49-50; Mitchell and Rook, 502-506. See Bibliography for complete references.

Celastrus scandens

Common Name(s) Bittersweet, American Bitter-sweet, False Bittersweet, Staff Tree, Waxwork
Family Celastraceae (Staff Tree)
Active Toxins See text, possibly alkaloids
Toxic Plant Parts Fruit, possibly entire plant

Celastrus scandens

This climbing vine is used outdoors as fence, trellis and wall covering. Its yellow-orange berries persist well into winter. These are frequently brought inside or purchased from florists for fall displays. This plant may reach 25 feet in length outdoors. Its leaves are ovate or lance-shaped, toothed and may reach four inches in length. It produces scarlet or crimson flowers, followed by the berries that are its principal attraction. Bittersweet contains an unknown toxin that causes vomiting and diarrhea when ingested. It may also act on the nervous system. Note that Bittersweet is also the common name of *Solanum dulcamara,* a nightshade containing the potent glyco-alkaloid solanine. *Solanum dulcamara* is not usually displayed indoors and does not have the berries characteristic of *Celastrus scandens.*

Recommendation Instruct children never to eat this or any nonfood plant. Display Bittersweet out of the reach of small children with care taken that berries do not fall to the floor.
References Bailey and Bailey, 239-240; Hardin and Arena, 95-96; Hart, 522-525; Lampe and McCann, 53; Levy and Primack, 114-115; Stephens, 154. See Bibliography for complete references.

Celosia species

Common Name(s) Celosia, Woolflower
Family Amaranthaceae (Amaranth)
Active Toxins See text
Toxic Plant Parts See text

Celosia is known for its dense wooly spikes of flowers. *Celosia argentea* produces such spikes in white or silvery-white; *Celosia cristata* produces feathery plumes in white, yellow, purple and shades of red. Both species have linear to lance-shaped leaves that may reach two inches in length. These plants are cultivated for use in the border outdoors and are also cultivated commercially for use by florists as cut flowers. No reports of adverse reactions from ingestion of these two species could be found. However, little information is available. They therefore should be regarded with caution.

Recommendation   Instruct children never to eat this or any nonfood plant. As a precaution, display *Celosia* out of the reach of small children.

References   Bailey and Bailey, 241-242; Micromedix, Inc. 1989 *Poisindex* references 3443978, 3443986. See Bibliography for complete references.

Centaurea cyanus

Common Name(s)   Bachelor's Button, Cornflower, Bluebottle
Family   Compositae (Composite)
Active Toxins   See text
Toxic Plant Parts   See text

Bachelor's Button is an easily-grown hardy annual found in the garden and flower border outdoors. It also grows wild along roadsides and at the edges of fields. It is cultivated commercially for its striking blue or blue-purple flowers, which are used by florists. This plant is a slender annual that grows to two feet in height. Both leaves and stems are covered with cottony hairs. Flower heads may reach one and one half inches across and are usually an unmistakable "Cornflower blue," although they may sometimes shade toward pink or purple. No reports of toxic ingestion of this plant could be found. However, because information on this plant is scarce, it should be regarded with caution.

Recommendation   Instruct children never to eat this or any nonfood plant. Display this plant out of the reach of small children.

References   Bailey and Bailey, 242-243; Micromedix, Inc. 1989 *Poisindex* reference 2597461; Mitchell and Rook, 194. See Bibliography for complete references.

Ceropegia woodii

Common Name(s)   Rosary Vine, Hearts Entangled, Hearts-on-a-String, String of Hearts, Heart Vine
Family   Asclepiadaceae (Milkweed)
Active Toxins   See text
Toxic Plant Parts   See text

Ceropegia woodii

Ceropegia is a genus of twining plants and subshrubs native to tropical Asia and Africa. *Ceropegia woodii* is a South African native that has delicate stems with heart-shaped leaves and grows out of a tuber. Its leaves may reach one inch in length and are dark green marbled with silvery white on the upper surface. Pink and purple tube-shaped flowers grow at the leaf axils during late summer. Another species in the *Ceropegia* genus, *Ceropegia distincta,* is thought to have been used as a hunting arrow poison in Africa, as well as for murder.

Other members of the Milkweed family are also known to be toxic. Accordingly, although there are no reports of toxic ingestion of this plant, it should be regarded with strong suspicion.

Recommendation Instruct children never to eat this or any nonfood plant. Display this plant out of the reach of small children.

References Bailey and Bailey, 252; Kingsbury (1964), 267-271; Micromedix, Inc. 1989 *Poisindex* reference 2454067. See Bibliography for complete references.

Chamaedorea elegans

Chamaedorea elegans

Common Name(s) Parlor Palm, Neanthe bella
Family Palmaceae (Palm)
Active Toxins See text
Toxic Plant Parts See text

Chamaedorea elegans (sometimes called by the invalid botanical name *Neanthe bella*) has a small, slow growth habit and indifference to abuse that has endeared it to indoor plantscapers. Its leaves are a deep green and grow from the top of a neat, green bamboo-like stem. These leaves grow in slightly irregular pairs on a long stalk and are divided into a number of leaflets (usually from 11 to 20). Each leaflet is about six inches long and one inch wide with a sharp tapering tip. Generally this plant grows to no more than five to six feet in height indoors. Because the plant is tolerant of cramped conditions when young, it is sometimes featured in dish and bottle gardens. The palm family as a whole has shown little toxicity and some palms have food uses, such as in the production of palm cooking oils. No evidence exists that this palm is toxic.

Recommendation Instruct children never to eat this or any nonfood plant. This plant is probably suitable for display in households with children.

References Bailey and Bailey, 255-256; Micromedix, Inc. 1989 *Poisindex* reference 2330176, 2331002. See Bibliography for complete references.

Chamaerops humilis

Common Name(s) European Fan Palm
Family Palmae (Palm)
Active Toxins See text
Toxic Plant Parts See text

Chamaerops humilis is the only palm native to Europe. Unlike many tropical palms, which cannot stand cool temperatures, this palm can thrive in cool winter rooms indoors. Its sharply-cut dark grey-green leaves are arranged in a dramatic fan that may reach two feet across. Stalks of this palm are woody and may become thorny with age. Ordinarily growing to about three feet, *Chamaerops humilis* can reach 20 feet under ideal conditions. The palm family as a whole has shown little toxicity and some palms have food uses, such as in the production of palm cooking oils. No evidence exists that any palm in the *Chamaerops* genus is toxic.

Recommendation Instruct children never to eat this or any nonfood plant. This plant is probably suitable for display in households with children. Any thorns or spikes that appear on the stalks should be trimmed.

References Bailey and Bailey, 257; see Micromedix, Inc. 1989 *Poisindex* reference 2329913. See Bibliography for complete references.

Chamaerops humilis

Chlorophytum comosum

Common Name(s) Spider Plant, Spider Ivy, Ribbon Plant, Walking Anthericum
Family Liliaceae (Lily)
Active Toxins See text
Toxic Plant Parts See text

This South African herb is an extraordinarily popular houseplant. *Chlorophytum comosum* forms attractive daylily-like leaves that are light green with a white or creamy stripe down the middle. The principal attraction of this plant is no doubt its unusual reproductive method. Spider Plants send up slender stalks of small white flowers, which are followed by small, new plants. As soon as a new plant weighs enough, the stem will bend over, bringing the base of the new plant in contact with soil so that it may root. Spider Plants are often displayed in hanging baskets so that the new plants drape over the edge of the basket. In its 1988 annual report, the American Association of Poison Control Centers National Data Collection System reported that there were 773 exposures to *Chlorophytum* during the reporting period. Most poison control center publications advise that these plants are harmless and there is in fact no evidence of any significant toxicity despite regular reports of ingestion of this plant.

Chlorophytum comosum

Recommendation Instruct children never to eat this or any nonfood plant. This plant is probably suitable for display in households with children.

References Bailey and Bailey, 265; Litovitz, et al., 525; Micromedix, Inc. 1989 *Poisindex* reference 2318891. See Bibliography for complete references.

Chrysalidocarpus lutescens

Chrysalidocarpus lutescens

Common Name(s) Areca Palm, Butterfly Palm, Cane Palm, Golden Butterfly Palm, Golden Feather Palm, Madagascar Palm
Family Palmaceae (Palm)
Active Toxins See text
Toxic Plant Parts See text
The many common names for this slow-growing palm point to its popularity. It grows in clumps and may generate as many as 25 separate plants in a single pot. Areca Palm fronds arch outward three to five feet on long stems. Fronds are arranged in opposite pairs and are curved and formed of stiff, yellow-green leaflets. The plant may reach substantial height and is frequently used as the tall component in interior plantscapes. This palm should not be confused with the palm from the *Areca* genus that is the source of the betel nut, *Areca catechu,* which is also sometimes called Areca Palm. The palm family as a whole has shown little toxicity and some palms have food uses, such as in the production of palm cooking oils. No evidence exists that this palm is toxic.
Recommendation Instruct children never to eat this or any nonfood plant. This plant is probably suitable for display in households with children.
References Bailey and Bailey, 266; Micromedix, Inc. 1989 *Poisindex* reference 2330507; Mitchell and Rook, 500. See Bibliography for complete references.

Chrysanthemum species

Common Name(s) Chrysanthemum, Mum, Pomp, Spider Mum, Boston Daisy, Marguerite Daisy
Family Compositae (Composite)
Active Toxins Sesquiterpene lactones
Toxic Plant Parts Leaves, stems, flowers
Over 160 species of *Chrysanthemum* are native to the Old World. Innumerable hybrids, many based on *Chrysanthemum indicum* are sold by florists as cut flowers. *Chrysanthemum* x *morifolium* is often forced into bloom by commercial growers and sold in pots by florists and nurseries for both indoor and outdoor display. Still other *Chrysanthemum* x *morifolium* cultivars, such as the Spider Mum, are sold as cut flowers. *Chrysanthemum frutescens,* known as the Marguerite Daisy or Boston Daisy, is a popular pot plant. Other species are common indoors as well. Mums, like many other members of the Composite family, contain substances known as sesquiterpene lactones. These are allergens, which cause allergic reactions in sensitized individuals. More than one exposure is frequently required before a person becomes sensitized. But once that happens, the

Chrysanthemum hybrid

reaction can become troublesome. Initially, sensitized individuals may note only a little redness or rash where they have handled Mums. With each re-exposure to Mum allergens, however, the reaction can become worse. Florists and others who handle Mums often may develop chronic skin rashes and eruptions. Mums are not generally regarded as toxic when eaten in small quantities. In fact, Mums are used in teas, soups and other foodstuffs in the Orient. In its 1988 annual report, the American Association of Poison Control Centers National Data Collection System reported that there were 800 exposures to *Chrysanthemum* during the reporting period.

Recommendation Instruct children never to eat this or any nonfood plant. The skin of infants and very young children may easily become irritated by Mums. Otherwise, however, these plants appear to present little risk. Provided care is taken to minimize exposure and the resultant risk of allergic reaction, these plants are probably suitable for display in households with children.

References Bailey and Bailey, 266-269; Hardin and Arena, 13; Lampe and McCann, 192; Litovitz, et al., 525; Mitchell and Rook, 195-200; Stoner and Rasmussen, 8-9. See Bibliography for complete references.

Cibotium species

Common Name(s) Tree Fern, Hawaiian Tree Fern, Mexican Tree Fern
Family Dicksoniaceae (Dicksonia)
Active Toxins See text
Toxic Plant Parts See text

Cibotium chamissoi, called Hawaiian Tree Fern, is frequently sold in four to eight foot trunks without leaves or roots. Those trunks send out tightly curled shoots called crosiers (because they resemble a bishop's staff) that uncurl to become four to six foot long fronds. These plants will live for years if set in water with rocks and pebbles to hold them erect. The closely-related Mexican Tree Fern, *Cibotium schiedei,* is usually sold without any visible trunk. Its airy fronds also unfold out of crosiers and may reach five feet across. No evidence exists that any *Cibotium* species is harmful if ingested.

Recommendation Instruct children never to eat this or any other nonfood plant. This plant is probably suitable for display in households with children.

References Bailey and Bailey, 270-271; Micromedix, Inc. 1989 *Poisindex* reference 2330572. See Bibliography for complete references.

Cibotium scheidei

Cissus rhombifolia

Common Name(s) Grape Ivy
Family Vitaceae (Grape)
Active Toxins See text
Toxic Plant Parts See text

Cissus rhombifolia

Plants called *Cissus* now once were classified in the same genus as the common grape, *Vitis,* because like the common grape they cling to any support with tiny tendrils. *Cissus rhombifolia,* known as Grape Ivy, is the species most often grown of this genus. Its 3-part, vaguely heart-shaped leaves have a metallic sheen when young. Later, they turn darker green, with rusty hairs on the veins underneath. This plant is widely favored because it tolerates low humidity, low light, and other abuse well. It is often grown in a hanging basket with leaves and stems left to trail over the side of the basket. Many poison control center publications treat Grape Ivy as non-poisonous. There is one 1973 report that the sap of this species irritates the skin, but otherwise no evidence exists of toxicity for this species. Other *Cissus* species have been alleged to be poisonous, however.

Recommendation Instruct children never to eat this or any nonfood plant. *Cissus rhombifolia* is probably suitable for display in households with children. Other *Cissus* species should be regarded with caution, however.

References Bailey and Bailey, 273-274; Micromedix, Inc. 1989 *Poisindex* reference 2453986; Mitchell and Rook, 721. See Bibliography for complete references.

Citrus species

Common Name(s) Citrus, Lime, Lemon, Meyer Lemon
Family Rutaceae (Rue)
Active Toxins Volatile oils
Toxic Plant Parts Fruit

Citrus aurantiifolia

Several *Citrus* species are regularly grown indoors, some for their edible fruit. They all have glossy lance-shaped or ovate foliage and, usually, produce fragrant blossoms. *Citrus aurantiifolia* (Lime) is a spiny, small tree that produces small limes. *Citrus limon* cv. 'Meyer' (Meyer Lemon) is a dwarf tree that grows lemons up to three inches in size. *Citrus limon* cv. 'Ponderosa' bears huge lemons—up to two pounds per lemon—and is often grown indoors in tubs or large pots. Some of these plants have spines that can pierce or scratch the skin. And the fruit of some, especially dwarf fruit, can be highly acidic and may therefore irritate the digestive tract of young children. Limes and other *Citrus* species also contain volatile oils that cause phytophotodermatitis—contact with these oils can sensitize the skin to ultraviolet light so that exposure to sunlight can cause redness and irritation of the skin.

Recommendation   Instruct children never to eat this or any nonfood plant. *Citrus* species with spines should be displayed out of the reach of small children to prevent injury to the skin. Alternatively, the spines may be nipped off. Fruiting trees may present some small risks if children play with or eat fruit. Parents may therefore want to display such trees out of reach or remove the fruit.

References   Bailey and Bailey, 275-276; Lampe and McCann, 199; Micromedix, Inc. 1989 *Poisindex* reference 3794769; Mitchell and Rook, 608-619. See Bibliography for complete references.

Clivia miniata

Clivia miniata

Common Name(s)   Kaffir Lily
Family   Amaryllidaceae (Amaryllis)
Active Toxins   Lycorine, an alkaloid
Toxic Plant Parts   Entire Plant

This flowering pot plant is a member of the Amaryllis family and was named after the Duchess of Northumberland, Charlotte Clive, who developed it in the 1860s as an indoor plant. It has shiny, dark-green, strap-shaped leaves up to two feet in length. These grow from the base of the plant and curve outward. Large flower stalks emerge in the spring and may reach 20 inches tall. These bear orange funnel-shaped flowers in clusters of 10 to 20. Blooming may continue through the summer. Kaffir Lily contains the alkaloid lycorine in small amounts. If ingested, the plant will produce nausea, vomiting and diarrhea.

Recommendation   Instruct children never to eat this or any nonfood plant. Kaffir Lilies should be displayed out of the reach of small children.

References   Bailey and Bailey, 287-288; Lampe and McCann, 58. See Bibliography for complete references.

Codiaeum variegatum

Codiaeum variegatum

Common Name(s)   Croton, Joseph's Coat, Garden Croton
Family   Euphorbiaceae (Spurge)
Active Toxins   Possibly tannin
Toxic Plant Parts   Latex

Croton is a small, colorful shrub native from Java to Australia and the South Sea islands. *Codiaeum variegatum* var. *pictum,* commonly called Joseph's Coat, is one of the most popular of the Crotons and is frequently grown indoors. This species has given rise to a large number of varieties with highly variable foliage and growth habits. Almost all varieties, however, have smooth, sturdy and highly colored leaves. Some poison control center publications report that Croton is non-toxic. But there are reports that the leaves and latex of Croton contain a substantial quantity of tannin, a substance which in strong concentrations can cause some dermatitis and digestive upset. There are reports of such reactions on contact with or ingestion of the latex of Croton. On the other hand, when taken in small doses, tannin has little effect. In fact, it is present in many teas. There are reports that whole leaves of Croton have been swallowed by children with no ill effect or only slight effect.

Recommendation Instruct children never to eat this or any nonfood plant. On balance, Croton should be regarded as a possible source of digestive upset and, for that reason, should be displayed out of the reach of small children.

References Bailey and Bailey, 291; Der Marderosian and Roia, in Kinghorn, at 106, 110-111; Mitchell and Rook, 264-268. See Bibliography for complete references.

Coffea arabica

Coffea arabica

Common Name(s) Coffee Plant
Family Rubiaceae (Madder)
Active Toxins Caffeine, coffee oils
Toxic Plant Parts Beans

Coffea arabica is the source of much of the high-quality coffee in the world. It is the only species of the *Coffea* genus that can be grown indoors. It rarely reaches more than four feet in height indoors and produces coffee beans indoors only after several years. As a pot plant, *Coffea arabica* reaches three to six feet in height. It generally grows from a single stem, which becomes thick and woody with age. Leaves are dark green, elliptic to ovate and pointed. Once the plants are four to five years old, they begin producing fragrant flowers in late summer. These are followed by fruit—the coffee beans for which the plant is known. Green coffee beans contain up to 2% caffeine, which can have a strong stimulant effect on small children. The beans also contain coffee oils, which can cause nausea and vomiting in small children if ingested.

Recommendation Instruct children never to eat this or any nonfood plant. Children should be kept away from coffee beans.

References Bailey and Bailey, 293-294; Micromedix, Inc. 1989 *Poisindex* reference 2454489; Mitchell and Rook, 603. See Bibliography for complete references.

Colchicum autumnale

Common Name(s)   Autumn Crocus Fall Crocus, Meadow Saffron, Mysteria, Wonder Bulb
Family   Liliaceae (Lily)
Active Toxins   Colchicine, an alkaloid
Toxic Plant Parts   Entire Plant

Colchicum autumnale is cultivated for its long, tubular white or purple flowers. It grows from a thickened underground stem called a corm, and has three to five strap-like leaves that reach to one foot in length. It is usually grown outdoors but is sometimes forced into flower indoors. Although sometimes called Crocus, *Colchicum* should not be confused with species from the *Crocus* genus. The poisonous properties of *Colchicum* have been known since the time of the Roman Empire. Eating any part of this plant can lead to immediate burning in the mouth and throat, intense thirst, nausea, abdominal pain, vomiting and severe diarrhea. Kidney damage may follow. Death is possible, principally through dehydration. This plant also may irritate the skin.

Recommendation   Instruct children never to eat this or any nonfood plant. Take care to display this plant completely out of the reach of small children. If that is not possible, do not keep it.

References   Bailey and Bailey, 294; Hardin and Arena, 43; Kingsbury (1964), 449-450; Levy and Primack, 46-47, 50-51; Lampe and McCann, 59-60; Mitchell and Rook, 441; Murray, et al., 528-532; Sauder, et al., 169-173; Stephens, 149; Woodward, 24. See Bibliography for complete references.

Colchicum autumnale

Coleus species

Common Name(s)   Coleus
Family   Labiatae (Mint)
Active Toxins   See text
Toxic Plant Parts   See text

Coleus is a fast-growing tender perennial that is typically bought in the spring and disposed of in the fall. It is grown both as a houseplant and outdoors for its bright, multi-colored foliage. Most varieties sold by florists and nurseries are hybrids derived from either *Coleus blumei* or *Coleus pumilus*. There is no typical growth pattern for *Coleus* hybrids. Leaves may be many different colors and shapes (ovate, heart-shaped, wing-shaped, elongated or deeply divided). All hybrids, though, produce leaves that are soft, pleasing to the touch and delicate. Insignificant blue flowers may be produced. Many poison control center publications list Coleus as harmless, and there appears to be no evidence to contradict this view.

Coleus x *hybridus*

Recommendation   Instruct children never to eat this or any nonfood plant. This plant is probably suitable for display in households with children.

References   Bailey and Bailey, 294-295; Micromedix, Inc. 1989 *Poisindex* reference 2319592; Mitchell and Rook, 360. See Bibliography for complete references.

Colocasia esculenta

Common Name(s)   Colocasia, Elephant's Ear
Family   Araceae (Arum)
Active Toxins   Raphides of calcium oxalate
Toxic Plant Parts   Leaves

Colocasia esculenta

Seven or eight species of *Colocasia* are native to Asia and Polynesia. At least one species is regularly cultivated for indoor use: *Colocasia esculenta*. *Colocasia esculenta* is grown as a food crop in Polynesia. Known as Taro, the plant's large, spherical underground tubers are a staple and are used in the creation of "poi." But the plant is also highly decorative and suitable for indoor cultivation. It produces large two foot-long leaves that are velvety green on their upper surface and crossed with lighter green veins. Many varieties of this species are available. Despite the fact that the tuber of this species is edible, leaves and perhaps other plant parts contain raphides of calcium oxalate. *Colocasia* is thus like other members of the Araceae (Arum) family such as *Arum, Alocasia,* and *Philodendron*. If eaten, *Colocasia* leaves may cause pain, swelling and irritation of the mouth, lips, and throat. They may also irritate the digestive tract, causing abdominal pain, nausea, vomiting and diarrhea. Ingestion of a significant amount may lead to swelling of the tongue, back of the mouth and throat. Such swelling can cause dangerous obstruction of airways. However, it is unlikely a child will consume an amount sufficient to cause such extreme swelling.

Recommendation   Instruct children never to eat this or any nonfood plant. *Colocasia* should be kept out of the reach of small children.

References   Bailey and Bailey, 296; Hardin and Arena, 48-51; Lampe and McCann, 60-61; see also Mitchell and Rook; Plowman, 97-122; Sakai and Hanson, 739-748; Sunell and Healy, 1029-1032. See Bibliography for complete references.

Columnea hirta

Common Name(s)   Goldfish Plant
Family   Gesneriaceae (Gesneriad)
Active Toxins   See text
Toxic Plant Parts   See text

This native of the Central American jungle has a trailing growth habit making it well-suited for hanging baskets. It produces spectacular fish-shaped vermilion flowers in great abundance, hence the name Goldfish Plant. Its leaves occur in pairs and are oblong, averaging one and one half inches long and three eighths inch wide. The stem and leaves of *Columnea hirta* are densely covered with fine hairs. Many poison control center publications treat this plant as harmless, a view that appears correct given the absence of any evidence of toxicity.

Recommendation Instruct children never to eat this or any nonfood plant. This plant is probably suitable for display in households with children.

References Bailey and Bailey, 297-298; Micromedix, Inc. 1989 *Poisindex* reference 2330233. See Bibliography for complete references.

Columnea hirta

Convallaria majalis

Common Name(s) Lily-of-the-Valley, Conval Lily, Mayflower

Family Liliaceae (Lily)

Active Toxins Digitalis-like glycosides, saponins

Toxic Plant Parts Entire plant, and vase water in which cuttings are kept

Lily-of-the-valley is a hardy perennial with hanging, bell-shaped white flowers. These flowers are small, generally less than one half inch long. Leaves are smooth, dark-green and lance-shaped, and typically reach eight inches in length. *Convallaria majalis* is sometimes kept inside to force blooming, and many garden centers sell specially prepared roots for such forcing. This plant contains a glycoside that acts much like digitalis, the drug used to treat heart ailments. When ingested, it may cause a slowing of the heart and heart rhythm disturbances that, in severe cases, can lead to death. The plant also contains irritant saponins that can cause burning in the mouth, nausea, vomiting and abdominal pain. Note that toxic glycosides in this plant are water-soluble and can migrate to vase water in which cuttings are kept. Poisonings have occurred from such vase water.

Convallaria majalis

Recommendation Instruct children never to eat this or any nonfood plant. In view of the cardiac effects of the glycosides in Lily-of-the-Valley, cuttings or potted blooms should be displayed out of the reach of small children.

References Bailey and Bailey, 308; Der Marderosian and Roia, in Kinghorn, at 112, and sources cited therein; Hardin and Arena, 43-44; Lampe and McCann, 62-63, and sources cited therein; Levy and Primack, 48-49; Mitchell and Rook, 442; Stephens, 140; Woodward, 2, 177. See Bibliography for complete references.

Cordyline terminalis

Common Name(s)   Ti Plant, Ti Log, Good Luck Plant,
Hawaiian Good Luck Plant, Tree-of-Kings, Dracaena
Family   Agavaceae (Agave)
Active Toxins   See text
Toxic Plant Parts   See text

Cordyline is a genus closely related to the *Dracaena*
genus. In fact, this plant is sometimes referred to by the
common name Dracaena and mistakenly designated
Dracaena terminalis. It produces leathery, lance-like
leaves similar to those of some *Dracaena* species.
Several varieties are available that produce leaves in
variegated colors, with stripes of maroon, red, purple,
white, pink and green. The basic species produces leaves
that are crimson-pink when young and that gradually
take on a purple tint as well as creamy white and green
streaks. Leaves may reach as much as two feet in length
and three to four inches in width. This plant is
sometimes sold as a novelty item because it can be
grown from a length of woody stem. Cut up pieces of
stem are packaged and sold as "Ti Log" or "Ti Plant"
along with instructions on how to root and grow the
cuttings. Many poison control center publications
report that this plant is harmless. There are reports that
Cordyline species contain calcium oxalate crystals. But
no evidence exists that they are present in sufficient
quantity to cause digestive upset or skin irritation.
Recommendation   Instruct children never to eat this
or any nonfood plant. This plant is probably suitable for
display in households with children.
References   Bailey and Bailey, 312; Micromedix, Inc.
1989 *Poisindex* reference 2318916; Mitchell and Rook,
50. See Bibliography for complete references.

Cordyline terminalis

Cosmos bipinnatus

Common Name(s)   Cosmos
Family   Compositae (Composite)
Active Toxins   See text
Toxic Plant Parts   See text

The *Cosmos* genus contains about 25 species of showy,
late-flowering annuals and perennials. These are native
from the southwestern United States to tropical America. *Cosmos bipinnatus* produces up to 4-inch-wide
flowers in white, pink, purple and sometimes yellow.
These come in anemone and double-flower forms and
are favored by florists for cut flowers. No evidence
exists that any *Cosmos* species is harmful if ingested and
patch testing for allergic reactions to this plant reveals
only occasional positive reactions.
Recommendation   Instruct children never to eat this
or any nonfood plant. This plant is probably suitable for
display in households with children.

References   Bailey and Bailey, 321; Micromedix, Inc. 1989 *Poisindex* reference 2337544; Mitchell and Rook, 201. See Bibliography for complete references.

Crassula argentea

Common Name(s)   Jade Plant, Jade Tree, Baby Jade, Dollar Plant, Cauliflower Ears, Chinese Rubber Plant, Dwarf Rubber Plant, Japanese Rubber Plant
Family   Crassulaceae (Orpine)
Active Toxins   See text
Toxic Plant Parts   See text

Crassula argentea, from South Africa, is an enormously popular houseplant. It has a thick, rubbery trunk and fleshy, oval leaves that take on a translucent, jade-like color, hence the name Jade Plant. This plant can reach several feet in height indoors. Jade Plant is tolerant of abuse and very long-lived. In its 1988 annual report, the American Association of Poison Control Centers National Data Collection System reported that there were 2,618 exposures to *Crassula* species during the reporting period. This plant is often shown in poison control center publications as non-toxic, a view that is confirmed by the absence of any substantial evidence of toxicity despite many reported ingestions.

Recommendation   Instruct children never to eat this or any nonfood plant. This plant is probably suitable for display in households with children.

References   Bailey and Bailey, 327; Lampe and McCann, 4-5; Litovitz, et al., 525; Micromedix, Inc. 1989 *Poisindex* reference 2319584. See Bibliography for complete references.

Crassula argentea

Crinum species

Common Name(s)   Crinum Lily, Spider Lily, Bengal Lily
Family   Amaryllidaceae (Amaryllis)
Active Toxins   Lycorine, an alkaloid
Toxic Plant Parts   Entire plant

Crinum Lily is one of the largest bulb plants used for indoor growing. Its bulbs are usually potted half in, half out of the soil. Magnificent white, pink or red lily-like flowers are borne on a three foot stalk. Leaves typically are sword-shaped or strap-like and may reach two to three feet in height. Among the most common species are *Crinum asiaticum* (Spider Lily), *Crinum kirkii, Crinum moorei* and *Crinum powellii*. All parts of the plant, especially the bulb, contain lycorine, an alkaloid that irritates the digestive tract. Ingestion of Crinum Lilies may cause nausea, vomiting and diarrhea. Some *Crinum* species have also been shown to irritate the skin on contact.

Recommendation Instruct children never to eat this or any nonfood plant. Crinum Lilies should be displayed out of the reach of small children.

References Bailey and Bailey, 333-334; Hardin and Arena, 48; Kingsbury (1964), 468; Lampe and McCann, 65-66; Levy and Primack, 49; Mitchell and Rook, 61. See Bibliography for complete references.

Cryptanthus species

Common Name(s) Earth Stars
Family Bromeliaceae (Bromelia or Pineapple)
Active Toxins See text
Toxic Plant Parts See text

Cryptanthus bivittatus

The *Cryptanthus* genus contains about twenty species of herbaceous plants which grow from stolons (stems which grow horizontally along the ground and take root). The name *Cryptanthus* means "hidden flower" and refers to the fact that these Bromeliads have flowers that are concealed beneath the leaves rather than growing erect above the leaves as with other Bromeliads. They are sometimes referred to as "Earth Stars." Several *Cryptanthus* species are common house plants. *Cryptanthus bivittatus* has arching, spiny leaves that may reach 4 inches long and are greenish brown with two pink stripes. *Cryptanthus acaulis,* known as the Starfish Plant, has small, wavy-edged leaves in varying shades of green and yellow arranged in a starfish-like rosette. *Cryptanthus bromelioides tricolor,* called Rainbow Star, has bright green leaves that are vivid rose at the base and on the margins and are edged and striped with ivory white. *Cryptanthus zonatus* 'Zebrinus', the Zebra Plant, has bronze leaves crossbanded with brown. The Bromeliad family as a whole exhibits low toxicity. As a result, many poison control centers treat the entire family as non-toxic. No evidence exists that plants in the *Cryptanthus* genus are toxic. Note that many Bromeliads have coarse or spiny leaves or bracts, which may pierce or scratch the skin.

Recommendation Instruct children never to eat this or any nonfood plant. Evaluate each Bromeliad plant for its potential to scratch or injure the skin. This may vary within a species or as a plant ages. Plants which do not pose undue risk of injury to children's skin are suitable for display in households with children.

References Bailey and Bailey, 339-340; Micromedix, Inc. 1989 *Poisindex* reference 2340521. See Bibliography for complete references.

Cycas revoluta

Common Name(s) Sago Palm, Japanese Sago Palm, Japanese Fern Palm, Funeral Palm
Family Cycadaceae (Cycad)
Active Toxins Probably alkaloids
Toxic Plant Parts Seeds, foliage

Cycas revoluta

Sago Palm is not a true palm, but rather is a member of the Cycad family, an ancient group of fern-like plants. Cycads such as the Sago Palm are among the most primitive living seed plants. They are the disappearing remnants of an ancient flora that was abundant during the Mesozoic era. Sago Palms are strikingly handsome, with fronds up to three feet long. Older plants develop trunks that can reach 10 feet in height. Sago Palm is the source of most funeral wreaths supplied by florists. It is also a frequent subject of Bonsai culture in Japan. Cattle grazing on *Cycas* species suffer damage to the nervous system and there are reports that *Cycas* seeds have caused paralysis and other serious systemic poisoning in humans. These reports warrant treating this plant with caution.

Recommendation Instruct children never to eat this or any nonfood plant. Display this plant out of the reach of small children.

References Bailey and Bailey, 350; Hardin and Arena, 41-42; Kingsbury (1964), 123. See Bibliography for complete references.

Cyclamen persicum

Common Name Cyclamen
Family Primulaceae (Primrose)
Active Toxins Cyclamine
Toxic Plant Parts Tuberous root, possibly other parts

Cyclamen persicum

Cyclamen persicum, and its many hybrids and cultivars, have striking rosettes of fleshy, heart-shaped dark green leaves and bright butterfly-like flowers held well above the leaves. The flowers appear from mid-autumn until mid-spring. Leaves and flowers arise from a fleshy tuber similar to that of the tuberous begonia. This species is the one most often sold by nurseries and florists. The tubers, and possibly other parts of the plant, of some species of *Cyclamen* contain cyclamine, a bitter-tasting substance that has a pronounced purging effect on the bowels and also can cause nausea, vomiting and pain in the gastrointestinal tract. Deaths have been recorded, probably as a result of dehydration. Patch testing of this plant to determine its potential for causing allergic responses has resulted in occasional positive responses. It is not a strong allergen.

Recommendation Instruct children never to eat this or any nonfood plant. Display this plant out of the reach of small children.

References Bailey and Bailey, 351-352; Micromedix, Inc. 1989 *Poisindex* reference 2453960; Mitchell and Rook, 545. See Bibliography for complete references.

Cymbidium hybrids

Cymbidium
'Gainesville' x 'Dan Carpenter'

Common Name(s) Cymbidium orchid
Family Orchidaceae (Orchid)
Active Toxins Quinones
Toxic Plant Parts Entire plant

Because they are easy to grow, *Cymbidium* orchids are perhaps the most popular of the orchids commonly kept as houseplants. They are also sold as cut flowers by florists. Most *Cymbidium* orchids kept indoors are crosses between dwarf species and standard orchids. The resulting foliage can reach two feet in height and spikes of flowers may reach three feet. The flowers come in all colors but blue and true red. *Cymbidium* orchids have been shown to contain quinones that cause rashes when they come in contact with the skin of some individuals. There are no reports on the effects of ingesting plants of this genus. The absence of data warrants caution.

Recommendation Instruct children never to eat this or any nonfood plant. As a precaution, display this plant out of the reach of small children.

References Bailey and Bailey, 353-354; Hausen and Shoji, 1206-1208. See Bibliography for complete references.

Cyperus alternifolius

Cyperus alternifolius

Common Name(s) Umbrella Plant, Dwarf Umbrella Plant, Umbrella Palm, Umbrella Sedge
Family Cyperaceae (Sedge)
Active Toxins See text
Toxic Plant Parts See text

The Sedge family, in which *Cyperus* species are found, is closely related to the grass family. *Cyperus papyrus* is the plant first used to make paper in Egypt. It is only occasionally cultivated indoors, since it reaches eight feet in height. Much more common as houseplants are *Cyperus alternifolius,* the Umbrella Plant, and *Cyperus alternifolius* 'Gracilis', a dwarf variety that only reaches about two feet in height. These are called Umbrella Plant because their leaves resemble an umbrella's ribs. Many poison control center publications treat what they call "Umbrella Plant" as non-poisonous without being specific as to the botanical name of the plant. Such treatment is probably not warranted for *Cyperus* species, because there is evidence that they contain volatile oils that cause vomiting or other irritation of the digestive tract and may also cause kidney damage if repeatedly consumed. Note that *Brassaia actinophylla,* often called Schefflera, is also sometimes called Umbrella Tree or Umbrella Plant.

Recommendation   Instruct children never to eat this or any nonfood plant. Display this plant out of the reach of small children.

References   Bailey and Bailey, 356; Micromedix, Inc. 1989 *Poisindex* reference 2461195; Mitchell and Rook, 248. See Bibliography for complete references.

Cyrtomium falcatum

Cyrtomium falcatum

Common Name(s)   Holly Fern, Japanese Holly Fern, Fish Tail Fern
Family   Polypodiaceae (Common Fern)
Active Toxins   See text
Toxic Plant Parts   See text

Cyrtomium falcatum, native to Asia, produces stiff fronds up to two feet in length growing from a silvery, thickened underground stem called a rhizome. Leaves are ovate, shiny, dark green, arranged pinnately in pairs, and vaguely resemble holly leaves. Crushed *Cyrtomium* rhizomes are used by Chinese herbalists, principally for treating worms in humans. The common fern family as a whole exhibits low toxicity, and no evidence exists that this plant is toxic.

Recommendation   Instruct children never to eat this or any nonfood plant. This plant is probably suitable for display in households with children.

References   Bailey and Bailey, 357; Micromedix, Inc. 1989 *Poisindex* reference 2330564; Rhee, Woo, Baek and Ahn, 277-284. See Bibliography for 99 complete references.

Dahlia hybrids

Common Name(s)   Dahlia
Family   Compositae (Composite)
Active Toxins   See text
Toxic Plant Parts   See text

Dahlias are native to Central and South America. About 25 species occur in nature. However, most of the plants sold in commerce in North America are hybrids probably derived from *Dahlia pinnata* and *Dahlia coccinea*. Dahlias grow from tuberous roots and develop brilliant semi-spherical flowers in many colors. They are usually grown outdoors, but are often cut for display in flower arrangements. They are also grown commercially for use by florists. The tubers of *Dahlia* species are sometimes used for food in Mexico, and also have been used as a homeopathic remedy for diabetes. However, there are no reported ingestions of most of the hybrids used by florists and gardeners. In view of the extensive hybridization of this plant and the scarcity of information on hybrids, caution is warranted.

Recommendation   Instruct children never to eat this or any nonfood plant. As a precaution, display this plant out of the reach of small children.

References   Bailey and Bailey, 360-361; Micromedix, Inc. 1989 *Poisindex* reference 2649064; Mitchell and Rook, 202. See Bibliography for complete references.

Daphne odora

Common Name   Daphne, Winter Daphne
Family   Thymelaeaceae (Mezereum)
Active Toxins   Mezerein, daphnetoxin, possibly other toxins
Toxic Plant Parts   Entire plant

Daphne odora 'Marginata'

Daphne odora is a winter-flowering woody plant that produces clusters of small pink or reddish flowers and is sometimes kept indoors as a flowering houseplant. Its leaves are leathery and shiny. The plant is also usually quite fragrant. *Daphne* species have been reported as toxic since the time of the ancient Greeks. All of the poisonous plant reference books of the 1700s and 1800s report *Daphne* as highly toxic, and experiments were carried out using *Daphne* as early as 1814. Of the *Daphne* species, *Daphne mezereum* is especially toxic, but all species are suspect. *Daphne* species contain many poisonous compounds, including mezerein, an intensely irritating, blistering resin, and daphin, a glycoside. Ingestion will produce a burning sensation, swelling, and possible blistering, of the lips, mouth and throat. Swallowing may be difficult, abdominal pain may be present and nausea, vomiting and diarrhea (possibly with blood) may follow. *Daphne* also may cause systemic damage to the kidneys. In severe poisonings, victims may show delirium, convulsions, and shock, possibly leading to death. Any ingestion of any *Daphne* species must be regarded as a medical emergency. Medical treatment should be sought immediately.

Recommendation   Instruct children never to eat this or any nonfood plant. *Daphne* species should not be kept in households with small children.

References   Bailey and Bailey, 362-363; Hardin and Arena, 93-94; Kingsbury (1964), 386-388; Lampe and McCann, 68-69; Levy and Primack, 88-90; Woodward, 3, 4. See Bibliography for complete references.

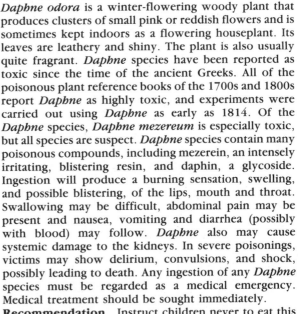

Davallia species

Common Name(s) Davallia, Deer's Foot Fern, Rabbit's Foot Fern, Ball Fern, Squirrel's Foot Fern
Family Polypodiaceae (Common Fern)
Active Toxins See text
Toxic Plant Parts See text

These Old World ferns are characterized by finely-divided foliage and stems or rhizomes (thickened root-like stems) that creep along the surface of pots. This creeping growth habit and a leaf size that rarely exceeds two to three feet make *Davallia* ideal for use in hanging baskets. *Davallia canariensis* (Deer's Foot Fern), *Davallia fejeensis* (Rabbit's Foot Fern), *Davallia mariesii* (Ball Fern) and *Davallia trichomanoides* (Squirrel's Foot Fern) are common as houseplants. No evidence exists that these ferns are toxic.

Recommendation Instruct children never to eat this or any nonfood plant. Davallia ferns are probably suitable for display in households with children.

References Bailey and Bailey, 365-366; Micromedix, Inc. 1989 *Poisindex* reference 2329187. See Bibliography for complete references.

Davallia trichomanoides

Delphinium species

Common Name(s) Delphinium, Larkspur
Family Ranunculaceae (Crowfoot or Buttercup)
Active Toxins Delphinine and other alkaloids
Toxic Plant Parts Entire plant, especially seeds and young plants

Many *Delphinium* species are grown in perennial outdoor gardens, either from seed or fleshy tuberous roots. They are also cultivated commercially for use by florists as cut flowers. They produce very showy long clusters of flowers, usually in white, blues and purples, and always with a characteristic spur or backward-projecting petal. Larkspurs have been recognized as poisonous from classical times. Its seeds have been used in powdered form as an insecticide for hundreds of years. Wild species have caused massive losses of livestock in the Western United States, but domestic species and hybrids also have shown toxicity. The alkaloids present in these plants can cause nausea, vomiting, and nervous symptoms, such as agitation and depression, and may be fatal if ingested in quantity.

Recommendation Instruct children never to eat this or any nonfood plant. *Delphinium* should be displayed out of the reach of small children.

References Arena, 549; Bailey and Bailey, 367-369; Hardin and Arena, 56-57; Micromedix, Inc. 1989 *Poisindex* reference 3124099; Mitchell and Rook, 581. See Bibliography for complete references.

Delphinium hybrid

Dendrobium species

Common Name(s) Dendrobium Orchid
Family Orchidaceae (Orchid)
Active Toxins Dendrobine and other alkaloids
Toxic Plant Parts Entire plant

Dendrobium primulinum

Perhaps 900 species of *Dendrobium* are found in nature, ranging from small creeping plants to giants taller than a man. *Dendrobium* orchids are extremely popular with florists for use in cut flower arrangements. Many of the orchids used by florists are hybrids taken from *Dendrobium phalaenopsis* and *Dendrobium nobile.* Hybrids from these species are also grown as potted plants at home. For centuries, *Dendrobium* orchids have been used in the Orient as homeopathic and folk remedies to improve appetite, stimulate saliva-tion and promote general health. It is also popular with Chinese opera singers to improve their voices. Only recently have the alkaloids responsible for *Dendrobium* orchids' medicinal properties been identified. It is clear that these alkaloids are active, but their mechanism is not yet well understood. Caution is warranted.

Recommendation Instruct children never to eat this or any nonfood plant. As a precaution, display this plant out of the reach of small children.

References Bailey and Bailey, 369-373; Wang, Zhao and Che, 796. See Bibliography for complete references.

Dianthus caryophyllus

Common Name(s) Carnation, Pink
Family Caryophyllaceae (Carnation)
Active Toxins Saponins
Toxic Plant Parts Entire plant

Dianthus caryophyllus

Dianthus caryophyllus is the species used for the florists' Carnation and has graced many a bouquet and buttonhole. It is also occasionally cultivated as a houseplant, although its somewhat difficult cultural requirements discourage this. This species produces long-stalked flowers in white, pink, red, purple and yellow, as well as in spots. Frequently, however, florists buy white Carnations and then color them by setting their stems in dyed water. Some species of Carnation are used in teas, soups and other food preparations in the Orient. In addition, oil of Carnation has been used in dentistry for decades with no apparent ill effect. However, *Dianthus* species have been reported to contain saponins that have the potential of damaging blood cells when ingested regularly or in quantity. Carnations can also cause skin rashes in some suscepti-ble individuals who come in contact with the plant. On balance, ingestion of small quantities of Carnation is unlikely to cause harm.

Recommendation   Instruct children never to eat this or any nonfood plant. This plant is probably suitable for display in households with children.

References   Bailey and Bailey, 376-380; Micromedix, Inc. 1989 *Poisindex* reference 2295305; Mitchell and Rook, 160. See Bibliography for complete references.

Dieffenbachia species

Common Name(s)   Dieffenbachia, Dumbcane, Dumb-cain, Dumb Plant, Mother-in-Law's Tongue Plant, Tuft Root

Family   Araceae (Arum)

Active Toxins   Proteolytic enzymes, raphides of calcium oxalate, probably other toxins

Toxic Plant Parts   Leaves, stems, latex

Dieffenbachia is a common commercial interior landscape plant and houseplant. It has been grown indoors for hundreds of years for its attractive foliage. A number of species of *Dieffenbachia* are available, including *Dieffenbachia amoena, Dieffenbachia bausei, Dieffenbachia candida, Dieffenbachia exotica, Dieffenbachia maculata* and *Dieffenbachia seguine*. In general, the plant produces elliptic, oblong leaves that are bright green, mottled with cream or yellow splotches. All *Dieffenbachia* species contain an extraordinarily potent combination of irritants that can cause serious tissue damage to the eyes and skin and to internal mucous tissue. The potency of the irritants in *Dieffenbachia* has been known for centuries. In his 1707 account of travel to Jamaica and Barbados, H. Sloane observed these characteristics of *Dieffenbachia:*

Dieffenbachia amoena

> "If one Cut this cane with a Knife, and put the tip of the Tongue to it, it makes a very painful Sensation, and occasions such a very great irritation on the salivary Duct, that they presently swell, so that the person cannot speak, and do nothing for some time but void Spittle in a great degree, what European Arums does in a lesser, and from this quality, and being jointed this *Arum* is called Dumb-Cane."

The name "Dumb-Cane" is still used today. The irritant qualities of *Dieffenbachia* have been employed for evil since the plant was discovered. Jamaican slaves were punished sometimes by rubbing their mouths with Dumb-Cane. And, during World War II, the Nazis experimented with *Dieffenbachia* using concentration camp inhabitants as their subjects.

Dieffenbachia exotica

The calcium oxalate raphides found in this plant and most members of the Arum (Araceae) family are sharp crystals, which puncture tissue. Some researchers theorize that proteolytic enzymes present in *Dieffenbachia* attack cells through the punctures caused by the crystals. This may account for why tissue damage caused by *Dieffenbachia* is more extensive than that caused by other plants in the Arum family that also contain calcium oxalate raphides, such as *Philodendron*. Chewing a *Dieffenbachia* leaf produces almost immediate pain, which can become intense. Swelling and blistering of tissue exposed to the plant toxins will almost certainly follow. Swelling and damage to vocal cords can occur, leading to loss of voice. Swelling of throat tissue may occur if significant amounts of plant material are eaten, and this swelling can block airways, leading to death. However, because of the immediate pain that results when this plant is chewed, children are unlikely to eat significant amounts. In addition to its irritant qualities, *Dieffenbachia* appears to cause systemic poisoning in its victims, damaging internal organs and, in severe poisonings, leading to death. The mechanism of this systemic poisoning is not clear. In its 1988 annual report, the American Association of Poison Control Centers National Data Collection System reported that there were 3,806 exposures to *Dieffenbachia* species during the reporting period.

Recommendation Instruct children never to eat this or any nonfood plant. Because this plant is often grown quite large, it may be difficult to display out of the reach of small children. If it cannot be put completely out of reach, it should not be kept in households with small children.

References Arditti and Rodriguez, 293-296; Bailey and Bailey, 383-385; Barnes and Fox, 173-181; Der Marderosian and Roia, in Kinghorn at 109, 123-124, Hardin and Arena, 48-51; Kuballa, 444-451; Lampe and McCann, 72-73; Levy and Primack, 68-71; Litovitz, et al., 525; Plowman, 97-122; Pohl, 812-813; Sakai and Hanson, 739-748; Stephens, 135; Woodward, 6, 53. See Bibliography for complete references.

Digitalis purpurea

Common Name(s) Foxglove, Digitalis, Fairy Bells, Fairy Cap, Thimbles, Fairy Thimbles, Folks Glove, Throatwort

Family Scrophulariaceae (Figwort)

Active Toxins Digitalis glycosides, saponins

Toxic Plant Parts Entire plant, including, possibly, vase water

Digitalis purpurea (Foxglove) is known for its beautiful tall columns of bell-shaped hanging flowers. These grow on stalks that average about two feet in height. Flowers come in purple, pink, white and, rarely, yellow. Foxglove is a common garden biennial or perennial. It is also cultivated commercially for use by florists as a cut flower. Foxglove has been used medicinally for over 700 years and was first listed in a written pharmacopoeia around the year 1200. Since at least 1785, Foxglove has been used as an herbal remedy for what was known as "dropsy" and certain heart problems. Recent research has shown that these early herbal remedies were, when expertly administered, extraordinarily useful in treating certain heart conditions. It is now known that this is due to the presence of certain cardioactive glycosides in Foxglove. One of those glycosides is now extracted from Foxglove and sold as the prescription drug digitalis. Ingestion of Foxglove leaves, flowers or other plant parts, even in small amounts, can lead to dangerous rhythm disturbances of the heart beat. In larger amounts, heart function can become depressed or disrupted completely, leading to death. In addition, since foxglove contains irritant saponins, ingestion can lead to burning in the mouth and throat, nausea, vomiting and abdominal pain. Foxglove poisonings still occur, sometimes by accidental ingestion of the plant and sometimes by ingestion of teas containing Foxglove. Although death from ingestion of Foxglove is rare, it has occurred in recent years, principally through ingestion of Foxglove herbal teas.

Digitalis purpurea

Recommendation Instruct children never to eat this or any nonfood plant. Digitalis should be displayed out of the reach of small children. If the plant cannot be put completely out of reach, remove it from the house.

References Bailey and Bailey, 385-386; Center for Disease Control, 257-259; Der Marderosian and Roia, in Kinghorn, at 113, and sources cited therein; Hardin and Arena, 145, Lampe and McCann, 73-74, and sources cited therein; Levy and Primack, 54-55; Radford et al. 540-544; Reitbrock and Woodcock, 267-269; Stephens, 102, Woodward, 7, 177. See Bibliography for complete references.

Dizygotheca elegantissima

Common Name(s) False Aralia
Family Araliaceae (Aralia or Ginseng)
Active Toxins See text
Toxic Plant Parts See text

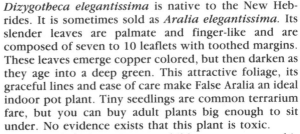

Dizygotheca elegantissima

Dizygotheca elegantissima is native to the New Hebrides. It is sometimes sold as *Aralia elegantissima*. Its slender leaves are palmate and finger-like and are composed of seven to 10 leaflets with toothed margins. These leaves emerge copper colored, but then darken as they age into a deep green. This attractive foliage, its graceful lines and ease of care make False Aralia an ideal indoor pot plant. Tiny seedlings are common terrarium fare, but you can buy adult plants big enough to sit under. No evidence exists that this plant is toxic.

Recommendation   Instruct children never to eat this or any nonfood plant. False Aralia is probably suitable for display in households with children.

References   Bailey and Bailey, 393; Micromedix, Inc. 1989 *Poisindex* reference 2318742. See Bibliography for complete references.

Dracaena species

Common Name(s)   Dracaena, Janet Craig Dracaena, Corn Plant, Massange's Dracaena, Dragon Tree, Red-margined Dracaena, Ribbon Plant, Belgian Evergreen

Family   Agavaceae (Agave)

Active Toxins   See text

Toxic Plant Parts   See text

Dracaena deremensis
'Warneckii'

The *Dracaena* genus produces some of the most reliable performers among houseplants. Tolerance for abuse, the ability to survive in low light conditions and low humidity, and the wide variety of striking forms available all make *Dracaena* species favorites of commercial plant interior designers. These plants are seen everywhere in offices, malls and homes. Among the several species commonly cultivated, four are extremely popular. *Dracaena deremensis* is usually sold in one of two cultivars. *Dracaena deremensis* 'Janet Craig' (Janet Craig Dracaena) produces a corn-like plant with dark green glossy leaves. *Dracaena deremensis* 'Warneckii' (Striped Dracaena) is similar to Janet Craig, but has lighter green leaves with creamy-white stripes down the centers of the leaves. *Dracaena fragrans* 'Massangeana' (Corn Plant, Massange's Dracaena) has leaves that look strikingly like those of corn. When young, the plant grows in rosette form from the soil, but it is usually sold with a portion of mature trunk rooted in soil. Leaves grow from the upper portions of the trunk, giving a palm-like effect. *Dracaena marginata* (Dragon Tree, Red-margined Dracaena) has narrow grayish green leaves with purple margins. The leaves grow from a cane-like trunk and drop off from the lower portions of the trunk as the plant matures, creating a very graceful palm-like effect. *Dracaena sanderana* (Ribbon Plant, Belgian Evergreen) resembles *Dracaena deremensis*

Dracaena fragrans
'Massangeana'

'Warneckii' except that the white stripe is on leaf margins instead of down the center of the leaf. Many poison control center publications treat all *Dracaena* species as nontoxic based on the relatively low incidence of symptoms that occur when these species are ingested. However, some species of *Dracaena* such as *Dracaena cylindrica* (which is not commonly sold as a houseplant) have been reported as causing stomach irritation. *Dracaena sanderana* has shown some evidence of alkaloid content and has produced significant deaths when administered experimentally to rats at very high doses (10% of body weight) during testing conducted in the 1970s. Other *Dracaena* species, however, have been used for medicinal purposes with no apparent harmful effect. On the whole, most *Dracaena* species appear *not* to present a high risk of adverse reactions, but caution should be exercised.

Recommendation Children should be taught never to eat this or any nonfood plant. Most Dracaenas are usually kept as floor plants, and are therefore accessible to children. Because they may irritate the digestive tract or cause other symptoms when eaten, they should be moved to a location out of the ready reach of small children.

References Bailey and Bailey, 398; Der Marderosian and Roia, in Kinghorn, 114, and sources cited therein; Micromedix, Inc. 1989 *Poisindex* references 2329210, 3347344. See Bibliography for complete references.

Dracaena marginata

Dyckia fosterana

Common Name(s) Dyckia
Family Bromeliaceae (Bromelia or Pineapple)
Active Toxins See text
Toxic Plant Parts See text

These Bromeliads grow stiff, spiny-margined leaves in rosette-shaped clumps that reach only four inches in height. They produce orange flowers that grow on one foot long spikes. The Bromeliad family as a whole exhibits low toxicity. As a result, many poison control centers treat the entire family as non-toxic. No evidence exists that this plant is toxic. However, its spiny leaves may pierce or scratch the skin.

Recommendation Instruct children never to eat this or any nonfood plant. Because this plant may injure the skin, it should be displayed out of the reach of small children.

References Bailey and Bailey, 404-405. See Bibliography for complete references.

Dyckia fosterana

Echeveria species

Common Name(s) Echeveria, Hen-and-Chicks, Hen-and-Chickens, Mexican Snowball, Pearl Echeveria, White Mexican Rose
Family Crassulaceae (Orpine)
Active Toxins See text
Toxic Plant Parts See text

The *Echeveria* genus produces small rosette-shaped succulents popular both as outdoor rock garden plants and as houseplants. They are native from Texas to Argentina, but are especially concentrated in Mexico. All species are generally known as Hen-and-Chicks. They stay small enough (2 to four inches across) to be kept in a dish garden or on a windowsill indefinitely. Occasionally, they send up slender stalks with small yellow or rose colored flowers. Two of the most popular species of this genus are *Echeveria elegans* and *Echeveria runyonii*. *Echeveria elegans* is sometimes called the Mexican Snowball, Pearl Echeveria or White Mexican Rose because its leaves are covered with a white dusty powder to such an extent that they appear almost white. *Echeveria runyonii* is similar to *Echeveria elegans,* except it lacks the dusty covering and is somewhat flatter. Many other species of *Echeveria* and a number of hybrids and cultivars are regularly cultivated. Many poison control center publications treat all *Echeveria* species as harmless. At least for *Echeveria elegans* and *Echeveria runyonii,* this view appears correct, since no evidence exists that they are harmful.

Recommendation Instruct children never to eat this or any nonfood plant. This plant appears suitable for display in households with children.

References Bailey and Bailey, 406-410; Micromedix, Inc. 1989 *Poisindex* reference 3347865. See Bibliography for complete references.

Echeveria runyonii

Epipremnum aureum

Common Name(s) Pothos, Devil's Ivy, Arum Ivy, Pothos Vine, Golden Pothos, Taro Vine, Solomon Island Ivy, Hunter's Robe, Variegated Philodendron, Golden Ceylon Creeper
Family Araceae (Arum)
Active Toxins Raphides of calcium oxalate
Toxic Plant Parts Entire plant

Epipremnum aureum, which is also sometimes still called by the invalid names *Scindapsus aureus, Pothos aureus* and *Raphidophora aurea,* is often mistaken for a member of the *Philodendron* genus because it has similar leaves and a vining growth habit. Pothos, however, usually can be distinguished by its heart-shaped leaves, which are mottled with cream-colored or yellow markings. Like other members of the Araceae (Arum) family such as *Arum, Alocasia,* and *Colocasia,* Pothos contains calcium oxalate raphides. Eating this plant can cause pain, swelling and irritation of the mouth, lips and throat. It can also irritate the digestive tract, causing abdominal pain, nausea, vomiting and diarrhea. Ingestion of a significant amount may lead to swelling of the tongue, back of the mouth and throat. Such swelling can cause dangerous obstruction of airways. However, because of the discomfort caused by eating this plant, it is unlikely a child will consume enough to cause such a severe reaction. Pothos has also been reported to cause skin rashes. In its 1988 annual report, the American Association of Poison Control Centers National Data Collection System reported that there were 2,382 exposures to Pothos during the reporting period.

Epipremnum aureum

Recommendation Instruct children never to eat this or any nonfood plant. Pothos should be kept out of the reach of small children.

References Bailey and Bailey, 431-432; Lampe and McCann, 77-78; Litovitz, et al., 525; Mitchell and Rook, 125 (article); see Hardin and Arena, 48-51.

Eucalyptus species

Common Name(s) Eucalyptus
Family Myrtaceae (Myrtle)
Active Toxins Eucalyptol, other volatile oils
Toxic Plant Parts Entire plant

Over 500 species of *Eucalyptus* are native to Australia and Tasmania. A few species are cultivated for use by florists in cut flower arrangements. Among those used by florists are *Eucalyptus perriniana* and *Eucalyptus gunnii.* The former, sometimes called Round-leaved Snow Gum, has round leaves that encircle their stems and become smaller toward the tip of the stem. The latter has lance-shaped hanging foliage that is blue-green in color. The leaves of both species contain aromatic oils that are released when the leaves are crushed. Eucalyptol and other Eucalyptus oils are used medicinally. But when a substantial quantity is consumed, they can cause nausea, vomiting and diarrhea. Eucalyptus leaves can also cause skin rashes.

Recommendation Instruct children never to eat this or any nonfood plant. Display this plant out of the reach of small children.

References Bailey and Bailey, 449-456; Kingsbury (1964), 371; Lampe and McCann, 194; Micromedix, Inc. 1989 *Poisindex* reference 2536709; Mitchell and Rook, 484-486, 514. See Bibliography for complete references.

Euonymus species

Common Name(s)   Euonymus
Family   Celastrus (Staff-Tree)
Active Toxins   Probably alkaloids, cardiac glycosides in some species
Toxic Plant Parts   Entire plant

Euonymus japonica

Several species of *Euonymus* are commonly cultivated as houseplants. *Euonymus fortunei,* known as Winter Creeper, is a slow-growing creeping or climbing plant with stems to 18 inches in length and dark green white-edged leaves that are sometimes tinged with red. *Euonymus japonica,* called Spindle Tree, is also cultivated as a houseplant and is available in many cultivars. The leaves of this plant are glossy green and frequently also contain yellow or cream colors. Several species of *Euonymus* have been reported to cause nausea, vomiting and diarrhea. One species, *Euonymus europaea,* is known to contain glycosides that affect the action of the heart and may cause convulsions and coma in high doses. That plant is not commonly kept indoors, however. Still, all *Euonymus* species warrant caution.
Recommendation   Instruct children never to eat this or any nonfood plant. *Euonymus* species should be displayed out of the reach of small children.
References   Bailey and Bailey, 459-460; Hardin and Arena, 95-96; Kingsbury (1964), 208; Lampe and McCann, 79-81, and references cited therein. See Bibliography for complete references.

Euphorbia lactea

Common Name(s)   Candelabra Cactus, Dragon Bones, Milk-Striped Euphorbia
Family   Euphorbiaceae (Euphorbia)
Active Toxins   Terpenes and diterpenes
Toxic Plant Parts   Latex (the milky sap beneath the skin)

Euphorbia lactea

Euphorbia lactea looks like a green candelabra and is often mistaken for a cactus. It grows to a height of three feet or taller, has milky-white streaks running along its leafless stems and is lined with thorns. The thorns are justification enough to keep this plant out of the reach of small children, but there is still another reason. Like many other *Euphorbia* species, this plant contains a highly caustic latex (the milky fluid beneath its skin). Complex terpenes in that latex can damage the skin and any moist mucous membrane with which it comes into contact. If it contacts the skin, it can cause severe skin rashes. If the latex reaches the eyes, it can cause severe inflammation or other damage. If swallowed, the latex can cause irritation of the digestive tract, nausea, vomiting and diarrhea.

Recommendation Instruct children never to eat this or any nonfood plant. Display this plant out of the reach of small children.

References Bailey and Bailey, 461-466; Crowder and Sexton, 476-484; Frohne and Pfander, 87-88; Kingsbury, 185-189; Lampe and McCann, 81-82; Levy and Primack, 96; Hardin and Arena, 112-116; Woodward, 12. See Bibliography for complete references.

Euphorbia milii

Common Name(s) Crown-of-Thorns, Christ Plant, Christ Thorn
Family Euphorbiaceae (Spurge)
Active Toxins Terpenes and diterpenes
Toxic Plant Parts Latex

The *Euphorbia* genus contains over 1600 species, with remarkable variation among species. Crown of Thorns is one of the most popular of the indoor *Euphorbias,* second perhaps only to *Euphorbia pulcherrima*—the Poinsettia. Crown of Thorns is a shrubby, flowering *Euphorbia* that can reach about three feet tall indoors. As its name suggests, Crown of Thorns is laden with thorns that can prick adults and injure small children. Its latex—the milky sap under the skin—contains a caustic, acrid substance that is intensely irritating. If it contacts the skin, it can cause severe skin rashes. If the latex reaches the eyes, it can cause severe inflammation or other damage. If swallowed, the latex can cause irritation of the digestive tract, nausea, vomiting and diarrhea.

Euphorbia milii
var. *splendens*

Recommendation Instruct children never to eat this or any nonfood plant. Display this plant out of the reach of small children.

References Bailey and Bailey, 461-466; Frohne and Pfander, 87-88; Hardin and Arena, 115-116; Kingsbury, 185-189; Lampe and McCann, 81-83; Levy and Primack, 94-95. See Bibliography for complete references.

Euphorbia pulcherrima

Common Name(s) Poinsettia, Christmas Flower, Christmas Star, Painted Leaf, Lobster Plant, Mexican Flameleaf
Family Euphorbiaceae (Spurge)
Active Toxins See text
Toxic Plant Parts See text

Euphorbia pulcherrima is the Poinsettia sold in huge numbers during the winter holidays. It has bright green ovate, lobed leaves, insignificant yellow flowers and bright red or pink bracts surrounding the flowers. Probably no decorative houseplant has been the subject of more controversy than the Poinsettia. For years, the plant has been listed in a number of poisonous plant reference books as potentially lethal. All of those references can be traced back to one account from 1919 reporting that a Hawaiian child died after eating Poinsettia. That account was plausible, because many species of the *Euphorbia* genus, to which Poinsettia belongs, produce an acrid, caustic latex (latex is the milky liquid beneath the skin of the plant). Some species of *Euphorbia* can be quite toxic; the irritant diterpenes in the latex can cause severe skin irritation and can damage mucous tissue in the digestive tract or elsewhere. Certain *Euphorbias* are therefore considered lethal.

In the 1970s, however, evidence emerged that Poinsettia was in fact *not* lethal. Several studies were performed on rats showing that large quantities of Poinsettia could be eaten without any sign of toxicity. Professional florist and nursery organizations and a host of other defenders then took up for Poinsettia, widely asserting that it had been falsely accused. One ardent defender went so far as to eat a Poinsettia on national television. Some authorities and many popular periodicals still report that Poinsettia is lethal. It is virtually certain, however, that claims that Poinsettia is lethal are incorrect.

Euphorbia pulcherrima

In its 1988 annual report, the American Association of Poison Control Centers National Data Collection System reported that there were 3,001 exposures to this species during the reporting period. Out of these many reported ingestions, there were no serious poisonings. However, reports surface from time to time in which nausea and vomiting result from exposure to Poinsettia. These may arise from any number of factors. Indeed, it is quite possible that parents, panicked at the ingestion of what they believe to be a "lethal" plant, induce a reaction in their children, even though the plant eaten is harmless (that is one reason why parents should try to be calm after a child has eaten a plant). Because it is possible that the plant may have some small effect on certain children, though, it seems best to exercise at least some caution.

Recommendation   Instruct children never to eat this or any nonfood plant. There is no reason to ban Poinsettia from households with children. But because it may irritate the digestive tract when eaten, it should be kept out of reach of small children. Note that other holiday plants may present substantially more danger. See listings for *Taxus* (Yew), *Ilex* (Holly) and *Phoradendron* (Mistletoe), for instance.

References   Bailey and Bailey, 461-466; Der Marderosian and Roia, in Kinghorn, at 115, and sources cited therein; Dominquez et al., 1184-1185; Edwards, 404;

Hardin and Arena, 115; Lampe and McCann, 81-83; Levy and Primack, 97; Stephens, 65-67; Stone and Collins, 301-302; compare Woodward, at 9. See Bibliography for complete references.

Euphorbia tirucalli

Common Name(s) Pencil Tree, Pencil Tree Cactus, Milkbush, Malabar Tree, India Tree Spurge, Monkey Fiddle
Family Euphorbiaceae (Spurge)
Active Toxins Terpenes and Diterpenes
Toxic Plant Parts Latex (the milky sap under the skin)

Euphorbia tirucalli

The *Euphorbia* genus contains over 1600 species, with remarkable variation among species. Pencil Tree is a shrubby *Euphorbia* that can reach six feet tall indoors. It has cylindrical, many-branched stems bearing tiny leaves that soon fall off, leaving the branches bare. These branches are bright green and pencil-like, hence the name Pencil Tree. The latex of this plant—the milky sap under the skin—contains a caustic, acrid substance that is intensely irritating. If it contacts the skin, it can cause severe skin rashes. If the latex reaches the eyes, it can cause severe inflammation or other damage. And if swallowed, the latex can cause irritation of the digestive tract, nausea, vomiting and diarrhea. This shrub grows vigorously, so it may be difficult to keep pruned and out of the reach of small children.

Recommendation Instruct children never to eat this or any nonfood plant. *Euphorbia tirucalli* should probably not be displayed in households with children because its size and growth habit make it difficult to keep away from children.

References Bailey and Bailey, 461-466; Crowder and Sexton, 476-484; Frohne and Pfander, 87-88; Hardin and Arena, 115-116; Kingsbury, 185-189; Lampe and McCann, 81-83; Levy and Primack, 94-95. See Bibliography for complete references.

X Fatshedera lizei

Common Name(s) Tree Ivy, Fat Lizzy, Ivy Tree, Botanical Wonder
Family Araliaceae (Ginseng)
Active Toxins See text
Toxic Plant Parts See text

x *Fatshedera lizei*

X Fatshedera lizei is an intergeneric hybrid cross between *Fatsia japonica* cv. 'Moseri' and *Hedera helix* var. *hibernica*. The combination of the genera names "*Fatsia*" and "*Hedera*" gave rise to the new genus *Fatshedera*. *Fatshedera lizei* is a weak-stemmed evergreen shrub of erect growth habit, that reaches three feet when fully grown. Leaves are leathery, bright green, broad and palmate, with three or five lobes. One of the parents of this hybrid, *Hedera helix,* is toxic if ingested. Ingestion of leaves or the bitter-tasting berries of that plant will cause a burning sensation in the mouth and may cause nausea, vomiting and diarrhea. There are no reports of the effects of ingestion of *Fatshedera lizei.* It is best to assume that it, too, is toxic.

Recommendation   Instruct children never to eat this or any nonfood plant. Display this plant out of the reach of small children.

References   Bailey and Bailey, 471; Micromedix, Inc. 1989 *Poisindex* reference 2549016. See Bibliography for complete references.

Fatsia japonica

Fatsia japonica

Common Name(s)   Fatsia, Japanese Fatsia, Formosa Rice Tree, Paper Plant, Glossy-Leaved Paper Plant
Family   Araliaceae (Aralia or Ginseng)
Active Toxins   See text
Toxic Plant Parts   See text

The *Fatsia* genus has only one species that is commonly cultivated. That species, *Fatsia japonica,* is an evergreen shrub native to Japan. It has shiny, deeply cut, dramatic leaves that can reach up to 15 inches across. It grows rapidly and may reach four feet or more in height. Fatsias are most often used as potted indoor specimen plants and in that capacity add an exotic, tropical accent to more common greenery. No evidence exists that Fatsias are toxic.

Recommendation   Instruct children never to eat this or any nonfood plant. This plant is probably suitable for display in households with children.

References   Bailey and Bailey, 471; Micromedix, Inc. 1989 *Poisindex* reference 2329260. See Bibliography for complete references.

Ficus benjamina

Common Name(s)   Fig, Weeping Fig, Java Fig, Benjamin Tree, Small-Leaved Rubber Plant
Family   Moraceae (Mulberry)
Active Toxins   See text
Toxic Plant Parts   See text

Weeping Fig is a graceful birch-like tree common in commercial interiors and as a houseplant. It can reach nearly 20 feet in height, and often is the dominant plant in atriums and other large, open indoor spaces. As a houseplant it is seldom sold more than eight feet in height and can be found as short as two feet tall. In its 1988 annual report, the American Association of Poison Control Centers National Data Collection System reported that there were 809 exposures to *Ficus benjamina* during the reporting period. Most poison control center publications treat *Ficus benjamina* as nontoxic, and there is no substantial evidence that this species of *Ficus* is harmful if ingested, despite many reported exposures. *Ficus carica,* the species from which we get food figs, is known to cause skin rashes, but no evidence exists that *Ficus benjamina* causes skin irritation.

Recommendation   Instruct children never to eat this or any nonfood plant. *Ficus benjamina* is probably suitable for display in households with children.

References   Bailey and Bailey, 477-479; Der Marderosian and Roia, in Kinghorn, at 116-117; Hardin and Arena, 14; Lampe and McCann, 5, 198; Litovitz, et al., 525. See Bibliography for complete references.

Ficus elastica

Common Name(s)   Rubber Plant, India Rubber Tree, Assam Rubber Plant
Family   Moraceae (Mulberry)
Active Toxins   See text
Toxic Plant Parts   See text

This is the old favorite Rubber Tree of Victorian parlors. It can reach eight feet in height if left unpruned. The plant's common names refer to the fact that the latex of this species was once used to produce an inferior grade of natural rubber. Generally, *Ficus elastica* has an unbranched stem and dark green, leathery, glossy oval leaves up to 12 inches long, with a prominent central vein. Young leaves are wrapped in a reddish sheath called a stipule. Several interesting newer varieties of *Ficus elastica* are available. *Ficus elastica 'Decora'* has large leaves that can reach up to 15 inches long. *Ficus elastica* 'Variegata' has long, narrow leaves flecked with bright green, grey and creamy yellow. In its 1988 annual report, the American Association of Poison Control Centers National Data Collection System reported that there were 783 exposures to *Ficus elastica* during the reporting period. Because there is a very low incidence of reported problems where this plant has been ingested, many poison control center publications treat this plant as harmless. That view has been confirmed by tests conducted in the 1970s using rats and mice. *Ficus carica,* the species from which we get food figs, is known to cause skin rashes, but no evidence exists that *Ficus elastica* causes skin irritation.

Recommendation   Instruct children never to eat this or any nonfood plant. Rubber Plant is probably suitable for display in homes with children.

Ficus elastica

References Bailey and Bailey, 477-479; Der Marderosian and Roia, in Kinghorn, at 116-117; Hardin and Arena, 14, 155; Litovitz, et al., 525. See Bibliography for complete references.

Ficus lyrata

Ficus lyrata

Common Name(s) Fiddle-Leafed Fig
Family Moraceae (Mulberry)
Active Toxins See text
Toxic Plant Parts Leaves
Ficus lyrata (which is sometimes sold as *Ficus pandurata*) is native to tropical West Africa. Indoors, this plant reaches to about five feet tall. Its shiny, leathery leaves are bright green with contrasting white veins. The leaves are pinched slightly in the middle, giving them some resemblance to the body of a fiddle, hence the name "Fiddle-Leafed Fig." These leaves may reach up to 16 inches long and nine inches wide. *Ficus lyrata* is well-known as a houseplant, but is not as widespread as *Ficus benjamina*. Testing done in the 1970s, which involved feeding an extract of the leaves of this species to rats, showed significant evidence of toxicity: all of the rats died. The doses used were very high (equal to 10% of body weight), but these results still warrant treating this plant with caution.
Recommendation Instruct children never to eat this or any nonfood plant. Display this plant out of the reach of small children.
References Bailey and Bailey, 477-479; Der Marderosian and Roia, in Kinghorn, at 106, 117. See Bibliography for complete references.

Fittonia verschaffeltii
var. *argyroneura*

Fittonia verschaffeltii

Common Name(s) Mosaic Plant, Silver Net Plant, Nerve Plant, Silver Fittonia, White-Leaf Fittonia, Silver Nerve, Silver Threads
Family Acanthaceae (Acanthus)
Active Toxins See text
Toxic Plant Parts See text
Fittonias are small, creeping plants that are sometimes kept as houseplants. They are more common as greenhouse plants, because of their preference for very warm, humid growing conditions. This plant bears ovate, somewhat pointed leaves from two to four inches long arranged in pairs. These leaves are criss-crossed with a net of purple veins. *Fittonia verschaffeltii* var. *argyroneura* has a network of white veins. No evidence exists that this plant is toxic.
Recommendation Instruct children never to eat this or any nonfood plant. This plant is probably suitable for display in households with children.

References   Bailey and Bailey, 480-481; Micromedix, Inc. 1989 *Poisindex* reference 2318800. See Bibliography for complete references.

Forsythia species
Common Name(s)   Forsythia, Golden Bells
Family   Oleaceae (Olive)
Active Toxins   See text
Toxic Plant Parts   See text
Forsythias are treasured for their brilliant yellow early spring flowers. They are common as landscape shrubs, but also are cultivated commercially for use by florists. In winter, commercially grown Forsythia are cut and their budded branches brought indoors to encourage early blooming. They are common fare in late winter and early spring flower arrangements. Several species and a number of hybrids are grown commercially. Perhaps the most common is *Forsythia x intermedia,* which is available in nearly a dozen cultivars. No evidence exists that Forsythia is toxic if ingested in small quantities.
Recommendation   Instruct children never to eat this or any nonfood plant. This plant is probably suitable for display in households with children.
References   Bailey and Bailey, 482-483; Micromedix, Inc. 1989 *Poisindex* reference 2318817. See Bibliography for complete references.

Freesia species
Common Name(s)   Freesia
Family   Iradaceae (Iris)
Active Toxins   See text
Toxic Plant Parts   See text
Freesias are commercially grown in huge quantities in the United States and Europe for use by florists in cut flower arrangements. Their flowers are delightfully fragrant and come in a wide variety of colors and patterns. Freesia rootstocks are sometimes potted and forced into bloom in late winter and early spring. About 20 species of Freesia are found in nature. Those sold by florists are usually *Freesia x hybrida* or one of its many cultivars. There are no reported toxic ingestions of Freesia, but information is scarce. It appears best to exercise caution, especially because some other members of the Iris family are toxic. Also, Freesia rootstocks may be coated with insecticidal or fungicidal dust that is toxic to humans.
Recommendation   Instruct children never to eat this or any nonfood plant. As a precaution, display this plant out of the reach of children.

Freesia x *hybrida*

References Bailey and Bailey, 487; Micromedix, Inc. 1989 *Poisindex* references 3565087, 3565095. See Bibliography for complete references.

Gardenia jasminoides

Gardenia jasminoides
Common Name(s) Gardenia, Cape Jasmine
Family Rubiaceae (Madder)
Active Toxins See text
Toxic Plant Parts See text
Discovered in China in the 1700s, the *Gardenia* genus now includes about 200 species. Gardenias are tender evergreen shrubs revered for their velvety white blossoms and their delightful fragrance. Gardenia foliage is likewise attractive—its leaves are a deep, glossy green. *Gardenia jasminoides* is the species most often grown indoors as a potted plant. Gardenia flowers have been used by herbalists to make jasmine tea, which is consumed without apparent harm. Gardenia fruits have been used for generations both as a dye and as a constituent in medicinal concoctions. There is some evidence that compounds in Gardenia fruits or leaves may cause a purging of the bowels. Caution is warranted around small children.
Recommendation Children should be taught never to eat this, or any, nonfood plant. As a precaution, display this plant out of the reach of small children.
References Bailey and Bailey, 495; Micromedix, Inc. 1989 *Poisindex* reference 3642398; Yamauchi, et al., 39-47. See Bibliography for complete references.

Gasteria liliputana

Gasteria species
Common Name(s) Gasteria, Spotted Gasteria, Dutchwings
Family Liliaceae (Lily)
Active Toxins See text
Toxic Plant Parts See text
Gasteria is a succulent member of the Lily family. Its odd, tongue-shaped leaves, which are flecked with raised white spots called tubercles, rise from the base of the plant and then separate into facing rows. *Gasteria maculata,* called Spotted Gasteria, has pointed leaves that reach two inches wide at the base and six inches long. The uppermost surface of each leaf is concave; the lower surface is convex. The entire plant is covered with grey-white warts. *Gasteria liliputana,* called Dutchwings, reaches no more than four inches tall. Its short two one half inch leaves are dark green spotted with white and spiral up from the base of the plant. No evidence exists that these plants are toxic.

Recommendation Instruct children never to eat this or any nonfood plant. These plants are probably suitable for display in households with children.

References Bailey and Bailey, 496-497; Micromedix, Inc. 1989 *Poisindex* reference 2329294. See Bibliography for complete references.

Gerbera jamesonii

Common Name(s) Gerbera Daisy, Transvaal Daisy, Barberton Daisy, African Daisy, Veldt Daisy
Family Compositae (Composite)
Active Toxins See text
Toxic Plant Parts See text

This African native produces large, colorful solitary flowers on long scapes. Perhaps 70 *Gerbera* species are known in nature, but only a few are cultivated commercially. Principal among those is *Gerbera jamesonii*. That species, available in many color forms, is the source of cut flowers for florists. Also, *Gerbera jamesonii* rootstocks are sometimes potted and forced into bloom indoors. Gerbera grows to 18 inches tall, has 10 to 12 inch leaves on six inch petioles and produces solitary flowers on long leafless stalks. Those flowers grow up to four inches wide and consist of a central head surrounded by one or more concentric rows of colored rays. Colors range through shades of yellow, salmon, pink and red. There are no reports of poisonings resulting from ingestion of Gerbera, but information is scant. Caution is therefore warranted.

Gerbera jamesonii

Recommendation Instruct children never to eat this or any nonfood plant. As a precaution, display this plant out of the reach of small children.

References Bailey and Bailey, 506-507; Micromedix, Inc. 1989 *Poisindex* reference 3526691. See Bibliography for complete references.

Gladiolus hybrids

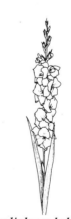

Common Name(s) Gladiolus, Glad, Corn Flag, Sword Lily
Family Iradaceae (Iris)
Active Toxins See text
Toxic Plant Parts Flowers

Glads are everywhere cultivated for garden display and for use indoors as cut flowers. The many varieties of *Gladiolus* now being sold are the product of so much hybridization that it is impossible to give them clear botanical names. There are, however, still in cultivation some of the original species used for hybridization. *Gladiolus gandavensis* and *Gladiolus primulinus,* for instance are still available. In general, Glads are tender perennial herbs with long sword-shaped leaves. They

Gladiolus x *hybridum*

grow to four feet or more in height and produce long, densely-flowered spikes of flowers in summer. Many colors are available. For years, there have been reports of various medicinal uses for Glads. For instance, they have been used as folk remedies for dysentery, diarrhea and colds. More recently, studies have been done on at least one of the original species—*Gladiolus gandavensis*. When experimental doses of *Gladiolus* flowers were administered to rats, a high percentage of them died. The experimental doses were high and represent far more than ordinarily would be eaten accidentally, but these results do indicate significant toxicity. Coupled with poison center reports indicating digestive upset when Glads are eaten, these results warrant treating Glads with caution.

Recommendation   Instruct children never to eat this or any nonfood plant. Display this plant out of the reach of small children.

References   Bailey and Bailey, 511-512; Der Marderosian and Roia, in Kinghorn, at 117; see also Watt and Breyer-Brandwijk and O'Leary. See Bibliography for complete references.

Gloriosa species

Common Name(s)   Glory Lily, Climbing Lily
Family   Liliaceae (Lily)
Active Toxins   Colchicine-like alkaloids
Toxic Plant Parts   Entire plant

Gloriosa is a vining plant with an intricate, lily-like flower that reaches up to four inches across. Half a dozen species are known, but two are regularly cultivated: *Gloriosa superba* and *Gloriosa rothschildiana*. The latter species is the one most often kept as a houseplant. The plant is grown indoors in pots with the vines trained up fibrous stakes or small trellises. This species climbs by means of tendrils which are long extensions of the plant's pointed leaf tips. Glory lilies contain alkaloids that cause gastric irritation and some stimulation of the nervous system. On ingestion, expect burning sensations in the mouth and throat, thirst, nausea, abdominal pain, vomiting and diarrhea. Shock due to fluid loss is possible, as is kidney damage. Deaths have been reported from ingestion of this plant.

Recommendation   Instruct children never to eat this or any nonfood plant. Glory Lily should be displayed out of the reach of small children. Because the plant is vining and may trail over, take special care to keep vines out of reach.

References   Bailey and Bailey, 514; Hardin and Arena, 44-46; Kingsbury (1964), 452-453; Lampe and McCann, 85-86, and references cited therein. See Bibliography for complete references.

Gloriosa superba

Grevillea robusta

Common Name(s) Silk Oak, Silky Oak
Family Proteaceae (Protea)
Active Toxins Phenol compounds
Toxic Plant Parts Possibly entire plant

The Silk Oak is native to Australia. In its native habitat, it is a fast-growing tree that can reach 150 feet tall. However, it is also widely cultivated as a potted plant three to five feet tall. Its 6- to 18-inch long leaves are fern-like and lacy. Unlike most ferns, however, this plant is tolerant of sun. *Grevillea robusta* has been reported to cause skin rashes on those coming in contact with the plant. There are no reports of ingestion of this plant, but in light of its irritating properties, it should be treated with caution.

Recommendation Instruct children never to eat this or any nonfood plant. Display this plant out of the reach of small children.

References Bailey and Bailey, 525; Micromedix, Inc. 1989 *Poisindex* reference 3598533. See Bibliography for complete references.

Grevillea robusta

Guzmania lingulata

Common Name(s) Guzmania
Family Bromeliaceae (Bromelia or Pineapple)
Active Toxins See text
Toxic Plant Parts See text

This Bromeliad has long strap-like leaves that may reach one and one half feet long. White flowers are borne above the rosette of leaves, followed by orange and red bracts, which may stay colorful for months. Many varieties and hybrids based on this species are available. The Bromeliad family as a whole exhibits low toxicity. As a result, many poison control centers treat the entire family as non-toxic. No evidence exists that this particular Bromeliad species is toxic. Note that many Bromeliads have coarse or spiny leaves or bracts, which may pierce or scratch the skin.

Recommendation Instruct children never to eat this or any nonfood plant. Evaluate each Bromeliad plant for its potential to scratch or injure the skin. This may vary within a species or as a plant ages. Plants which do not pose undue risk of injury to children's skin are suitable for display in households with children.

References Bailey and Bailey, 529; Micromedix, Inc. 1989 *Poisindex* reference 2337297. See Bibliography for complete references.

Guzmania lingulata

Gynura aurantiaca

Common Name(s) Purple Passion, Velvet Plant, Purple Velvet Plant, Royal Velvet Plant

Gynura aurantiaca

Family Compositae (Composite)
Active Toxins See text
Toxic Plant Parts See text
Gynura aurantiaca, a popular native of the Old World tropics, is a stout, branchy plant with new leaves and stems completely covered with short, strikingly purple hairs. Older leaves lose some of their hairs and become dark green with purple hairs along veins and at leaf edges. The velvety effect of the hairs covering this plant has given rise to the common name "Velvet Plant." The stems of this plant are erect when young, but clamber over as the plant grows. They may reach several feet in length. *Gynura aurantiaca* produces small, yellow, unpleasant-smelling flowers in the spring. Most poison control center publications treat this plant as harmless, a view borne out by the absence of any evidence of toxicity.
Recommendation Instruct children never to eat this or any nonfood plant. This plant is probably suitable for display in households with children.
References Bailey and Bailey, 531; Micromedix, Inc. 1989 *Poisindex* reference 2329335. See Bibliography for complete references.

Gypsophyla paniculata

Gypsophila paniculata
Common Name(s) Baby's Breath, Gypsophila
Family Caryophyllaceae (Pinks)
Active Toxins Saponins
Toxic Plant Parts See text
Gypsophila paniculata is the Baby's Breath popular with florists as an accompaniment to roses and other cut flowers. It produces a spray of tiny white, pink or reddish flowers on a diffuse array of small branches. *Gypsophila paniculata* 'Compacta' is the dwarf form of Baby's Breath. This and other species of *Gypsophila* are also popular outdoor rock garden perennials. *Gypsophila* species contain saponins and have been used in medicinal tinctures. The claimed medicinal properties of *Gypsophila* have led some scientists to conduct studies on rats using extracts of the plant. From these, it appears likely that the plant does not present a serious threat of poisoning. There have been no reported ingestions of Gypsophila by humans, however, to verify this. Saponins present in the plant may have some irritating properties if eaten in sufficient quantity. Also, workers exposed to *Gypsophila* on a regular basis have shown allergic reactions. On balance, caution is advised.
Recommendation Instruct children never to eat this or any nonfood plant. As a precaution, this plant should be displayed out of the reach of small children.

References   Bailey and Bailey, 531-532; Micromedix, Inc. 1989 *Poisindex* reference 2319518; Mitchell and Rook, 160.   See Bibliography for complete references.

Haworthia species

Common Name(s) Haworthia, Zebra Haworthia, Wart Plant, Windowed Haworthia
Family   Liliaceae (Lily)
Active Toxins   See text
Toxic Plant Parts   See text

There are perhaps as many as 160 species of *Haworthia,* which are succulents native to South Africa. The *Haworthia* genus includes a striking variety of forms and colorations.   Perhaps the best known species for indoor cultivation is *Haworthia fasciata,* commonly called Zebra Haworthia.   This small plant has thick leaves arranged in rosette form. The plant takes its common name from the white crosswise banding on its dark green leaves.   Also sometimes cultivated indoors are *Haworthia attenuata* (called the Wart Plant for its raised white bumps) and *Haworthia cuspidata* (called Windowed Haworthia because the tips of its soft triangular leaves are translucent).   There are no reports on the effect of ingesting *Haworthia* species.   Because some other members of the Lily family are toxic, it is best to exercise caution.

Haworthia fasciata

Recommendation Instruct children never to eat this or any nonfood plant. As a precaution, display these plants out of the reach of children.

References   Bailey and Bailey, 540-543. See Bibliography for complete references.

Hedera helix

Common Name(s)   Ivy, English Ivy
Family   Araliaceae (Ginseng)
Active Toxins   Saponins
Toxic Plant Parts   Leaves and berries

There are five species in the genus *Hedera,* but *Hedera helix* is the species most commonly cultivated as a houseplant.   It is a climbing evergreen plant with a woody stem.   Young leaves are three- or five-lobed and grow on branches that have aerial roots that attach to any moist surface.   Older leaves lack lobes.   This plant produces dark berries, but rarely does so indoors. *Hedera helix* has more than 200 cultivars.   It is used often in basket and dish garden plantings, as well as in terrariums. Florists sometimes add it to arrangements to provide greenery. *Hedera helix* has been known to be toxic since the time of the Greeks.   Ingestion of leaves or the bitter-tasting berries of this plant will cause a burning sensation in the mouth and may cause nausea,

Hedera helix

vomiting and diarrhea. Ingestion of large quantities of *Hedera helix* may lead to labored respiration, convulsions and coma. Contact with the plant may also cause skin rashes. In its 1988 annual report, the American Association of Poison Control Centers National Data Collection System reported that there were 744 exposures to Hedera species during the reporting period.

Recommendation Instruct children never to eat this or any nonfood plant. Display this plant out of the reach of small children.

References Bailey and Bailey, 544-545; Hardin and Arena, 106-107; Kingsbury (1964), 371-372; Lampe and McCann, 87-88; Levy and Primack, 73-74; Litovitz, et al., 525; Woodward, 14. See Bibliography for complete references.

Hibiscus rosa-sinensis

Common Name(s) Hibiscus, Chinese Hibiscus, Hawaiian Hibiscus, Rose-of-China, China Rose, Blacking Plant

Family Malvaceae (Mallow)

Active Toxins See text

Toxic Plant Parts See text

This tropical evergreen shrub may reach 30 feet in height outdoors, but rarely exceeds five feet indoors. It is noted for its Hollyhock-like flowers, which may be single or double in shades from yellow, through salmon to pink or red. Under proper culture, the plant is almost ever-blooming. Most *Hibiscus rosa-sinensis* varieties have large-toothed, ovate, glossy leaves, which can reach six inches in length outdoors, but rarely exceed half that indoors. *Hibiscus rosa-sinensis* cv. 'Cooperii', however, has attractive variegated leaves. *Hibiscus rosa-sinensis* has been used by Oriental herbalists for a number of purposes. In experiments seeking to explore its medicinal properties, it has been shown to cause abortions in pregnant mice at relatively high doses. However, it has apparently shown no other toxic effects. In the southeastern United States in particular, where it is grown outdoors, reported ingestions are common. Those reports yield little or no evidence of toxicity, however. There are old reports, now apparently discredited, that this plant contains cardiac glycosides that lower the blood pressure. On balance, this plant appears innocuous.

Recommendation Instruct children never to eat this or any nonfood plant. This plant is probably suitable for display in households with children.

References Agarwal and Rastogi, 41-42; Bailey and Bailey, 561-562; Pakrashi et al., 523-536; Tan, 247-248. Bibliography for complete references.

Hibiscus rosa-sinensis

Hippeastrum species and hybrids

Common Name(s)   Amaryllis, Barbados Lily
Family   Amaryllidaceae (Amaryllis)
Active Toxins   Lycorine and other alkaloids
Toxic Plant Parts   Entire plant, especially bulb

The *Hippeastrum* genus has about 75 species of herbaceous bulbed plants. Several species and many hybrids of *Hippeastrum* are grown outdoors in gardens and as potted plants for their spectacular and quite large flowers. In the north, the outdoor *Hippeastrum* species are brought indoors for the winter. Most often, however, the large bulbs of *Hippeastrum* are sold in the fall for forcing of winter flowers. First, sword-like leaves emerge from the bulb. These may reach 12 to 18 inches in height, or more. After the leaves are well up, a large-diameter cylindrical stalk emerges. This may reach 24 inches tall and eventually produces several attractive lily-like flowers reaching up to six inches across. Sometimes a second flower stalk will follow the first. Most of the bulbs sold for winter forcing are hybrids, some with quite complex parentage. The most common parent species for hybridization are *Hippeastrum aulicum, Hippeastrum elegans, Hippeastrum puniceum, Hippeastrum reginae, Hippeastrum reticulatum* and *Hippeastrum striatum*. Plants in the *Hippeastrum* genus contain lycorine and other related alkaloids. When ingested, the plant, especially the bulb, may produce nausea and persistent vomiting and diarrhea.

Hippeastrum x *hybridum*

Recommendation   Instruct children never to eat this or any nonfood plant. Display this plant out of the reach of small children.
References   Bailey and Bailey, 564-565; Der Marderosian and Roia, in Kinghorn, at 106, 117-118; Hardin and Arena, 48; Lampe and McCann, 31. See Bibliography for complete references.

Howea species

Common Name(s)   Sentry Palm, Howea Palm, Belmore Sentry Palm, Curly Palm, Flat Palm, Forster Sentry Palm, Thatch-Leaf Palm
Family   Palmaceae (Palm)
Active Toxins   See text
Toxic Plant Parts   See text

The *Howea* genus yields two species commonly grown indoors: *Howea belmoreana,* called the Belmore Sentry Palm or Curly Palm, and *Howea forsterana,* called the Flat Palm, Forster Sentry Palm or Thatch-Leaf Palm. Both species are also called Kentia Palms, Howea Palms or Sentry Palms. Both grow from a single trunk and have long feathery leaves composed of many slender leaflets.

Howea belmoreana

Both can grow to considerable height. The growth habit of *Howea belmoreana* is spreading. *Howea forsterana,* the more common of the two species, is taller and more upright. Newer leaves at the top are larger, giving this species something of a vase shape as it ages. The palm family as a whole has shown little toxicity, and some palms have food uses, such as in the production of palm cooking oils. No evidence exists that palms from the *Howea* genus are toxic.

Recommendation Instruct children never to eat this or any nonfood plant. These plants are probably suitable for display in households with children.

References Bailey and Bailey, 574; Micromedix, Inc. 1989 *Poisindex* reference 2329377. See Bibliography for complete references.

Hoya carnosa

Hoya carnosa

Common Name(s) Wax Plant, Honey Plant
Family Asclepiadaceae (Milkweed)
Active Toxins See text
Toxic Plant Parts See text

Hoyas, from south China and Australia, are twining plants with thick leaves on branching vines. *Hoya carnosa* is the species most commonly kept as a houseplant. It is a succulent shrub with trailing or climbing stems and ovate to oblong leaves that reach up to three inches in length. If properly cared for, this species can produce intensely fragrant, pinkish-white flowers, each with a red star shape in the middle. Many poison control center publications treat Hoya or Wax Plant as nontoxic. Evidence of ingestion of this plant is scarce, but appears to support the view that this plant is not harmful if small quantities are ingested. However, there is evidence that this plant contains an allergen that can sensitize persons handling the plant and cause skin rashes if exposure is repeated.

Recommendation Instruct children never to eat this or any nonfood plant. This plant is probably suitable for display in households with children.

References Bailey and Bailey, 574-575; Micromedix, Inc. 1989 *Poisindex* reference 2657174; Rothe, 250-252. See Bibliography for complete references.

Hyacinthus orientalis

Common Name(s) Hyacinth, Dutch Hyacinth, Garden Hyacinth
Family Liliaceae (Lily)
Active Toxins Probably alkaloids
Toxic Plant Parts Entire plant, especially bulbs

Hyacinths are popular with florists as a late winter and early spring cut flower. *Hyacinthus orientalis* is the species most often sold. It is a perennial flowering plant that reaches up to 18 inches in height. It usually produces four to six strap-like leaves, which have upturned margins and reach up to one foot long. Intensely fragrant flowers, up to one inch wide and often double-petaled and nodding, grow densely at the end of a hollow stalk. Flowers are available in a range of reds, blues and whites. Bulbs are sometimes purchased separately and kept refrigerated to force rooting and early blooming. This can lead to the assumption by children that the bulbs are food. Handling the bulbs without gloves can lead to skin rashes or other irritation. Ingestion has been reported to cause abdominal cramping, nausea, vomiting, diarrhea and purging of the bowels.

Recommendation Instruct children never to eat this or any nonfood plant. Bulbs should be stored and plants displayed out of the reach of small children.

References Bailey and Bailey, 577; Hardin and Arena, 46; Kingsbury (1964), 453; Lampe and McCann, 194. See Bibliography for complete references.

Hydrangea macrophylla

Common Name(s) Hydrangea, Hills-of-Snow, Hortensia, French Hydrangea
Family Saxifragaceae (Saxifrage)
Active Toxins Cyanogenic glycosides
Toxic Plant Parts Flower Buds

Hydrangea macrophylla

Perhaps 80 species of *Hydrangea* are found in nature. Among those cultivated, *Hydrangea macrophylla* is most popular for indoor culture. It is frequently sold potted and blooming in spring (starting at Easter) and early summer. *Hydrangea macrophylla* is a deciduous shrub that reaches up to eight feet in height outdoors, but the potted plants sold for indoor use are generally no more than two feet in height. This plant has large leaves that are ovate with toothed margins and reach up to six inches in length. Flowers grow in a flat-topped, several-branched showy cluster and come in a range of white, pinks and blues. Flower color depends in part on soil acidity, so as soil acidity changes in a potted plant from year to year, flower color will change also. Poisonings have resulted from eating the flower buds. It is believed that they contain cyanogenic glycosides that produce toxic cyanide compounds, which are activated by acid in the stomach and may have no effect for several hours. They can cause sweating, abdominal pain, vomiting and diarrhea. Cyanosis may develop, causing the lips and other parts of the body to become blue from lack of oxygen. In severe poisonings (where substantial quantities are ingested), convulsions, coma, and death may result.

Recommendation Instruct children never to eat this or any nonfood plant. *Hydrangea* should be displayed out of the reach of small children. Care should be taken that expended flowers do not drop within reach of children. Do not keep the plant in households with children unless you are certain that the plant and all fallen material can be kept completely away from children.

References Bailey and Bailey, 578-579; Der Marderosian and Roia, in Kinghorn, at 118; Hardin and Arena, 78-79; Lampe and McCann, 94-95; Stephens, 151; Woodward, 17. See Bibliography for complete references.

Hypoestes phyllostachya

Hypoestes phyllostachya

Common Name(s) Polka-Dot Plant, Pink Polka-Dot Plant, Measles Plant, Flamingo Plant, Freckle Face
Family Acanthaceae (Acantha)
Active Toxins See text
Toxic Plant Parts See text

As its common names suggest, this shrub has highly decorative leaves spotted with pink. They are ovate, about two inches long and one inch wide, and dark green with pink patches and bright red veining. The branches are also red. In spring, insignificant small lavender flowers appear. No evidence exists that this plant is toxic if ingested.

Recommendation Instruct children never to eat this or any nonfood plant. This plant is probably suitable for display in households with children.

References Bailey and Bailey, 586; Micromedix, Inc. 1989 *Poisindex* reference 2330796. See Bibliography for complete references.

Ilex aquifolium

Ilex species

Common Name(s) Holly, American Holly, English Holly
Family Aquifoliaceae (Holly)
Active Toxins Alkaloids, glycosides, saponins, terpenoids
Toxic Plant Parts Berries, perhaps leaves

American Holly *(Ilex opaca)* and English Holly *(Ilex aquifolium)* are both used as holiday decorations indoors. Leaves of both species are thick, leathery, glossy dark green and have spines at intervals around the leaf margins. Both species also produce bright red berries. Berries and leaves contain caffeine, theobromine (a caffeine-like alkaloid) glycosides, triterpenes and saponins. In small doses, Holly may stimulate the nervous system. Early American settlers, in fact, used *Ilex vomitoria* to make yaupon tea. During the Civil War, when coffee was unavailable, southerners used yaupon tea as a substitute. In larger doses, *Ilex opaca* and *Ilex aquifolium* cause digestive upset and depress the nervous system. Poisoning causes nausea, persistent vomiting and sometimes diarrhea. The berries are a special danger to small children and may prove fatal if enough are eaten and symptoms are not treated. Some estimates put the fatal dose at twenty berries, but this is not a reliable gauge in small children. In its 1988 annual report, the American Association of Poison Control Centers National Data Collection System reported that there were 2,337 exposures to *Ilex* species during the reporting period.

Recommendation Instruct children never to eat this or any nonfood plant. Because the red berries are especially attractive to young children, extra care should be taken to insure that children cannot reach Holly displayed indoors. Parents should also be aware that the berries may fall off even if the plant is displayed in a high location.

References Bailey and Bailey, 589-593; Hardin and Arena, 95; Lampe and McCann, 97; Levy and Primack, 124-125; Woodward, 82. See Bibliography for complete references.

Ilex opaca

Iris species

Common Name(s) Iris, Flag, Fleur-De-Lis
Family Iridaceae (Iris)
Active Toxins Possibly glycosides, irritant resins
Toxic Plant Parts Rootstock and leaves

There are probably upward of 200 species of *Iris* and many more hybrids. Almost all of these may be used as cut flowers and some may be grown as potted plants. In recent times, Irises have been the subject of extensive hybridization and many horticultural varieties now available cannot be referred to any specific species. Irises generally grow from either a thickened underground stem called a rhizome or a bulb and are available in a vast variety of colors and flower forms. Leaves generally are linear or sword shaped. The rootstock of *Iris x germanica, Iris x germanica* var. *florentina* and *Iris pseudoacorus* have been shown to cause pain in the digestive tract, nausea, vomiting and diarrhea when eaten. The toxin involved is not known, but glycosides and resins are present in the rootstock. There are also reports that the rootstocks cause skin irritation. It is prudent to assume that all *Iris* rootstocks will cause such distress, although that has not been shown. Leaves and

Iris hybrid

flowers have not been implicated in most of these reports, but it should be assumed that they too will cause at least mild distress when eaten.

Recommendation   Instruct children never to eat this or any nonfood plant. *Iris* should be kept out of the reach of small children.

References   Bailey and Bailey, 598-606; Hardin and Arena, 14; Kingsbury (1964), 471-472; Lampe and McCann, 98; Woodward, 19-22. See Bibliography for complete references.

Jasminum species

Common Name(s)   Jasmine, Jessamine, Poet's Jessamine, Angel Wing Jasmine, Windmill Jasmine, Star Jasmine, Confederate Jasmine, Winter Jasmine, Arabian Jasmine

Family   Oleaceae (Olive)

Active Toxins   See text

Toxic Plant Parts   See text

Jasminum species are erect, climbing shrubs famous for their fragrant blossoms. They most often have small, shiny, dark-green leaves and white or yellow tubular flowers appearing in clusters at the branch tips or leaf axils. Those commonly kept indoors include *Jasminum officinale* (Poet's Jessamine), *Jasminum nitidum* (Angel Wing Jasmine, Windmill Jasmine, Star Jasmine, Confederate Jasmine), *Jasminum polyanthum* (Winter Jasmine) and *Jasminum sambac* (Arabian Jasmine). There are no reports that these species are harmful if ingested. There are, however, reports that some *Jasminum* species cause skin rashes if they come in contact with skin. Note that plants other than *Jasminum* species are also called Jasmine or Jessamine. *Gelsemium sempervirens,* for instance, is called Yellow Jessamine, Carolina Yellow Jasmine and Yellow False Jasmine. It contains substances that exert a strychnine-like action and is considered highly toxic. *Cestrum* species such as *Cestrum parqui, Cestrum nocturnum* and *Cestrum diurnum* are also called Jessamine and are reported to be toxic. Plants of several other genera are also called Jasmine from time to time. Because of the number of different genera that are called by the common names Jasmine and Jessamine, great care should be taken in identifying plants called by these names.

Recommendation   Instruct children never to eat this or any nonfood plant. *Jasminum* species are probably suitable for display in households with children, provided care is taken to avoid repeated skin contact.

Jasminum officinale

References Bailey and Bailey, 611-612; Kingsbury (1964), 278; Lampe and McCann, 84-85; Micromedix, Inc. 1989 *Poisindex* references 2625246, 3248600, 3248758, 3751375. See Bibliography for complete references.

Jatropha multifida

Jatropha multifida

Common Name(s) Coral Plant, Physic Nut
Family Euphorbiaceae (Spurge)
Active Toxins Jatrophin, a plant lectin
Toxic Plant Parts Seeds, possibly other parts of plant
Jatropha multifida is a highly toxic plant that is often kept as a houseplant. It is an attractive plant, with large, almost circular leaves that are very deeply cut into as many as 11 lobes. The common name "Coral Plant" comes from the showy clusters of coral-red flowers that are nearly ever-blooming. This plant produces a bright yellow, three-sided fruit, with each side containing one seed. The seeds, and possibly other parts of this plant, contain jatrophin, a plant lectin that inhibits protein synthesis in the intestine wall. Ingestion of plant material can cause rapid onset of nausea, vomiting and diarrhea. Ingestion can lead to serious systemic poisoning and even death, with just one seed posing a serious threat of severe poisoning in children. Children find the yellow fruit of this plant attractive. Note that, even if this plant is displayed out of reach, its fruit and seeds may fall to the ground. Obviously, seeds should not be permitted to form on any plant kept in households with children.
Recommendation Because of the risk of serious poisoning or death posed by this plant, it probably should not be kept in households with children.
References Bailey and Bailey, 612; Hardin and Arena, 117-118; Kingsbury (1964), 191-192; Lampe and McCann, 98-100; Levy and Primack, 79-80. See Bibliography for complete references.

Kalanchoe blossfeldiana

Kalanchoe blossfeldiana

Common Name(s) Kalanchoe
Family Crassulaceae (Orpine)
Active Toxins See text
Toxic Plant Parts See text
Kalanchoe blossfeldiana is an herbaceous perennial with an erect, branching growth habit. It grows to a height of 12 inches indoors. It is cultivated for its attractive, long-lasting flowers. Leaves are fleshy and ovate to elliptic with toothed edges and average between two and three inches in diameter. Tubular red flowers are carried in clusters on leafless stems. Most poison control centers treat Kalanchoes as nontoxic.

However, some investigators report toxins known as bufadienolides in *Kalanchoe* species. Given the absence of information on Kalanchoes and the possibility that active toxins are present, caution is advised.

Recommendation Instruct children never to eat this or any nonfood plant. As a precaution, display this plant out of the reach of small children.

References Bailey and Bailey, 620-623; Cheek and Shull, 194-195; Micromedix, Inc. 1989 *Poisindex* reference 2697518. See Bibliography for complete references.

Lantana camara

Lantana camara

Common Name(s) Lantana, Yellow Sage
Family Verbenaceae (Verbena)
Active Toxin sProbably alkaloids
Toxic Plant Parts Immature fruit, leaves

Lantana is a low-growing shrub native to the West Indies. These plants are common outdoors, but are also sold by florists and nurseries for indoor growth. Indoors, they may reach up to four feet in height. Leaves are rough-textured and elliptic, with toothed margins.   Under the right conditions, Lantana will produce spectacular tubular flowers that grow from the leaf axils and may bloom almost continuously.   The flowers change color as they age.   Outdoors and occasionally indoors, the plant will also produce a berry that is greenish when young and turns blue-black when mature. Ingestion of immature fruit (which appear to exhibit the highest toxicity of any plant part) or leaves of this plant can cause digestive upset, vomiting, diarrhea, weakness, circulatory collapse and, in severe poisonings, damage to the liver and other internal organs and death. Lantana grows wild in the Southeastern United States and is a common cause of poisoning in children. Child fatalities have been reported.

Recommendation Instruct children never to eat this or any nonfood plant. This plant should not be kept in households with children, unless it can be put completely out of reach.

References Bailey and Bailey, 635; Hardin and Arena, 135-136; Kingsbury (1964), 296-298; Lampe and McCann, 104; Levy and Primack, 123-124. See Bibliography for complete references.

Lathyrus odoratus

Common Name(s) Sweet Pea
Family Leguminosae (Pea or Pulse)
Active Toxins Beta-aminopropionitrile
Toxic Plant Parts Seeds

Sweet Peas are grown outdoors as annuals for their delicate and highly fragrant flowers. They are also cultivated commercially and sold by florists in cut flower arrangements. Leaves of this plant are elliptic and reach up to two inches long. Flowers grow one to four on a stalk and may reach up to two inches across. Flowers are available in a wide range of colors. From the time of Hippocrates, *Lathyrus* species have been known causes of widespread poisonings and loss of life. These poisonings have been associated with conditions of drought, famine and poverty, which force upon the victims a steady diet of *Lathyrus* seeds. Over the past several decades, a great deal of experimental work has been done confirming the long-term toxic effects of *Lathyrus*. From these experiments, it appears that modest amounts of the seeds of *Lathyrus* species in the diet do not cause much problem. However, diets consisting of more than about 25% *Lathyrus* seed will produce a paralytic syndrome, weak pulse, respiratory depression, convulsions and, in severe cases, death. Symptoms do not appear until several weeks after the seeds are introduced into the diet. However, once symptoms begin to appear, paralysis comes on very quickly.

Lathyrus odoratus

Recommendation Instruct children never to eat this or any nonfood plant. Despite the known toxicity of this plant, its effects do not appear unless large quantities of seed are eaten over a period of time. Provided care is take to avoid regular consumption, this plant would appear suitable for display in households with children.

References Bailey and Bailey, 638; Kingsbury (1964), 326-331; Micromedix, Inc. 1989 *Poisindex* reference 2278061. See Bibliography for complete references.

Laurus nobilis

Common Name(s) Laurel, Sweet Bay
Family Lauraceae (Laurel)
Active Toxins See text
Toxic Plant Parts See text

Laurus nobilis is the Laurel of antiquity, from the leaves of which crowns were once woven for heroes. The plant has single woody stems when young, which branch as the plant ages. Leaves are leathery, lance-like with wavy edges and reach three to four inches long. Yellow-green flowers appear in the spring, and if female plants are pollinated, berry-like fruits follow. When crushed, the aromatic leaves of Sweet Bay yield an essential oil that has been used as a flavoring in cooking for centuries. Oil from the fruits is used externally by herbalists to ease sprains and bruises. When taken internally, it is reputed to cause vomiting. If eaten whole, the tough and leathery leaves may obstruct airways in small children. Several such cases have been reported. If ingested, however, the plant is probably innocuous.

Recommendation   Instruct children never to eat this or any nonfood plant. This plant is probably suitable for display in households with children, provided care is taken to keep young children from inhaling leaves.

References   Bailey and Bailey, 639; Micromedix, Inc. 1989 *Poisindex* reference 2688484. See Bibliography for complete references.

Liatris spicata

Common Name(s)   Liatris, Blazing Star, Gay-Feather
Family   Compositae (Composite)
Active Toxins   See text
Toxic Plant Parts   See text

Liatris is a popular outdoor plant used in the wild garden and border. *Liatris spicata* is often used by florists in cut flower arrangements for its lavender spikes of feathery flowers. Unlike most spike flowers, *Liatris* species flower from the top of the spike downward. Outdoors, *Liatris spicata* grows to about five feet tall. Its leaves are lance-shaped or linear and may reach 16 inches in length. Flower spikes come in shades of lavender and purple and may reach one to two feet or longer in length. Some species of *Liatris* contain volatile oils that have been used in perfumes and chewing and smoking preparations. There are no reports of toxic ingestion of *Liatris spicata*. However, information is scarce. It is therefore best to treat this plant with caution.

Recommendation   Instruct children never to eat this or any nonfood plant. As a precaution, display this plant out of the reach of small children.

References   Bailey and Bailey, 655; Micromedix, Inc. 1989 *Poisindex* reference 2336512. See Bibliography for complete references.

Ligustrum japonicum

Common Name(s)   Wax-Leaved Privet, Luster-Leaved Privet, Japanese Privet, Wax-Leaved Ligustrum
Family   Oleaceae (Olive)
Active Toxins   Glycosides and other irritants
Toxic Plant Parts   Entire plant

Long reserved for outdoor gardens in the South, Wax-Leaved Privet is now often seen as a houseplant. It can be used in dish gardens, or as a larger potted plant, or as a four to six foot floor plant. The plant is an evergreen shrub with waxy, glossy, leathery leaves that may reach three inches or more in length. These leaves

Ligustrum japonicum

are pointed and ovate. Poisoning has been reported in children who have ingested *Ligustrum vulgare,* called Common Privet, which is closely related to Wax-Leaved Privet. Ingestion can lead to nausea, vomiting and diarrhea, all of which may persist for several days. Fatalities have been reported in children, probably as a result of dehydration brought on by vomiting and diarrhea.

Recommendation Instruct children never to eat this or any nonfood plant. Display this plant out of the reach of small children.

References Bailey and Bailey, 657-658; Hardin and Arena, 124; Kingsbury (1964), 261-262; Lampe and McCann, 107-108. See Bibliography for complete references.

Lilium species and hybrids

Common Name(s) Lily, Tiger Lily
Family Liliaceae (Lily)
Active Toxins See text
Toxic Plant Parts Bulbs, possibly other parts

Lilium hybrid

About 90 species of *Lilium* exist in nature. However, for many years, Lilies were seldom cultivated because the culture of the natural species was so difficult. All of that changed with the work of Jan De Graaf, a Dutch-born hybridizer who introduced to the world a host of strong, glorious Lily hybrids based on a few of the original species. There are now hundreds of hybrids in cultivation created using his original techniques. In addition, a few of the old species, such as *Lilium tigrinum* (Tiger Lily), are still seen. In general, Lilies grow from a bulb and produce a tall, unbranched stem with many alternating leaves. Flowers are solitary, often large and take on a characteristic Lily form. Flowers are often spotted and are available in a vast range of colors (except blue). Little or no information exists on many of the hybrids now in cultivation. However, several of the original *Lilium* species have been found to contain alkaloids, especially in the bulbs, which can cause nausea, vomiting and diarrhea if ingested. Lily bulbs are also known to cause skin rashes on the hands and fingers of plant workers handling them. The affliction is known as "lily fingers."

Recommendation Instruct children never to eat this or any nonfood plant. Display this plant out of the reach of small children.

References Bailey and Bailey, 658-664; Lampe and McCann, 191, 194. See Bibliography for complete references.

Limonium sinuatum

Common Name(s)   Statice, Sea Lavender
Family   Plumbaginaceae (Plumbago or Leadwort)
Active Toxins   See text
Toxic Plant Parts   See text

Limonium sinuatum

Limonium sinuatum is extremely popular as a cut flower used by florists. Flowers are almost always sold without leaves. Flowers are spikes densely clustered with airy, small, delicate flowers. The outer part of the flower (called the calyx) is blue or lavender and the center ring of petals is white. These flowers are notable in that they retain both their form and their color when dry. Hence they are frequently sold as components in dried arrangements.   Little information is available about Statice. Some studies have reported the presence of possibly toxic glucosides in *Limonium sinuatum,* but there are no reports documenting the effects of ingestion. Caution is therefore warranted.

Recommendation   Instruct children never to eat this or any nonfood plant. As a precaution, display this plant out of the reach of small children.

References   Bailey and Bailey, 664-666; Micromedix, Inc. 1989 *Poisindex* references 3351379, 3351543; Ross and Bishay, 91-95.   See Bibliography for complete references.

Lithops species

Common Name(s)   Lithops, Living Stones, Stoneface, Flowering Stones, Mimicry Plant
Family   Aizoaceae (Carpetweed)
Active Toxins   See text
Toxic Plant Parts   See text

Lithops lesliei

The *Lithops* genus produces some of the most interesting and unusual specimens among houseplants. These are succulents native to South Africa that are very slow-growing and are tolerant of high temperatures. Two of the most common species are *Lithops lesliei* and *Lithops fulleri*. Both are remarkable in their resemblance to stones. Each plant is formed of two thick, semicircular fleshy leaves that are fused together with a crevice between them along the upper side.   These leaves are stemless and lie just on top of the soil. *Lithops lesliei* leaves are rosy grey to dark greenish grey, with rusty spots on top. *Lithops fulleri* leaves are dove-grey on the sides and rust brown to light brown on top, with lighter spots.   Both species produce flowers from between the leaves in the fall. The leaves shrivel after flowering, and two new leaves form. No evidence exists that these plants are toxic.

Recommendation   Instruct children never to eat this or any nonfood plant. This plant is probably suitable for display in households with children.
References   Bailey and Bailey, 671-672; Micromedix, Inc. 1989 *Poisindex* reference 2329418. See Bibliography for complete references.

Livistona chinensis

Common Name(s)   Chinese Fan Palm, Chinese Fountain Palm
Family   Palmae (Palm)
Active Toxins   See text
Toxic Plant Parts   See text

Livistona chinensis

Native to Asia, Indonesia and the South Pacific, this is a durable palm the leaves of which form huge semicircles resembling open fans.   The leaves are divided into deeply incised segments that are pointed at the tips. On young plants, the leaves may be one foot to 18 inches across. As the plant matures, the leaves increase in size. Thread-like fibers hang between the segments of each leaf. Thick one inch spines cover the lower half of each stalk.   The palm family as a whole has shown little toxicity and some palms have food uses, such as in the production of palm cooking oils. No evidence exists that this palm is toxic.
Recommendation   Instruct children never to eat this or any nonfood plant. Because of the potential for injury from the spines on this plant, it should be displayed out of the reach of small children.
References   Bailey and Bailey, 673-674. See Bibliography for complete references.

Maranta leuconeura

Common Name(s)   Prayer Plant, Ten Commandments, Rabbit's Tracks Plant, Massange's Arrowroot
Family   Marantaceae (Maranta or Arrowroot)
Active Toxins   See text
Toxic Plant Parts   Leaves

Maranta leuconeura

Maranta leuconeura, from Brazil, is an herbaceous evergreen plant. It has ovate leaves up to about five inches long. The plant generally grows to about eight inches in height. *Maranta leuconeura* is commonly available in two varieties. *Maranta leuconeura* 'Kerchoviana' has broad bright green leaves with rows of brownish to dark green blotches on either side of the leaf midrib. Because those blotches resemble animal tracks, this variety is sometimes called Rabbit's Tracks Plant. *Maranta leuconeura* var. *leuconeura,* sometimes called Massange's Arrowroot, has broad leaves with veins arranged in a striking fishbone pattern. Each leaf has parallel stripes of silver and pink from the midrib to the leaf margins. The leaf surface is feathered with silver along the main rib, shading into brown to blue-green at the edges. *Maranta leuconeura* has strong circadian cycles of daily movement. During the day, the leaves of this plant are flat. At night, however, they turn upward like praying hands, hence the name Prayer Plant. Many regional poison control center publications list Prayer Plant as non-toxic. Those references are apparently based on the relatively low incidence of serious symptoms reported in connection with ingestion of *Maranta leuconeura* and on its medicinal uses. However, when scientists studied the toxicity of this plant in the mid-1970s by administering large doses to rats, the rats died. Although it is extremely unlikely that children could consume as much as the rats were administered, the test results suggest the presence of an active toxin.

Recommendation Instruct children never to eat this or any nonfood plant. Because of the possible presence of an active toxin, Prayer Plant should be kept out of the reach of small children.

References Bailey and Bailey, 712-713; Der Marderosian and Roia, in Kinghorn, at 107, 119; Micromedix, Inc. 1989 *Poisindex* reference 2329434. See Bibliography for complete references.

Matthiola incana

Matthiola incana

Common Name(s) Stock
Family Cruciferae (Mustard)
Active Toxins See text
Toxic Plant Parts See text

Matthiola incana, known as Stock, is a biennial or perennial herbaceous plant native to Southern Europe. Stock is a popular outdoor garden plant that is also sometimes brought indoors. It is also grown commercially for use by florists in cut flower arrangements. The plant grows to about two and one half feet in height. It has oblong to lance-shaped leaves that reach to about four inches in length. Stock produces extremely fragrant flowers on three to four inch stalks. Its flowers may be single or double and range in color from white through red, blue and yellow. There are no reports of toxic ingestion of this plant, but information is scarce. Caution is therefore warranted.

Recommendation Instruct children never to eat this or any nonfood plant. As a precaution, display this plant out of the reach of small children.

References Bailey and Bailey, 718; Micromedix, Inc. 1989 *Poisindex* reference 36597734. See Bibliography for complete references.

Mimosa pudica

Common Name(s) Sensitive Plant, Touch-Me-Not, Action Plant, Humble Plant, Shame Plant, Live-and-Die Plant
Family Leguminosae (Pea or Pulse)
Active Toxins See text
Toxic Plant Parts See text

Mimosa pudica

Mimosa pudica has small, locust-like leaves arranged pinnately in pairs along the leaf petioles. The plant is not particularly attractive, but is kept indoors as a curiosity because of its sensitivity to touch. When the finely divided leaflets are touched, they immediately fold up, hence the common name "Sensitive Plant." Some poison control center publications treat this plant as nontoxic, a view that appears confirmed by the absence of any evidence of toxicity. However, as the plant ages, it will develop spines that can puncture or scratch the skin.

Recommendation Instruct children never to eat this or any nonfood plant. When young, this plant is probably suitable for display in households with children. As spines develop, they should either be nipped off or the plant should be moved out of the reach of very young children.

References Bailey and Bailey, 734; Micromedix, Inc. 1989 *Poisindex* reference 2330978. See Bibliography for complete references.

Monstera deliciosa

Common Name(s) Monstera, Ceriman, Swiss-Cheese Plant, Breadfruit Vine, Hurricane Plant, Mexican Breadfruit, Fruit-Salad Plant, Window Plant, Split-Leaf Philodendron, Cut-Leaf Philodendron
Family Araceae (Arum)
Active Toxins Raphides of Calcium Oxalate
Toxic Plant Parts Entire plant

Monstera deliciosa

Monstera deliciosa is a jungle vine from tropical regions of South and Central America. Its 8- to 12-inch roughly circular leaves are perforated and lobed in a variety of patterns, accounting for several of the plant's common names Swiss-Cheese Plant, Window Plant and Hurricane Plant. Young plants lack the perforations of adult plants and are sometimes confused with and sold as *Philodendron pertusum*. Older plants are sometimes called Cut-Leaf or Split-Leaf Philodendron. Like other members of the Araceae (Arum) family such as *Arum, Alocasia, Colocasia* and *Philodendron,* the leaves of plants in the *Monstera* genus contain calcium oxalate raphides. If eaten by a child, these plants can cause pain, swelling and intense irritation of the mouth, lips and throat. They can also irritate the digestive tract, causing abdominal pain, nausea, vomiting and diarrhea. Ingestion of a significant amount may lead to swelling of the tongue, back of the mouth and throat. Such swelling can cause dangerous obstruction of airways. However, because of the immediate discomfort caused by eating this plant, it is unlikely a child will consume enough to cause such a severe reaction.

Recommendation Instruct children never to eat this or any nonfood plant. Display this plant out of the reach of small children.

References Bailey and Bailey, 739-740; Der Marderosian and Roia, in Kinghorn, at 107, 119; Hardin and Arena, 48-51; Lampe and McCann, 119. See Bibliography for complete references.

Myrtus communis

Myrtus communis

Common Name(s) Myrtle, Dwarf Myrtle, German Myrtle, Polish Myrtle

Family Myrtaceae (Myrtle)

Active Toxins Tannin, volatile oils

Toxic Plant Parts Entire plant

Myrtus communis is a many-branched evergreen shrub that may reach three feet in height indoors. The most-frequently cultivated variety is *Myrtus communis* 'Microphylla.' Its one inch leaves are lance-shaped with a pointed tip. When crushed, they release aromatic oils with a characteristic Myrtle scent. The white or pinkish flowers are one inch wide and bloom through the summer. Myrtle has been cultivated for centuries in the Mediterranean and its oils used in perfumery and herbal medicine. There is reason to believe the plant is somewhat toxic. The seeds that follow flowering have a high tannin content and may therefore cause nausea and vomiting if eaten in quantity. There are also reports that the aromatic oils are toxic.

Recommendation Instruct children never to eat this or any nonfood plant. Display this plant out of reach of children.

References Bailey and Bailey, 752; Micromedix, Inc. 1989 *Poisindex* reference 3047572; Uehleke and Brinkschulte-Freitas, 335-342. See Bibliography for complete references.

Narcissus species

Common Name(s) Narcissus, Daffodil, Jonquil, Paperwhite

Family Amaryllidaceae (Amaryllis)

Active Toxins Lycorine and other alkaloids

Toxic Plant Parts Bulbs, possibly other plant parts

There are about 26 species of *Narcissus*. However the species of this genus hybridize readily in nature and have been the subjects of extensive hybridization by horticulturalists and commercial growers. Hundreds of hybrids and cultivars are sold commercially. Many hybrids are favored by florists for their striking flowers. In addition many *Narcissi* are well-suited for winter forcing of flowering and are therefore kept potted indoors. *Narcissi* are classified into 11 groupings by students of the genus. Hybrids in three of those groupings are especially common indoors. Small-cupped *Narcissi,* known as Paperwhites, are regularly sold for forcing early flowers indoors. Trumpet *Narcissi* include the bright yellow, cream-colored and mixed color trumpet-shaped Daffodil hybrids often used by florists. Jonquil *Narcissi* include hybrids with pale yellow trumpet-like flowers with somewhat shorter central tubes than those species called Daffodils. *Narcissus* bulbs contain the alkaloid lycorine, as well as other alkaloids. During World War II, Dutch farmers fed *Narcissus* bulbs to livestock due to a shortage of feed. This resulted in poisoning and death of livestock. Ingestion of bulbs by humans even in small amounts can cause nausea, persistent vomiting and occasionally diarrhea, which may lead to dangerous dehydration in young children. Nervous symptoms such as trembling and convulsions may also occur. If bulbs are eaten in quantity, death is possible. Because bulbs are sometimes kept in the refrigerator to facilitate forcing, children may mistake them for foodstuffs. *Narcissi* have also been shown to cause rashes where the skin has come in contact with the plant.

Recommendation Instruct children never to eat this or any nonfood plant. These plants and especially their bulbs should be displayed and stored out of the reach of small children.

References Bailey and Bailey, 754-756; Hardin and Arena, 48; Kingsbury (1964), 468; Lampe and McCann, 121, 192. See Bibliography for complete references.

Narcissus x *hybridum*
(Tazetta Paperwhite)

Narcissus x *hybridum*
('King Alfred' Daffodil)

Neoregelia species

Common Name(s) Neoregelia, Blushing Bromeliad, Painted Fingernail
Family Bromeliaceae (Bromeliad or Pineapple)
Active Toxins See text
Toxic Plant Parts See text

Neoregelias are generally erect Bromeliads and frequently have colorful foliage. Many bear their blossoms low, well within the rosettes formed by the leaves. The most common species in this genus is *Neoregelia carolinae*. This plant has hard, glossy leaves in bright,

Neoregelia carolinae
'Meyendorffii Flandria'

almost metallic, green, copper and red. The leaves are arranged in a flat rosette. Foliage, especially toward the center of the rosette, changes color when the plant is in flower. *Neoregelia carolinae* 'Tricolor' has leaves striped along their length with rose-tinted white and green. *Neoregelia carolinae* 'Meyendorffii' is sometimes called Blushing Bromeliad because as it flowers, the leaves, especially near the center of the rosette, blush red. One species, *Neoregelia spectabilis* is known as "Painted Fingernail" because it has green leaves tipped with bright red. The Bromeliad or Pineapple family as a whole is relatively innocuous and no evidence exists that *Neoregelia* species are toxic. Note that many Bromeliads have coarse or spiny leaves or bracts, which may pierce or scratch the skin.

Recommendation Instruct children never to eat this or any nonfood plant. Evaluate each Bromeliad plant for its potential to scratch or injure the skin. This may vary within a species or as a plant ages. Plants which do not pose undue risk of injury to children's skin are suitable for display in households with children.

References Bailey and Bailey, 761-762; Micromedix, Inc. 1989 *Poisindex* reference 2329450. See Bibliography for complete references.

Nephrolepis exaltata 'Bostoniensis'

Nephrolepis exaltata

Common Name(s) Boston Fern, Sword Fern
Family Polypodiaceae (Common Fern)
Active Toxins See text
Toxic Plant Parts See text

Nephrolepis exaltata has nearly a dozen variants, most of which are known as Boston Ferns or Sword Ferns. *Nephrolepis exaltata* grows from an upright thickened underground stem called a rhizome, the tip of which usually projects above the surface of the soil. Leaves are curving, pinnate and divided into feathery segments called pinnae, which are joined along a central axis. Spores appear on the undersides of the leaves. The variety known commonly as Boston Fern (*Nephrolepis exaltata* 'Bostoniensis') is among the most popular indoor ferns because of its tolerance of abuse. The 'Bostoniensis' variety is more graceful and drooping than *Nephrolepis exaltata* itself. Most often, these ferns are displayed in hanging baskets, out of the reach of children. Studies done with *Nephrolepis exaltata* 'Scottii' suggest that these ferns cause little or no reaction when ingested. These studies, coupled with experience with other members of the common fern family, provide good evidence that these ferns are relatively harmless.

Recommendation Instruct children never to eat this or any nonfood plant. *Nephrolepis exaltata* 'Bostoniensis' and closely related varieties are suitable for display in homes with children.

References Bailey and Bailey, 764; DiPalma, 254; Hardin and Arena, 41; Der Marderosian and Roia, in Kinghorn at 107, 119; Micromedix, Inc. 1989 *Poisindex* references 2318859, 2329468. See Bibliography for complete references.

Nerine sarniensis

Common Name(s) Nerine Lily, Guernsey Lily
Family Amaryllidaceae (Amaryllis)
Active Toxins Lycorine and possibly other alkaloids
Toxic Plant Parts Bulb, possibly other parts
Nerine Lilies are cultivated commercially for use as cut flowers and are sometimes grown in pots indoors. The plants grow from bulbs and may reach 18 inches in height. Flowers appear on an erect stalk and take a spare, lily-like form. Flowers are usually pink or red. Nerine bulbs and possibly other plant parts contain the alkaloid lycorine, as well as other alkaloids. Ingestion of bulbs by humans can cause nausea, persistent vomiting and occasionally diarrhea, which may lead to dangerous dehydration in young children. Nervous symptoms such as trembling and convulsions may also occur. If bulbs are eaten in quantity, death is possible.
Recommendation Instruct children never to eat this or any nonfood plant. Display this plant out of the reach of small children.
References Bailey and Bailey, 765; Micromedix, Inc. 1989 *Poisindex* reference 2462359. See Bibliography for complete references.

Nerium oleander

Common Name(s) Oleander
Family Apocynaceae (Dogbane)
Active Toxins Glycosides affecting the heart, similar to digitalis
Toxic Plant Parts The entire plant is highly toxic. Also toxic are nectar, smoke from burning, vase water and honey made from flowers.
Nerium oleander is an evergreen, many-branched shrub popular as an outdoor landscape plant. It is frequently kept indoors in tubs or brought indoors in winter to prevent freezing, and is also sometimes kept as a small houseplant. This plant has leathery, lance-shaped leaves that reach about 10 inches long outdoors and six inches long indoors. The flowers range from yellow, through rose-pink and red-purple to white, and consist of a tube that opens into five flattened lobes. Because of its

Nerium oleander

poisonous properties, Oleander was the murder weapon featured in the mystery novel *"A Is For Alibi"* by Sue Grafton. The plant contains cardiac glycosides, which can seriously or fatally disrupt heart function. Ingestion can cause pain in the mouth and throat, nausea, vomiting, diarrhea, dizziness, slowed pulse, heart rhythm disturbances, impaired or arrested respiration, unconsciousness and death. One leaf has been reported to be a fatal dose for an adult. Very serious poisonings have resulted from eating roasted meat skewered on branches. Children have been poisoned from merely chewing leaves and flowers. Poisoning is also possible from vase water in which Oleander stems have been kept.

Recommendation Oleander may be acceptable as a landscape plant if children are kept away from it. However, it should not be allowed inside households with small children because of its high toxicity. Even if the plant is displayed out of reach, one fallen leaf chewed by a child may prove dangerous.

References Bailey and Bailey, 765; Der Marderosian and Roia, in Kinghorn at 19-20, and references cited therein; Hardin and Arena, 129-131; Lampe and McCann, 121-123; Levy and Primack, 84-85; Radford et al., 540-544; Stephens, 83-84; Szabuniewicz et al., 12-21; Woodward, 31. See Bibliography for complete references.

Nicotiana species

Common Name(s) Dwarf Nicotiana, Flowering Tobacco
Family Solanaceae (Nightshade)
Active Toxins Nicotine or related alkaloids
Toxic Plant Parts Entire plant

Nicotiana alata

Nicotiana tabacum is the common tobacco plant, and is not usually cultivated indoors. However, smoking and chewing tobaccos derived from that species are kept indoors. In addition, several other species of *Nicotiana* are available in flower and plant shops for use as either bedding plants or houseplants. One such species is *Nicotiana alata,* called Dwarf Nicotiana or Flowering Tobacco. It grows to two or three feet tall indoors and has ovate or elliptic deep green leaves that may reach eight inches in length. *Nicotiana alata* produces red or rose-colored flowers. Any species of *Nicotiana,* including *Nicotiana tabacum,* should be kept away from children. Nicotine and related alkaloids present in *Nicotiana* are highly toxic. Nicotine is so potent that it is sometimes used as an insecticide. The scientific literature is full of reports of poisonings, especially from *Nicotiana tabacum.* Accounts include: the death of a child from blowing soap bubbles through a tobacco pipe; a variety of deaths from, for instance, the accidental swallowing of snuff, and from the use of tobacco brews as enemas; the case of a smuggler who hid among tobacco leaves, perspired enough to activate the nicotine and thereby absorbed a lethal dose through the skin; and the death reported in the American Association of Poison Control Centers 1988 annual report which involved a young man who consumed a small quantity of concentrated nicotine alkaloids and died almost immediately. Ingestion of any *Nicotiana* species may result in nausea, sweating, vision disturbances, vomiting, dizziness, vascular collapse, failure of respiration and convulsions, and possibly death.

Recommendation Instruct children never to eat this or any nonfood plant. All *Nicotiana* species and all tobacco products should be kept far out of the reach of young children.

References Bailey and Bailey, 766; Gehlbach et al., 478-480; Hardin and Arena, 140; Keeler, in Kinghorn, 66-67; Lampe and McCann, 123-124; Manoguerra and Freeman, 861-864; Oberst and McIntyre, 338-340. See Bibliography for complete references.

Nidularium species

Common Name(s) Nidularium, Blushing Cup, Blushing Bromeliad

Family Bromeliaceae (Bromelia or Pineapple)

Active Toxins See text

Toxic Plant Parts See text

Nidularium billbergioides

Plants in the *Nidularium* genus are epiphytic—that is, they can grow upon other woody plants. Among the most common species are *Nidularium billbergioides* and *Nidularium fulgens*. Both species have shiny, strap-like leaves arranged in a rosette. When the plants are about to flower, these leaves turn rosy near their base. *Nidularium billbergioides* usually has eight leaves, more or less, which reach up to one foot in length. These have minute spines along their margins. The bracts of this species grow out about nine inches from the base of the plant and are generally yellow to pink. *Nidularium fulgens* (sometimes called Blushing Cup or Blushing Bromeliad) has pale green leaves with darker green patches. These may reach one foot in length and are up to two inches wide. They, also have spiny margins. The central "cup" of leaves on this plant turns brilliant red just before the plant is about to flower, hence the common names. This plant likewise develops scarlet bracts. The Bromeliad or Pineapple family as a whole is relatively innocuous. As a result, many poison control centers treat the entire family as non-toxic. No evidence exists that *Nidularium* species are toxic. These Bromeliads have coarse or spiny leaves and bracts, however, which may pierce or scratch the skin.

Recommendation Instruct children never to eat this or any nonfood plant. These plants are probably suitable for display in households with children, provided care is taken to prevent injury from coarse bracts and spines.
References Bailey and Bailey, 766-767. See Bibliography for complete references.

Olea europaea

Olea europaea

Common Name(s) Olive
Family Oleaceae (Olive)
Active Toxins Allergens
Toxic Plant Parts Oil, bark, wood, pollen
Olea europaea, the common olive tree, has been cultivated for millennia for its oil and fruit. It is also grown both indoors and out for the ornamental properties of its foliage. As a pot plant, Olive can reach six feet or more. Its leathery leaves are two to three inches long and elliptic to lance-shaped. Leaves are dark green above and silvery green below. The plant occasionally produces small, fragrant white flowers, but generally does not bear fruit indoors. Olive oil, wood and pollen contain oleic acid and other allergens that may cause skin rashes or other allergic symptoms in sensitized individuals. The oil has also caused rashes and irritation of the skin and eyes on contact. However, oil will probably not be produced indoors. There are no reports that the plant is otherwise harmful.
Recommendation Instruct children never to eat this or any nonfood plant. This plant is probably suitable for display in households with children.
References Bailey and Bailey, 781; Micromedix, Inc. 1989 *Poisindex* reference 3598401. See Bibliography for complete references.

Ornithogalum species

Common Name(s) Star-of-Bethlehem, Wonderflower, African Wonderflower, Chincherinchee, Nap-at-Noon, Summer Snowflake, Dove's Dung
Family Liliaceae (Lily)
Active Toxins Cardiac glycosides
Toxic Plant Parts Entire plant, but especially bulb
Two species of *Ornithogalum* are commonly kept

indoors. Both are sometimes called Star-of-Bethlehem. *Ornithogalum thyrsoides* (also called Wonderflower, African Wonderflower and Chincherinchee) is commonly cultivated for use by florists as a cut flower. It reaches two feet in height and has long, narrow lance-shaped leaves that may reach one foot in length and two inches in width. Its flowers are cream-colored or white, are three fourths inch across and are carried in clusters on long stalks. *Ornithogalum umbellatum* (also called Nap-at-Noon, Summer Snowflake and Dove's Dung) is smaller, reaching perhaps one foot in height. Its leaves are up to one foot long, but are only one half inch in width. They are bisected by a broad, white mid-vein. Flowers are white with green and somewhat larger than those for *Ornithogalum thyrsoides,* reaching perhaps one inch across. Both plants grow from onion-like bulbs. These bulbs, but also other parts of this plant, contain highly toxic glycosides, which affect the heart. Ingestion can cause irritation of the mouth and throat, nausea, vomiting, abdominal pain and diarrhea. Symptoms can also include heart malfunction, slowing and rhythm disturbances. Fatalities have resulted from ingestion of this plant.

Ornithogalum umbellatum

Recommendation Instruct children never to eat this or any nonfood plant. Display this plant out of the reach of small children.

References Bailey and Bailey, 800-801; Kingsbury (1964), 22, 456-457; Lampe and McCann, 125-126; Levy and Primack, 46. See Bibliography for complete references.

Osmanthus species

Common Name(s) Osmanthus, Fragrant Olive, Tea Olive, Sweet Olive, Holly Olive, Chinese Holly, False Holly

Family Oleaceae (Olive)

Active Toxins See text

Toxic Plant Parts See text

The *Osmanthus* genus, which is native mostly to Asia, has 30 to 40 species of evergreen shrubs. Two *Osmanthus* species are sometimes kept indoors as potted plants, *Osmanthus fragrans* (called Fragrant Olive, Tea Olive or Sweet Olive) and *Osmanthus heterophyllus* (called Holly Olive, Chinese Holly or False Holly). *Osmanthus fragrans* has a spherical, compact growth habit and reaches five feet or so indoors. Its 3- to 4-inch leaves are ovate, leathery, glossy and light green. It produces small, highly-scented flowers in spring and again in autumn. These flowers are used in China to add

Osmanthus fragrans

scent to tea and are also used in perfumery. *Osmanthus heterophyllus* reaches three to four feet indoors and has leaves strikingly similar to Holly. These leaves are glossy, leathery green and about three inches in length. These have sharp spines sparsely around the margins. This species produces small white flowers only once a year, in the autumn. Many cultivars of this species are available, most of them producing variegated leaves. Information on *Osmanthus* species is scarce, but there are no reports of adverse reactions on ingestion of these plants. Still, caution is warranted.

Recommendation Instruct children never to eat this or any nonfood plant. As a precaution, display this plant out of the reach of small children.

References Bailey and Bailey, 802-803; Micromedix, Inc. 1989 *Poisindex* reference 3613969. See Bibliography for complete references.

Oxalis species

Common Name(s) Oxalis, Shamrock, Regnell's Oxalis, Bowie Oxalis, Good Luck Plant
Family Oxalidaceae (Wood Sorrel)
Active Toxins Oxalic Acid
Toxic Plant Parts Probably entire plant

The Wood Sorrel family contains over 900 species in about 10 genera. More than 800 of those species fall in the *Oxalis* genus. A number of *Oxalis* species are well-suited for indoor use. Among the most common are *Oxalis regnellii,* called Shamrock or Regnell's Oxalis, *Oxalis bowiei,* called Bowie Oxalis, and *Oxalis deppei,* called Good Luck Plant. *Oxalis regnellii* is typical of the members of the genus grown indoors in that it grows from a thickened stem called a rhizome and produces clover-like trifoliate leaves. *Oxalis regnellii* grows to about eight inches tall. Three leaves grow at the end of a thin stem and several such stems may grow from the same rhizome. These leaves are triangular, dark green above and reddish purple below. The plant produces small, white star-shaped flowers almost year round. At night, both leaves and flowers fold up. While some species of *Oxalis* have been cultivated for food, many contain a sufficient quantity of oxalic acid to be of concern. Unlike calcium oxalate, oxalic acid is water soluble and presents a risk of systemic poisoning if enough is ingested. Some *Oxalis* species have caused poisonings in livestock, but there are no reported human poisonings. Where a large quantity of oxalic acid is present in an ingested plant, symptoms might include nausea and vomiting, kidney inflammation, loss of kidney function and, in severe poisonings, death from kidney failure. The absence of reliable information and

Oxalis regnellii

the potential for harm if large amounts of oxalic acid are present warrant caution.

Recommendation   Instruct children never to eat this or any nonfood plant. These plants should be displayed out of the reach of small children.

References   Bailey and Bailey, 805-806; Kingsbury (1964), 33-36, 200-201; Micromedix, Inc. 1989 *Poisindex* reference 3070565. See Bibliography for complete references.

Paeonia lactiflora

Common Name(s)   Peony
Family   Paeoniaceae (Peony)
Active Toxins   See text
Toxic Plant Parts   Roots, possibly other plant parts

Peonies are among the most popular of flowering plants. Some of the cultivars now in use have been cultivated continuously for centuries. Peonies are popular landscape plants, but they are also cultivated commercially for use by florists and are sometimes potted and forced into bloom indoors. The most common Peony for floral use is *Paeonia lactiflora*. This species has also given rise to hundreds of cultivars. It grows from a horizontal, thickened underground stem called a rhizome and may reach three feet in height. Its leaves are primarily lance-shaped to elliptical and may sometimes be lobed. Flowers are generally at least double and may reach four inches across. These flowers are very highly scented and may be white, pink, red or shades in between. The roots of *Paeonia lactiflora* and other Peony species have been used in Chinese herbal medicine for centuries. Their active constituents are the subject of considerable study. There are reports that ingestion of Peony roots has caused paralysis. Dutch floral workers have also been reported to get skin rashes from handling Peonies. Caution is warranted.

Paeonia lactiflora

Recommendation   Instruct children never to eat this or any nonfood plant. As a precaution, display this plant out of the reach of small children.

References   Bailey and Bailey, 810-811; Bruynzeel, 152-153; Micromedix, Inc. 1989 *Poisindex* references 3273929, 2295320. See Bibliography for complete references.

Pandanus veitchii

Common Name(s)   Screw Pine
Family   Pandanaceae (Screw Pine)
Active Toxins   See text
Toxic Plant Parts   See text

Pandanus veitchii

Pandanus is a diverse genus that includes more than 650 species. Among those species are the Breadfruit of Malaysia and the Philippines *(Pandanus odoratissimus)* and many species the leaves of which are used for mats, thatched roofs and the like. One species, *Pandanus veitchii,* is popular with florists and as an indoor pot plant. It is an evergreen with a woody stem terminating in a spray of sword-shaped, stalkless leaves about three feet in length. The leaves are green with lengthwise white striping and sharply spiny edges. Mature plants develop thick aerial roots. No evidence exists that this plant is toxic. However, there is some risk that spines may scratch or pierce the skin.

Recommendation Instruct children never to eat this or any nonfood plant. This plant is probably suitable for display in households with children, provided care is taken to prevent injury to the skin from leaf edges.

References Bailey and Bailey, 815-816; see Micromedix, Inc. 1989 *Poisindex* reference 2329492. See Bibliography for complete references.

Passiflora species

Common Name(s) Passionflower, Blue Passionflower, Red Passion-flower, Red Granadilla

Family Passifloraceae (Passionflower)

Active Toxins Alkaloids, cyanogenic compounds

Toxic Plant Parts Entire plant

The *Passiflora* genus has about 400 species of climbing vines. Many are grown as ornamentals. Several species, however, are important agricultural and commercial crops. These yield flavorings, perfume ingredients and fruits known as Passionfruits. Several *Passiflora* species are regularly grown indoors. Among the most popular are *Passiflora caerulea* (Blue Passionflower), the hybrid *Passiflora x alatocaerulea,* and *Passiflora coccinea* (Red Passionflower or Red Granadilla). All of these produce large flowers up to four inches across in colors from white to pink to blue and purple. Flowers generally consist of five sepals and five petals within which is a corona of filaments. Vines are thin with clinging tendrils and leaves are generally dark green and glossy. While some species of *Passiflora* are food plants, there are well-documented reports and empirical test results showing that some species contain toxic alkaloids and cyanogenic compounds. Reports of human ingestion of these species are sparse, but caution is warranted.

Recommendation Instruct children never to eat this or any nonfood plant. As a precaution, display these plants out of the reach of small children.

References   Bailey and Bailey, 825-826; Fischer et al.,
42-45; Oga et al., 303-306; Speroni and Minghetti,
488-491. See Bibliography for complete references.

Pedilanthus tithymaloides

Common Name(s)   Devil's Backbone, Redbird Slip-
perflower, Redbird Cactus, Slipper Plant, Christmas
Candle, Fiddle Flower, Japanese Poinsettia, Ribbon
Cactus
Family   Euphorbiaceae (Euphorbia)
Active Toxins   Euphorbol, proteolytic enzymes
Toxic Plant Parts   Latex, possibly other plant parts
Pedilanthus tithymaloides is a succulent shrub native to
dry tropical regions. It can grow to six feet in height
outdoors, but typically is no more than half that height
indoors. Its leaves are ovate, may reach three or more
inches in length, and alternate in simple form up the
stem of the plant. Leaves generally have a thickened
midrib and may be tinged in red. Small bird-like red
flowers occasionally appear at the tips of the stems.
Several subspecies and cultivars are available, including
variegated cultivars. The latex (the milky liquid beneath
the skin) of this plant contains euphorbol and possibly
other terpenes, as well as proteolytic enzymes. The latex
is caustic, acrid and intensely irritating to eyes, mucous
tissue and open wounds. Ingestion can cause abdominal
pain, nausea and vomiting (which may be protracted).
Recommendation   Instruct children never to eat this
or any nonfood plant. Display this plant out of the reach
of small children.
References   Bailey and Bailey, 832; Dutta and Dhar,
223-224; Lampe and McCann, 128; Lim and Soepadmo,
412. See Bibliography for complete references.

Pedilanthus tithymaloides

Pelargonium hybrids

Common Name(s)   Geranium, Storksbill
Family   Geraniaceae (Geranium)
Active Toxins   See text
Toxic Plant Parts   See text
Pelargonium species are the ''Geraniums'' of florists and
nurserymen. These are the popular annual or perennial
house and bedding plants seen nearly worldwide. They
must be distinguished from plants of the *Geranium*
genus, which are annual or perennial landscape plants
called Cranesbill. There are about 280 *Pelargonium*
species, most native to South Africa. Innumerable
hybrids of these species exist. Generally, most cultivated
hybrids are derived from *Pelargonium x domesticum*,
Pelargonium x hortorum, *Pelargonium x peltatum*,
and from a diverse group of highly-scented *Pelargonium* species. Perhaps most common indoors are

Pelargonium x domesticum and *Pelargonium peltatum*. The former is a hybrid complex with a number of species in its parentage and many fancy-named cultivars. They are sub-shrubs 12 to 16 inches high with slender, many-branched stems that are woody at the base. Leaves are rough to the touch, round and have wavy or lobed fine-toothed margins. When crushed, the leaves emit a characteristic "Geranium" smell. Flowers grow in clusters of about 10 stalks and have five petals, two of which are larger and darker than the others. Flowers come in white, pink, red or purple.

Plants in the *Pelargonium peltatum* group have long, slender trailing stems that are quite delicate. Leaves vary by cultivar. Some are rounded, others are lobed, some are hairy and some are smooth. Flower stalks are about eight inches high and bear small 5-petaled flowers (occasionally flowers are doubles). Flowers bloom from spring to fall. Many poison control center publications report that "Geraniums" are non-toxic without specifying genus or species. Some *Pelargonium* species are used in African folk medicine and have been shown to be pharmacologically active. Other species are the source of perfume oils, tooth powders and ointments. There are no reports of toxic reactions on ingestion of the commonly cultivated species. However, there are occasional reports that *Pelargonium* species cause skin rashes in some individuals. Information is probably too sparse to justify declaring all *Pelargonium* species non-toxic. Caution is therefore warranted.

Recommendation Instruct children never to eat this or any nonfood plant. As a precaution, display this plant out of the reach of small children.

References Bailey and Bailey, 832-836; Micromedix, Inc. 1989 *Poisindex* reference 2340539. See Bibliography for complete references.

Pellaea rotundifolia

Common Name(s) Button Fern, Pellaea
Family Polypodiaceae (Common Fern)
Active Toxins See text
Toxic Plant Parts See text

In the wild, Pellaeas or Cliff-Brake ferns grow on rocks. *Pellaea rotundifolia* is one of the few species grown indoors. It has thin, dark stems that grow from an underground rootstock. From these stems, unusual fronds grow, consisting of a strong central filament to which small leathery, round leaves are attached. These leaves are about one half inch in diameter. The leaflets on sterile fronds are toothed; those on fertile fronds are rounded such that they conceal the spore cases. No evidence exists that this fern is toxic.

Pellaea rotundifolia

Recommendation Instruct children never to eat this or any nonfood plant. This fern is probably suitable for display in households with children.
References Bailey and Bailey, 836; Micromedix, Inc. 1989 *Poisindex* reference 2337510. See Bibliography for complete references.

Pellionia daveauana
Common Name(s) Trailing Watermelon Begonia
Family Urticaceae (Nettle)
Active Toxins See text
Toxic Plant Parts See text
Pellionia daveauana, from Vietnam and Malaysia, is a creeping or trailing herbaceous plant that is often kept in hanging baskets indoors or used as a planter ground cover. Its succulent stems may reach two feet in length. It has close-set pairs of bronze-green leaves edged in brownish purple and with a broad central stripe of pale green. Leaf undersides are pinkish. No evidence exists that this plant is toxic.
Recommendation Instruct children never to eat this or any nonfood plant. This plant is probably suitable for display in households with children.
References Bailey and Bailey, 836; Micromedix, Inc. 1989 *Poisindex* reference 2329525. See Bibliography for complete references.

Pellionia daveauana

Peperomia species
Common Name(s) Peperomia, Emerald Ripple Peperomia, Green Ripple Peperomia, Little Fantasy Peperomia, Watermelon Peperomia, Watermelon Begonia, Baby Rubber Plant, American Rubber Plant, Pepper-Face
Family Piperaceae (Pepper)
Active Toxins See text
Toxic Plant Parts See text
Peperomia is a variable genus of succulent plants. More than 1,000 species occur in nature and perhaps two dozen of those are regularly sold. Without question, the most popular *Peperomia* species is *Peperomia caperata,* known as Emerald Ripple Peperomia, Green Ripple Peperomia and Little Fantasy Peperomia. It is a small, bushy, herbaceous plant with fleshy, heart-shaped leaves that are one to one and one half inches across. These are carried on pink stalks and are bright green and wrinkled or convoluted. The plant grows to only about six inches tall and has spikes of white flowers that bloom from early summer to fall. Also popular are *Peperomia argyreia,* known as Watermelon Peperomia or Watermelon Begonia and *Peperomia obtusifolia,* known as Baby Rubber Plant, American Rubber Plant or

Peperomia caperata
'Emerald Ripple'

Peperomia argyreia

Pepper-Face. *Peperomia argyreia* grows to about 12 inches tall and has tufted leaves with watermelon-like markings. Leaves grow on red or pink stalks. The plant also may produce a white flower spike. *Peperomia obtusifolia* has smooth, fleshy, rounded leaves that are dark green with purple shading. These reach three or more inches long indoors. This plant grows to about 10 inches tall. Most poison control center publications treat Peperomia as nontoxic. At least with respect to *Peperomia obtusifolia,* this view has been confirmed in testing conducted with mice in the 1970s. While those studies of *Peperomia obtusifolia* suggested that alkaloids were present in the plant, they also showed that administering plant extract doses of up to 10% of body weight produced no mortality. Although *Peperomia* species are quite common, there are no reports of toxic ingestions, suggesting that all or most *Peperomia* are indeed harmless.

Recommendation   Instruct children never to eat this or any nonfood plant. These plants are probably suitable for display in households with children.

References   Bailey and Bailey, 843-845; Der Marderosian and Roia, in Kinghorn at 109, 120; Micromedix, Inc. 1989 *Poisindex* references 3734632, 3734640, 3734658, 3734682, 3734708. See Bibliography for complete references.

Philodendron species

Common Name(s)   Philodendron, Heart-Leaf Philodendron
Family   Araceae (Arum)
Active Toxins   Raphides of calcium oxalate
Toxic Plant Parts   Leaves

Philodendron bipinnatifidum

From the more than 200 species of *Philodendron* native to Central and South America, thousands of hybrids have been developed. Most *Philodendron* species are climbers with aerial roots and very decorative foliage. In many species of *Philodendron,* there are striking differences between juvenile leaves and those of adult plants. However, many *Philodendron* species never reach their adult stage in the conditions of the average home. Far more *Philodendron* species are available than can be discussed here. However, three species that are quite common and are representative of the diversity found in this genus are *Philodendron bipinnatifidum, Philodendron scandens* and the hybrid *Philodendron* 'Burgundy' *Philodendron bipinnatifidum* is a non-climbing species that may reach three to four feet in height indoors. The leaves grow on stalks up to two feet long. As the plant ages, a short stem develops from which leaf stalks grow.

Philodendron bipinnatifidum leaves are dark green and average about 18 inches in length. They are wide, arrow-shaped and very deeply incised—almost down to the central vein. The leaves of juvenile plants are heart-shaped and only slightly notched. Adult leaves develop after several years. *Philodendron bipinnatifidum* is botanically very close to *Philodendron selloum,* and the names of the two species are frequently interchanged. *Philodendron scandens,* called Heart-Leaf Philodendron, is perhaps the most common *Philodendron* species in indoor cultivation. It is a climber with thin stems that can become quite long, certainly five feet or more. Leaves are heart-shaped, pointed and deep, glossy green and may grow up to four inches long. Many plants sold as *Philodendron oxycardium* and *Philodendron cordatum* are actually *Philodendron scandens.* The 'Burgundy' *Philodendron* is a hybrid derived from many species. It is a slow-growing climber that can reach six feet tall or more indoors. The stem has aerial roots. Leaves are arrow-shaped and may reach up to one foot long indoors. Leaves are pink when young and then become green above and dark burgundy below as they age. Note that one plant frequently called the Cut-Leaved or Split-Leaved Philodendron is not a member of the *Philodendron* genus at all. Rather, it is *Monstera deliciosa.*

Philodendron scandens, the Heart-Leaf Philodendron, is probably eaten by children more than any other houseplant. In its 1988 annual report, the American Association of Poison Control Centers National Data Collection System reported that there were 6,252 exposures to *Philodendron* species during the reporting period, nearly twice the number of exposures to the second-ranked plant *(Dieffenbachia).* Most of these ingestions involved *Philodendron scandens.* Like other members of the Araceae (Arum) family such as *Arum, Alocasia* and *Colocasia,* the leaves of plants in the *Philodendron* genus contain calcium oxalate raphides. If eaten by a child, these plants can cause pain, swelling and intense irritation of the mouth, lips and throat. Calcium oxalate raphides can also irritate the digestive tract, causing abdominal pain, nausea, vomiting and diarrhea. Ingestion of a significant amount may lead to swelling of the tongue, back of the mouth and throat. Such swelling can cause dangerous obstruction of airways. However, because of the immediate discomfort caused by eating these plants, it is unlikely a child will consume enough to cause such a severe reaction.

Recommendation Instruct children never to eat this or any nonfood plant. All *Philodendron* species should be kept out of the reach of small children.

Philodendron scandens

References   Ayres and Ayres, 330-333; Bailey and Bailey, Dorsey, 329-330; Hardin and Arena, 48-51; Lampe and McCann, 130-131; Levy and Primack, 68-71; Litovitz, et al., 525; Plowman, 97-122; Woodward, 182. See Bibliography for complete references.

Phlox paniculata

Common Name(s)   Phlox
Family   Polemoniaceae (Phlox)
Active Toxins   See text
Toxic Plant Parts   See text

Phlox paniculata

The *Phlox* genus contains about 60 species and many hybrids, most cultivated as outdoor flower garden subjects. *Phlox paniculata,* and its hybrids, are cultivated commercially for use by florists as cut flowers. It has thin elliptic or lance-shaped leaves up to six inches long. Flowers are about one inch across and have five petals. Colors range from white through salmon and scarlet to lilac and purple. No evidence exists that this plant is toxic.

Recommendation   Instruct children never to eat this or any nonfood plant. This plant is probably suitable for display in households with children.

References   Bailey and Bailey, 861-862; Micromedix, Inc. 1989 *Poisindex* reference 2319063. See Bibliography for complete references.

Phoenix roebelenii

Common Name(s)   Pygmy Date Palm, Miniature Date Palm, Roebelin Palm
Family   Palmae (palm)
Active Toxins   See text
Toxic Plant Parts   See text

Phoenix roebelenii

Several species of *Phoenix* palms are cultivated indoors. Perhaps the most common and certainly the most elegant is *Phoenix roebelenii,* the Pygmy Date Palm. This palm has delicate, graceful arching fronds and can grow to four feet, with an even wider spread. *Phoenix loureiri* is sometimes confused with *Phoenix roebelenii.* Spines develop on the latter as it ages and have caused nasty injuries in nursery workers handling such palms. The palm family as a whole has shown little toxicity and some palms have food uses, such as in the production of palm cooking oils. No evidence exists that this palm is toxic.

Recommendation   Instruct children never to eat this or any nonfood plant. This plant is probably suitable for display in households with children. If spines develop, they should be nipped off or the plant should be moved out of reach.

References   Bailey and Bailey, 862-863; Mitchell and Rook, 505. See Bibliography for complete references.

Phoradendron serotinum

Common Name(s)   Mistletoe (American)
Family   Loranthaceae (Mistletoe)
Active Toxins   Phoratoxin, a toxic lectin
Toxic Plant Parts   Berries, leaves and stems

Phoradendron serotinum (also sometimes called *Phoradendron flavescens)* is the Mistletoe popular in North America during the winter holidays. Mistletoe has thick, leathery leaves and white translucent berries. In its natural habitat, Mistletoe is a parasite of deciduous trees in the southeastern United States. Traditionally, the leaves and berries were knocked out of high branches and brought inside for holiday display. Now the plants are cultivated commercially for use by florists in wreathes and other holiday decorations. If ingested, the leaves, stems and berries can cause gastric upset, nausea, vomiting and diarrhea. There has been at least one reported fatality, resulting when a tea brewed from Mistletoe berries was ingested. *Viscum album* is known as European Mistletoe and has been reported as poisonous.

Phoradendron serotinum

Recommendation   Instruct children never to eat this or any nonfood plant. Mistletoe should be kept out of the reach of small children. Care should be taken that leaves and berries not fall within reach of children.
References   Bailey and Bailey, 864; Hardin and Arena, 98-100; Kingsbury (1964), 383-385; Lampe and McCann, 131-132. See Bibliography for complete references.

Phyllostachys aurea

Common Name(s)   Bamboo, Yellow Bamboo
Family   Gramineae (Grass)
Active Toxins   See text
Toxic Plant Parts   See text

The *Phyllostachys* genus consists of about 30 species of tall, evergreen bamboo grasses that grow from thickened underground stems called rhizomes. *Phyllostachys aurea* and other species of the *Phyllostachys* genus are sometimes grown in greenhouses, atriums and, occasionally, indoors. *Phyllostachys aurea* grows to about 20 feet high outdoors and to a diameter of over one inch. Indoor dimensions are less, by perhaps half. The entire genus, and this species in particular, has edible shoots. Hence, this bamboo is likely harmless if ingested.

Phyllostachys aurea

Recommendation   Instruct children never to eat this or any nonfood plant. This plant is probably suitable for display in households with children.

References   Bailey and Bailey, 866-867. See Bibliography for complete references.

Pilea species

Pilea cadierei

Common Name(s)   Pilea, Aluminum Plant, Watermelon Pilea, Friendship Plant, Panamiga, Artillery Plant
Family   Urticacae (Nettle)
Active Toxins   See text
Toxic Plant Parts   See text

Pilea is a genus containing many popular houseplants. Among them are *Pilea cadierei, Pilea involucrata* and *Pilea microphylla. Pilea cadierei,* called Aluminum Plant and Watermelon Pilea, is one of the most common houseplants. It grows to about 10 inches tall. Its leaves are cut by three conspicuous sunken veins, giving the leaves a quilted look. The quilted portions appear to have been brushed by aluminum paint, hence the name Aluminum Plant. *Pilea involucrata,* called Friendship Plant or Panamiga, is an easy-to-grow six to eight inch plant with two- to three-inch hairy copper-colored leaves. These leaves generally have reddish or purple undersides. Often plants sold as *Pilea spruceana* are in fact *Pilea involucrata. Pilea microphylla,* called Artillery Plant, is so-named because its flowers forcefully eject their pollen. This plant is a succulent annual or short-lived perennial that has many-branched, fleshy stems covered with bright green leaves. These ovate leaves are tiny, reaching less than three eighths inch in diameter. Many poison control center publications treat at least *Pilea cadierei,* and sometimes other *Pilea* species as nontoxic. However, in studies done in the mid-1970s with laboratory rats, *Pilea cadierei* showed evidence of toxicity attributable to the presence of alkaloids. When administered high doses of plant extract, half the rats tested died. Those doses were approximately 10 per cent of body weight. To duplicate such a dose, a child would have to eat several complete plants—which is extremely unlikely. Human ingestions of *Pilea cadierei* have been reported, but there is no record of any serious illness or death resulting from such ingestions. There is less information on other *Pilea* species, but, in general, there are no reports of toxic effects resulting from ingestion. On balance, plants in this genus are probably harmless under normal circumstances. However, because there is some evidence of toxicity, caution is advised.

Pilea involucrata

Recommendation   Instruct children never to eat this or any nonfood plant. As a precaution, display plants of the *Pilea* genus out of the reach of children.

References Bailey and Bailey, 872-873; Dipalma, 254; Der Marderosian and Roia, in Kinghorn, at 107, 120; Micromedix, Inc. 1989 *Poisindex* references 3734583, 3734609, 3734624. See Bibliography for complete references.

Pittosporum tobira

Pittosporum tobira

Common Name(s) Pittosporum, Japanese Pittosporum, Australian Laurel, Mock Orange, House-Blooming Mock Orange
Family Pittosporaceae (Pittosporum)
Active Toxins See text
Toxic Plant Parts See text
Pittosporum tobira is an evergreen, winter-flowering shrub or small tree that is cultivated outdoors, grown as a houseplant, shaped into miniature bonsai trees and cut for use in floral arrangements. It is many-branched and has woody stems. Indoors, it rarely reaches more than five feet in height. It has glossy, leathery, oval or teardrop-shaped leaves and highly scented yellow flowers that bloom in early to mid-summer. No evidence exists that this plant is toxic.
Recommendation Instruct children never to eat this or any nonfood plant. This plant is probably suitable for display in households with children.
References Bailey and Bailey, 880-881; Lampe and McCann, 5; Micromedix, Inc. 1989 *Poisindex* reference 2331124. See Bibliography for complete references.

Platycerium bifurcatum

Platycerium bifurcatum

Common Name(s) Staghorn Fern, Elk's Horn Fern, Antelope Ears
Family Polypodiaceae (Common Fern)
Active Toxins See text
Toxic Plant Parts See text
There are about 17 species of *Platycerium*. The most common species for indoor use is *Platycerium bifurcatum* and its many cultivars. This is an epiphytic fern, meaning that in nature it grows on another plant without drawing nourishment. Usually Staghorn ferns are found in nature attached to tree bark. *Platycerium bifurcatum* has two types of fronds, sterile and fertile. One sterile frond enfolds the base of the plant. When it dries out, it is replaced by a new frond. Fertile fronds are slightly erect or drooping and up to three feet long. These are divided into narrow segments, giving the fronds an overall appearance not unlike a stag's horn. Spores develop at the tip of the lower side of the fertile fronds. There are no reports of toxic effects resulting from ingestion of this plant. This, coupled with experi-

ence with other members of the common fern family, suggests that these ferns are relatively harmless.

Recommendation   Instruct children never to eat this or any nonfood plant. This plant is probably suitable for display in households with children.

References   Bailey and Bailey, 883-884; Micromedix, Inc. 1989 *Poisindex* reference 3508509. See Bibliography for complete references.

Plectranthus coleoides

Plectranthus species

Common Name(s)   Swedish Ivy, Swedish Begonia, Prostrate Coleus, Spur Flower
Family   Labiatae (Mint)
Active Toxins   See text
Toxic Plant Parts   See text

The *Plectranthus* genus contains about 250 species of herbaceous plants and shrubs. Most common indoors is *Plectranthus australis.* From Australia, it is a semi-erect plant, with stems that may reach two to three feet in length. Leaves are fleshy and broadly ovate, reaching perhaps one to two inches in diameter. Leaves have scalloped edges and are generally bright green. This species flowers only occasionally indoors, producing small pale purple flowers. *Plectranthus coleoides,* from India, is also common indoors. It is a graceful trailing plant with fleshy, almost square herbaceous stems that also can reach up to three feet in length. Heart-shaped bright green leaves may reach three inches in length and are soft and hairy with toothed margins. The cultivar *Plectranthus coleoides* 'Marginatus' is more widely available than the underlying species. It has white borders around its bright green leaves. *Plectranthus coleoides* sometimes produces inconspicuous pale purple tubular flowers in summer. Many poison control center publications list Swedish Ivy as nontoxic and all available evidence appears to confirm this view.

Recommendation   Instruct children never to eat this or any nonfood plant. This plant is probably suitable for display in households with children.

References   Bailey and Bailey, 885; Lampe and McCann, 3; Micromedix, Inc. 1989 *Poisindex* reference 2318875. See Bibliography for complete references.

Pleomele reflexa (Dracaena reflexa)

Common Name(s)   Pleomele
Family   Agavaceae (Agave)
Active Toxins   See text
Toxic Plant Parts   See text

Pleomele reflexa is a name of no botanical standing. What is most often sold as *Pleomele reflexa* is actually called *Dracaena reflexa*. Nurseries, plantsmen and florists have ignored this fact, however, and this plant is almost always sold as *Pleomele reflexa*. Whatever it is called, the plant is extremely popular with interior plantscape designers because of its tolerance of low light and low humidity. It is a branched shrub, usually kept trimmed to under five feet in height, although in nature it can reach 30 feet. Its leaves are linear or lance-shaped, dark green and often "reflexed" (curved or bent backward). This is an extremely variable species, with many cultivars. Despite reported ingestions, no evidence exists that it is toxic.

Pleomele reflexa

Recommendation Instruct children never to eat this or any nonfood plant. This plant is probably suitable for display in households with children.

References Bailey and Bailey, 398; Micromedix, Inc. 1989 *Poisindex* references 2329591, 2331158. See Bibliography for complete references.

Podocarpus macrophyllus

Common Name(s) Southern Yew, Japanese Yew, Buddhist Pine
Family Podocarpaceae (Podocarpus)
Active Toxins See text
Toxic Plant Parts Entire plant

The *Podocarpus* genus contains about 75 species of coniferous trees and shrubs native to temperate zones and mountainous regions of the tropics, especially in the Orient. Most ornamental species are grown outdoors. *Podocarpus macrophyllus,* however, is often kept as an indoor plant. It is usually pruned to keep it a small tree under six feet in height, although if left unpruned it will grow much higher. Its upright stems bear many lateral branches with horizontal or drooping growth habit. These horizontal twigs are crowded and leafy. Leaves are three to four inches long and are only about three eighths inches in width. They have prominent central veins on both upper and lower surfaces and are sometimes wavy or folded near the tip. Generally, no flowers are produced indoors. If ingested, this plant may produce nausea, vomiting and diarrhea, sometimes persistent. More severe symptoms may result if fluid loss is not corrected. This plant, which is sometimes called a Yew, should not be confused with Yews of the *Taxus* genus, which are even more toxic.

Podocarpus macrophyllus

Recommendation Instruct children never to eat this or any nonfood plant. Display this plant out of the reach of small children.

References Bailey and Bailey, 890-891; Micromedix, Inc. 1989 *Poisindex* reference 2377202. See Bibliography for complete references.

Polianthes tuberosa

Polianthes tuberosa

Common Name(s) Tuberose
Family Agavaceae (Agave)
Active Toxins Lycorine, an alkaloid
Toxic Plant Parts Entire plant

Polianthes tuberosa is widely grown commercially, both for use as a cut flower by florists and as a source of perfume oils. It is a species unknown in the wild. *Polianthes tuberosa* grows from an elongated bulb-like base. It has very narrow leaves that may reach one and one half feet long. Flowers are waxy-white or pale pink, very fragrant and appear in pairs on an erect stem. The bulb and possibly other parts of this plant contain lycorine, an alkaloid. Deaths and severe poisonings have been reported in livestock eating this plant. Ingestion of bulbs or other plant parts by humans may cause nausea, persistent vomiting and occasionally diarrhea, which may lead to dangerous dehydration in young children. Nervous symptoms such as trembling and convulsions may also occur. If bulbs are eaten in quantity, death is possible.

Recommendation Instruct children never to eat this or any nonfood plant. Display this plant out of the reach of small children.

References Bailey and Bailey, 893; Micromedix, Inc. 1989 *Poisindex* reference 2462416. See Bibliography for complete references.

Polypodium aureum

Polypodium aureum

Common Name(s) Rabbit's-Foot Fern, Hare's-Foot Fern, Golden Polypodium
Family Polypodiaceae (Common Fern)
Active Toxins See text
Toxic Plant Parts See text

This fern grows from surface-creeping rootstocks and is native to tropical regions from Florida to Argentina. Its fronds have deeply cut, wavy edges and may reach up to two feet long indoors. They grow twice as long in a properly humid environment with proper care. Many cultivars of this species are available. Note that ferns in the genus *Davallia* are also called Rabbit's-foot Ferns. There are no reports of toxic effects resulting from ingestion of this plant. This, coupled with experience with other members of the common fern family, suggests that these ferns are relatively harmless.

Recommendation Instruct children never to eat this or any nonfood plant. This plant is probably suitable for display in households with children.

References Bailey and Bailey, 897-898. See Bibliography for complete references.

Polyscias species

Common Name(s) Aralia, Geranium-Leaf Aralia, Wild Coffee or Coffee Tree
Family Araliaceae (Aralia)
Active Toxins Saponins
Toxic Plant Parts Entire plant

The *Polyscias* genus consists of about 80 species of small shrubs and trees native to Polynesia and tropical Asia. Several species are grown indoors. Two of the most popular are *Polyscias balfouriana* and *Polyscias guilfoylei*. The former, called the Balfour Aralia, is an erect, much-branching shrub that is usually kept to three feet or less indoors. Stems are green and spotted with grey. Leaves are glossy, and boldly green. Leaf shape varies with age: young plants have nearly round leaves; older plants have deeply incised margins and multi-part leaves. Variegated varieties of this species are common. *Polyscias guilfoylei,* called Geranium-Leaf Aralia, Wild Coffee or Coffee Tree, also is usually kept under three feet indoors, has long pinnate leaves (reaching up to 16 inches in length), with three or more saw-toothed leaflets. The end leaflet is usually longer. Dark green leaves are usually white-edged. Some species of *Polyscias* (e.g. *Polyscias guilfoylei)* are reported to contain saponins. In substantial dosage, these can irritate the gastrointestinal tract, causing nausea, vomiting and perhaps diarrhea. Contact with these plants has also been reported to cause skin rashes.

Recommendation Instruct children never to eat this or any nonfood plant. Display these plants out of the reach of small children.

References Bailey and Bailey, 899; Micromedix, Inc. 1989 *Poisindex* reference 3289794. See Bibliography for complete references.

Polyscias balfouriana

Protea species

Common Name(s) Protea
Family Proteaceae (Protea)
Active Toxins See text
Toxic Plant Parts See text

About 100 species of *Protea* are native to South Africa and some tropical regions of Africa. Within the last 20 years or so, many species of *Protea* have become very popular subjects in modern flower arranging. Commercial cultivation of *Protea* is thus on the rise and the large, unusual and very striking flower heads of *Protea* are increasingly common in flower arrangements. Flower characteristics vary. Perhaps typical is *Protea grandiceps*. It has stalkless, elliptic, leathery leaves with reddish margins arranged around the stem, topped by a flower head that may reach six inches across. The flower head is rounded at the apex and covered with a peach-colored, white, purple or black beard. Little information is available about the toxicity of *Protea* species. Thus, although there are no reports of toxic ingestions of *Protea,* caution is appropriate.

Recommendation   Instruct children never to eat this or any nonfood plant. As a precaution, display this plant out of the reach of small children.

References   Bailey and Bailey, 916-917. See Bibliography for complete references.

Pteris cretica

Common Name(s)   Cretan Brake, Brake Fern, Table Fern, Dish Fern

Family   Polypodiaceae (Common Fern)

Active Toxins   See text

Toxic Plant Parts   See text

Pteris cretica

The *Pteris* genus is full of handsome, easily-cared-for plants that are known for their forking or cresting fronds. Their compact size makes them well-suited for table tops and shelves. Several species are available. Perhaps the most popular is *Pteris cretica.* It grows from a thickened underground stem called a rhizome into one of two types: sterile or fertile. Fronds of each are overall about 12 inches long and may get as wide as eight inches, but they are deeply divided into pinnae or leaflets. Fronds consist of two or more pairs of opposite, ribbon-like pinnae, each up to four inches long and one inch wide. Fertile fronds have spore-cases on the edges of their undersides. Many cultivars of this species are available. Little information is available about ferns of the *Pteris* genus, but as a whole the Common Fern family exhibits low toxicity. Care should be taken that the plants of the *Pteris* genus are not confused with those of the *Pteridium* genus and especially with *Pteridium aquilinum* (which was once called *Pteris aquilina*). That plant, which is called Bracken Fern and sometimes also Brake or Brake Fern, has been shown to be toxic to range animals and carcinogenic to animals and humans. However, it is not cultivated commercially and not generally kept as a houseplant.

Recommendation   Instruct children never to eat this or any nonfood plant. This plant is probably suitable for display in households with children.

References   Bailey and Bailey, 925; see Micromedix, Inc. 1989 *Poisindex* reference 2337510. See Bibliography for complete references.

Rhapis excelsa

Rhapis excelsa

Common Name(s) Lady Palm, Slender Lady Palm, Broad-leaved Lady Palm, Bamboo Palm, Fern Rhapis, Miniature Fan Palm
Family Palmae (Palm)
Active Toxins See text
Toxic Plant Parts See text
Rhapis excelsa is a small, bushy palm that can reach five or six feet in height indoors. It has dark-green, fan-like leaves that are cut very deeply into three to 10 separate segments, each with a blunt tip. These segments may be almost a foot in length and up to two inches wide and frequently curve or droop. *Rhapis excelsa* is sometimes also sold as *Rhapis flabelliformis.* The palm family as a whole has shown little toxicity and some palms have food uses, such as in the production of palm cooking oils. No evidence exists that this palm is toxic.
Recommendation Instruct children never to eat this or any nonfood plant. This plant is probably suitable for display in homes with children.
References Bailey and Bailey, 946-947; Micromedix, Inc. 1989 *Poisindex* reference 2331223. See Bibliography for complete references.

Rhododendron species

Rhododendron x *hybridum*
(Azalea)

Common Name(s) Azalea, Rhododendron
Family Ericaceae (Heath)
Active Toxins Grayanotoxins (andromedotoxin) and glycosides
Toxic Plant Parts Leaves, flowers, honey made from nectar
The *Rhododendron* genus comprises about 600 species and many hybrids. Azaleas were once classified in a separate *Azalea* genus, but botanical housekeepers decided that there was no scientific basis for the separate genus and so swept all Azaleas into the *Rhododendron* genus. Azaleas of North American origin are generally deciduous; those from Asia are evergreen. Most Rhododendrons are evergreen. Many Azalea cultivars and a few Rhododendrons are available from florists and nurseries as blooming houseplants. Most species in the *Rhododendron* genus have simple, shiny green leaves that are alternate or sometimes crowded together toward the ends of branches. Stems are woody or slightly woody. Flowers bloom in many colors and usually appear as terminal clusters. The poisonous characteristics of *Rhododendron* led the Delaware Indians to use it as a suicide potion. This fatal potency is attributable to grayanotoxins and a glycoside that act on the heart. Initial symptoms include a burning sensation in the mouth. This may be followed by nausea, vomiting, abdominal pain, diarrhea and a prickling sensation

in the skin. The victims may experience headache, weakness, vision disturbances, slowed heartbeat, very low blood pressure and, in severe poisonings, convulsions, coma and death. Rhododendrons and Azaleas have caused severe poisonings in children eating the leaves. Note that poisoning may also result from sucking flower nectar or eating honey made from *Rhododendron* nectar. In its 1988 annual report, the American Association of Poison Control Centers National Data Collection System reported that there were 955 exposures to *Rhododendron* species during the reporting period.

Recommendation   Instruct children never to eat this or any nonfood plant. Members of the *Rhododendron* genus should be kept out of the reach of small children. Parents should also see that no fallen leaves or flowers will be within reach. If that cannot be assured, the plant should not be kept inside.

References   Bailey and Bailey, 949-965; Hardin and Arena, 122-123; Lampe and McCann, 142-143; Leach, 215-237; Levy and Primack, 86-87; Litovitz, et al., 525; Woodward, 42. See Bibliography for complete references.

Rhoeo spathacea

Rhoeo spathacea

Common Name(s)   Moses-in-the-Cradle, Moses-in-the Bulrushes, Man-in-a-Boat, Two-Men-in-a-Boat, Three-Men-in-a-Boat, Boat-Lily, Oyster Plant, Purple-leaved Spiderwort, Moses-on-a-Raft

Family   Commelinaceae (Spiderwort)

Active Toxins   See text

Toxic Plant Parts   Leaves, possibly other plant parts

The *Rhoeo* genus has just one species *Rhoeo spathacea*. This plant, which is native to the West Indies, Guatemala and Mexico, is usually kept for its attractive foliage. Leaves are pointed, up to one foot long and three inches wide, and are dark green above and purple below. Most of the names of this plant stem from the small white flowers that appear in boat-shaped purple bracts that emerge at the plant's base. The plant is used medicinally in Cuba because of its astringent properties. It is said to stop the flow of blood in small cuts. In Mexico, the plant is used in cosmetics to heighten skin color by irritating the skin mildly. Reports of the effects of ingestion are scarce. Because of the plant's known irritant properties and the absence of other data, caution is warranted.

Recommendation   Instruct children never to eat this or any nonfood plant. Display this plant out of the reach of small children.

References   Bailey and Bailey, 966; Micromedix, Inc., 1989 *Poisindex* reference 2477952. See Bibliography for complete references.

Ricinus communis

Common Name(s) Castor Bean, Castor Oil Plant, Palma Christi
Family Euphorbiaceae (Spurge)
Active Toxins Ricin, a phytotoxin
Toxic Plant Parts Seeds, possibly leaves

Ricinus communis is a native of tropical Africa cultivated in several varieties for the oil found in its leaves and for its bold foliage. It is common outdoors, both as a specimen plant and, in some areas, as a weed. It is also occasionally kept as a houseplant. *Ricinus communis* is an annual that may reach 15 feet tall outdoors. Leaves are broad and lobed, with from five to 11 lobes, and may reach as much as three feet across outdoors. Flowers are without petals and have many stamens and branching filaments. Seeds, and possibly leaves, of the Castor Bean contain ricin, a potent toxin that inhibits protein synthesis in the intestine wall.

Ricinus communis

Some authorities estimate that as little as one milligram of ricin is sufficient to kill an adult, a fact which, if true, would make ricin one of the most lethal poisons known. Ricin was reportedly the weapon chosen by Bulgarian assassins some years ago, when a vocal BBC critic of the Bulgarian government was murdered. The poison was reportedly injected in pellet form, delivered when the victim was stuck with the tip of an umbrella.

Ricin appears to operate by causing an allergy-like reaction to proteins normally present in the body. The first symptoms may not appear until hours after ingestion. Burning sensations in the mouth and throat may appear, followed by nausea, vomiting, diarrhea, abdominal pain, thirst, intestinal dysfunction, liver dysfunction and death. Ricin is present in greatest concentration in the seeds of the castor bean. Seeds are contained in spiny, walnut-sized fruits at the top of the plant. As few as one seed may be sufficient to kill a child; from two to five seeds may kill an adult. The seeds are covered with a hard coat that prevents absorption of much ricin. Hence, most poisonings occur only where the seeds have been well chewed. The plant may be prevented from generating seeds if the flower tops or immature fruits are cut off before seed formation. Castor bean seeds are the source of castor oil. Because ricin is not soluble in the oil, and in any event is rendered ineffective by heating, oil that has been properly extracted and heated should not contain harmful quantities of active ricin.

Recommendation Instruct children never to eat this or any nonfood plant. Because ricin is so toxic, castor bean plants should not be kept in households with children. If the plant is outside near households with children, either in the wild or in cultivation, care should be taken to prevent the formation of seeds.

References Bailey and Bailey, 971; Balint, 77-102; Hardin and Arena, 119-121; Kopferschmidt, 239-242; Lampe and McCann, 144-145; Levy and Primack, 52-54; Stephens, 70; Woodward, 25-26, 52. See Bibliography for complete references.

Rivina humilis

Common Name(s) Rouge Plant, Blood Berry, Baby Pepper, Coral Berry (see also *Ardisia crenata* and *Aechmea fulgens* 'Discolor', also called Coral Berry)
Family Phytolaccaceae (Pokeweed)
Active Toxins Probably triterpenes
Toxic Plant Parts Leaves, roots, possibly berries

Rivina humilis, a relative of the common Pokeweed, is an erect plant with spreading branches and slender-stalked, pointed, oval leaves. It is known for clusters of orange or crimson berry-like fruits that follow white or pink blossoms. The berries are quite short-lived. Ingestion of this plant causes slight distress in the digestive tract, including some nausea, vomiting and diarrhea. Note that Ardisia crenata and *Aechmea fulgens* 'Discolor' are also called Coral Berry.

Recommendation Instruct children never to eat this or any nonfood plant. Display this plant out of the reach of small children.

References Bailey and Bailey, 971; Lampe and McCann, 145-146; Lampe and Fagerstrom, 27, 31-34. See Bibliography for complete references.

Rosa species

Rosa hybrid

Common Name(s) Rose
Family Rosaceae (Rose)
Active Toxins See text
Toxic Plant Parts See text

More than 100 species of *Rosa* exist in nature, but that is only the beginning. There are now more than 20,000 cultivars and hybrids and several hundred new ones are introduced each year. Most of these are prickly shrubs, which may sometimes have climbing or trailing habits. Most Rose species are grown in the yard or garden, but the Rose is also unquestionably the world's most popular cut flower. Some *Rosa* species, such as *Rosa chinensis* 'Minima', are also grown indoors as potted plants. Rose petals and Rose hips (the small, fleshy fruit of the Rose) are sometimes used in herbal teas and remedies and Rose hips are sometimes also sold as natural sources of Vitamin C. The petals of some Rose species yield a volatile oil used in perfumery. There have been reports that some Rose species, such as *Rosa odorata,* may cause skin rashes in some individuals. Otherwise the plant appears to have little or no toxic effect.

Recommendation Instruct children never to eat this or any nonfood plant. Many Rose species, of course, have thorns and hence can prick the skin. Roses otherwise are suitable for display in homes with children.

References Bailey and Bailey, 974-983; Micromedix, Inc. 1989 *Poisindex* reference 2462424. See Bibliography for complete references.

Rumohra adiantiformis

Rumohra adiantiformis

Common Name(s) Leatherleaf Fern, Leather Fern, Iron Fern
Family Polypodiaceae
Active Toxins See text
Toxic Plant Parts See text

Rumohra adiantiformis is the florists' Leatherleaf Fern, as distinguished from *Dryopteris marginalis,* the Leatherleaf Woodfern, which is not usually cultivated indoors. Since the 1970s, the florists' Leatherleaf has become the most common filler and background material for bouquets and floral arrangements. Once cut, it remains green and attractive for weeks. This plant grows to about three feet in height. Leaves are broadly triangular and leathery and are divided into a number of pinnae or leaflets. Those at the base of the leaf are triangular, while those further from the base become oblong. There have been no reported ingestions of Leatherleaf. Other members of the same family are generally considered harmless. The plant has been reported to cause occasional allergic skin rashes among floral workers, but spore allergies are suspected as the cause. *Rumohra adiantiformis* is also sometimes sold as *Polystichum adiantiforme* and *Polystichum capense.*

Recommendation Instruct children never to eat this or any nonfood plant. This plant is probably suitable for display in households with children.

References Bailey and Bailey, 988; Hausen and Schultz, 325-329. See Bibliography for complete references.

Ruscus aculeatus

Common Name(s) Ruscus, Butcher's Broom, Box Holly
Family Liliaceae (Lily)
Active Toxins See text
Toxic Plant Parts See text

Ruscus aculeatus is an evergreen shrub native to Mediterranean countries. It is grown outdoors in the southern United States and is also cultivated commercially for use by florists as cut greens in flower arrangements and, as components in dried, artificially colored winter decorations. *Ruscus aculeatus* has shiny, dark-green cladophylls (flattened stem segments that look like leaves). These are ovate, with pointed tips and may reach from one to two inches in length and average one half inch in width at the base. *Ruscus aculeatus* has been used medicinally by herbalists for years as a diuretic and anti-inflammatory agent. In the United States, powdered extracts of the plant are sold in natural food stores. Recently, *Ruscus aculeatus* has been discovered as the source of active vascular drugs. Reports of the effects of ingestion of the plant are scarce, but because potential cardiac or vascular effects are possible, caution is warranted.

Recommendation   Instruct children never to eat this or any nonfood plant. As a precaution, display this plant out of the reach of small children.

References   Bailey and Bailey, 989; Elsohly, 1623-1624, and articles cited therein. See Bibliography for complete references.

Saintpaulia ionantha

Saintpaulia ionantha

Common Name(s)   African Violet
Family   Gesneriaceae (Gesneriad)
Active Toxins   See text
Toxic Plant Parts   See text

Originally collected in Africa in the late 1800s, this plant is extremely popular for its long-lasting blooms. There are thousands of named African violets available, most being hybrids derived from *Saintpaulia ionantha*. These are small, herbaceous perennial plants that grow to no more than six inches or so in height. They have fleshy, heart-shaped, hairy leaves arranged in a rosette around the base of the plant. Flowering may occur at any time and flowers are available in a wide range of colors. Toxicity information is available on only a few *Saintpaulia* hybrids. Testing conducted in the 1970s on *Saintpaulia ionantha* cv. 'Ocean Waves' indicated that there may be alkaloids present in that cultivar. However, when the plant was administered to laboratory rats in quite high doses, there was no indication of toxicity. Many ingestions of African violets by children have been reported to poison control centers. For instance, in its 1988 annual report, the American Association of Poison Control Centers National Data Collection System reported that there were 1,252 exposures to *Saintpaulia* species during the reporting period, but no confirmed fatalities or serious illnesses have been associated with ingestion of this plant. Thus, there is little or no evidence that this plant is toxic. Patch testing performed using African Violets has shown only modest potential for causing allergic reactions.

Recommendation Instruct children never to eat this or any nonfood plant. African violets are probably suitable for display in households with small children.

References Bailey and Bailey, 994; Der Marderosian and Roia, in Kinghorn, at 121, and sources cited therein; Dipalma, 254; Lampe and McCann, 4; Mitchell and Rook, 316; Litovitz, et al., 525. See Bibliography for complete references.

Sansevieria species

Common Name(s) Mother-in-Law Tongue, Snake Plant
Family Agavaceae (Agave)
Active Toxins Saponins
Toxic Plant Parts Entire plant mildly toxic

A member of the Agave family, *Sansevieria* is one of the hardiest and hence most popular of indoor plants. *Sansevieria trifasciata* is probably the most common species. It has stiff, waxy, fleshy leaves that are sharply lance-shaped. These leaves grow from the tip and may reach three feet or more in length. Leaves are dark green and, especially in cultivars, are often mottled with lighter green or streaked with creamy yellow. This plant is sometimes reported as nontoxic, based probably on its use as a medicinal plant by herbalists in some parts of the world. It has been used as a remedy for hemorrhoids and intestinal parasites, for instance. Studies of *Sansevieria trifasciata* 'Laurentii' and *Sansevieria thyrsiflora* were conducted during the 1970s. In those studies, plant material was administered to rats and mice by various means. While the doses administered were high—ten per cent of body weight—the investigators found that significant numbers of the rats and mice died. Other investigators report finding saponins in *Sansevieria,* and it seems likely that in extremely high doses, these could cause the deaths reported in the studies. Most of the human ingestions of this plant that have been reported have not resulted in any symptoms. Thus, it appears likely that the plant is generally harmless in low doses. Ingestions of large amounts may cause nausea, vomiting and other distress in the digestive tract, probably as a result of saponins.

Recommendation Instruct children never to eat this or any nonfood plant. While it is unlikely a child would

Sansevieria trifasciata
'Laurentii'

eat quantities of *Sansevieria* equivalent to doses used in testing, test results must still be taken as some indication of toxicity. This plant therefore should be kept out of the reach of small children.

References Bailey and Bailey, 1002-1003; Der Marderosian and Roia, in Kinghorn, at 122, and sources cited therein; Micromedix, Inc. 1989 *Poisindex* reference 4016641. See Bibliography for complete references.

Sarracenia leucophylla

Common Name(s) Lace Trumpet, Pitcher Plant
Family Sarraceniaceae (Pitcher Plant)
Active Toxins See text
Toxic Plant Parts See text

Sarracenia leucophylla is an herbaceous, carnivorous perennial that grows naturally in the swamps of Georgia, Florida and Mississippi. It is also sometimes grown indoors as a curiosity and is cultivated commercially for use in cut flower arrangements. The principal attraction of this plant is its odd-shaped leaves, which form a pitcher-shaped or trumpet-shaped nearly erect tube. This tube is wavy-margined and white or light lavender with a network of darker purple veins. The leaf tube is capped with an upright lid or wing on one side. Each leaf, because of its unusual shape and its coloration, is often mistaken for a flower. In nature, insects fall into the tube, are trapped inside and are digested. No evidence exists that this plant is toxic, except to the small creatures who happen to fall in its pitcher.

Recommendation Instruct children never to eat this or any nonfood plant. This plant is probably suitable for display in households with children.

References Bailey and Bailey, 1006-1007; Micromedix, Inc. 1989 *Poisindex* reference 2329640. See Bibliography for complete references.

Sarracenia leucophylla

Scabiosa caucasica

Common Name(s) Scabiosa
Family Dipsacaceae (Teasel)
Active Toxins See text
Toxic Plant Parts See text

There are about 80 species of *Scabiosa,* most of them native to the Mediterranean region. *Scabiosa caucasica* is grown in flower gardens, but is also cultivated commercially for use by florists. It is a perennial herbaceous plant that reaches two feet in height. Flowers are carried on long, thick stems that may reach 18 inches in height. At the top of the stem is a flattened head about one to two inches across covered with dozens of small cup-shaped flowers, each with four or five petals. Flowers are generally light blue or pale lavender. No evidence exists that *Scabiosa caucasica* is toxic.

Recommendation Instruct children never to eat this or any nonfood plant. This plant is probably suitable for display in homes with children.

References Bailey and Bailey,1013-1015; Micromedix, Inc. 1989 *Poisindex* reference 2319120. See Bibliography for complete references.

Schlumbergera species

Common Name(s) Christmas Cactus, Thanksgiving Cactus
Family Cactaceae (Cactus)
Active Toxins See text
Toxic Plant Parts See text

Schlumbergera bridgesii is an epiphytic (meaning that it grows on other plants without feeding on them) cactus that is extremely popular as a potted plant. The stems of this plant arch outward to about one foot in length. Stems are formed of flattened, crab leg-like joints with a few prominent teeth. The flowers appear in early winter (sometimes around Christmas) and may be red, pink, yellow or white. *Schlumbergera truncata* is a close relative very similar in appearance and growth habit. *Schlumbergera truncata* is called Thanksgiving Cactus; its flowers bloom a few weeks before those of the Christmas Cactus. Many poison control center publications report that these plants are nontoxic and the absence of any evidence of toxicity appears to confirm this view.

Recommendation Instruct children never to eat this or any nonfood plant. These plants are probably suitable for display in households with children.

References Bailey and Bailey, 1018-1019; Micromedix, Inc. 1989 *Poisindex* reference 2329773. See Bibliography for complete references.

Schlumbergera bridgesii

Sedum morganianum

Common Name(s) Burro's Tail, Donkey's Tail, Sedum
Family Crassulaceae (Orpine)
Active Toxins See text
Toxic Plant Parts See text

Sedum morganianum is a fascinating plant. Its tear-shaped leaves overlap so closely that hanging stems of the plant appear to form thick braids up to 18 inches long. The effect is not unlike the tangled knots of a

Sedum morganianum

burro's tail, hence the name. The leaves are heavy and not firmly attached. They can be expected to come off in curious little hands or to fall to the floor if jarred. Most poison control centers report this plant to be nontoxic and in fact no evidence exists that the plant is toxic. Its leaves are tempting morsels, however, and parents may therefore want to treat it with caution.

Recommendation Instruct children never to eat this or any nonfood plant. This plant is probably suitable for display in households with children, but it is bound to attract attention if kept within reach.

References Bailey and Bailey, 1023-1030; Micromedix, Inc. 1989 *Poisindex* reference 2329666. See Bibliography for complete references.

Sempervivum tectorum

Common Name(s) Hen-and-Chickens, Common Houseleek, Roof Houseleek, Old-Man-and-Woman
Family Crassulaceae (Orpine)
Active Toxins See text
Toxic Plant Parts See text

Sempervivum tectorum

About 40 species of *Sempervivum* are found in nature, mainly in Europe and western Asia. The most widely cultivated species is *Sempervivum tectorum*. It has been grown for hundreds of years, both outdoors (in European countries it is even grown as a roof covering) and as a potted plant. This plant grows in rosettes of 50 to 60 leaves, with rosettes reaching one to three inches across. Leaves are green and often have purple tips. This plant propagates by growing new, smaller rosettes adjacent to the parent rosette, hence the common name Hen-and-Chickens. Many poison control center publications report that this plant is nontoxic. There are no reports of toxic effects resulting from ingestion. It seems likely this plant is relatively harmless.

Recommendation Instruct children never to eat this or any nonfood plant. This plant is probably suitable for display in households with children.

References Bailey and Bailey, 1032-1034; Micromedix, Inc. 1989 *Poisindex* reference 3353036. See Bibliography for complete references.

Senecio species

Common Name(s) Senecio, Parlor Ivy, Natal Ivy, Wax Vine
Family Compositae (Composite)
Active Toxins Possibly alkaloids
Toxic Plant Parts Entire plant

The *Senecio* genus is one of the largest genera of flowering plants, with from 2,000 to 3,000 species throughout the world. These species may differ greatly within the genus. Some are herbaceous plants with large leaves. Others are succulents sometimes mistaken for cacti. The popular *Senecio x hybridus* hybrids are herbaceous plants cultivated for their excellent flowers. They generally are crosses of *Senecio cruentus* and *Senecio heritieri,* but other crosses are found as well. *Senecio x hybridus* plants grow to a height of from 12 inches to 20 inches. They have daisy-like blooms that are red, blue, lilac, violet or white and that flower in late winter or early spring. Another popular *Senecio* species is *Senecio macroglossus.* Known as Parlor Ivy, Natal Ivy or Wax Vine, it is a slender evergreen climber with waxy, roughly triangular leaves that may reach two inches in width. *Senecio macroglossus* 'Variegatum' is a variegated cultivar with green and yellow markings. Several species in the *Senecio* genus are known to be highly toxic, causing abdominal pain, enlarged liver, liver dysfunction, darkly-stained urine, apathy, lethargy and possibly death. There are no reports of such reactions to *Senecio macroglossus* or *Senecio x hybridus.* However, information on these species is scarce. In light of the toxicity of other *Senecio* species, these plants should be treated with extreme caution.

Senecio macroglossus

Recommendation Instruct children never to eat this or any nonfood plant. Do not keep these plants in households with children, unless they can be displayed completely out of the reach of children.

References Bailey and Bailey, 1034-1038; Center for Disease Control, 257-259; Micromedix, Inc. 1989 *Poisindex* reference 2479677. See Bibliography for complete references.

Setcreasea pallida cv. 'Purple Heart'

Common Name(s) Purple Heart
Family Commelinaceae (Spiderwort)
Active Toxins See text
Toxic Plant Parts See text

The *Setcreasea* genus has only one species that is cultivated indoors, *Setcreasea pallida.* 'Purple Heart' is the cultivar most often sold. Often, however, it is sold under the name *Setcreasea purpurea.* This is a trailing herbaceous plant with deep purple stems and leaves. The leaves are oblong and lance-shaped and their stalkless base enfolds the stem of the plant. Leaves may reach six inches in length and are covered with fine

Setcreasea pallida

down. The plant produces small pink flowers in summer. There have been reports that the juice of *Setcreasea* species produces intense stinging and a rash when it comes in contact with skin. There are few reported ingestions of this plant on which to base a judgment, so caution is warranted.

Recommendation Instruct children never to eat this or any nonfood plant. Display this plant out of the reach of small children.

References Bailey and Bailey, 1040; Micromedix, Inc. 1989 *Poisindex* reference 2725260. See Bibliography for complete references.

Solanum pseudocapsicum

Solanum pseudocapsicum

Common Name(s) Jerusalem Cherry
Family Solanaceae (Nightshade)
Active Toxins Solanine, a glyco-alkaloid, and possibly other alkaloids
Toxic Plant Parts Fruit, possibly other parts

Solanum pseudocapsicum is an Old World shrub that is popular for its bright, cherry-like fruit. It is often sold by florists at full fruit around Christmas, and for that reason is often called the Jerusalem Cherry. It has pointed ovate leaves two to three inches long that are glossy above. Its most notable feature is its scarlet fruit, which is spherical and can reach an inch across. This fruit, and possibly other parts of the plant, contain solanine, a highly toxic glyco-alkaloid. In addition, all plant parts probably contain other toxic alkaloids and, possibly, saponins. Ingestion of *Solanum pseudocapsicum* can lead to a burning sensation in the mouth and throat, followed by gastric irritation, fever and diarrhea. In severe poisonings, symptoms may include altered pulse rate, dilation of the pupils, difficulty breathing, shock, coma, paralysis and, in rare cases, death. Children appear to be more susceptible to solanine poisoning than do adults. This plant should not be confused with plants of the *Capsicum* genus, the red peppers of which are similar to the fruits of *Solanum pseudocapsicum*.

Recommendation Instruct children never to eat this or any nonfood plant. Display this plant out of the reach of small children.

References Bailey and Bailey, 1054-1056; Hardin and Arena, 143-144; Lampe and McCann, 157-160; Levy and Primack, 66-67. See Bibliography for complete references.

Solanum tuberosum

Common Name(s)   Potato, White Potato
Family   Solanaceae (Nightshade)
Active Toxins   Solanine, a glyco-alkaloid, and other toxins
Toxic Plant Parts   Leaves, uncooked sprouts and sun-greened tuber skin

Solanum tuberosum is the common white potato found in groceries and kitchens everywhere. It is occasionally the subject of household science projects and hence may sometimes be grown indoors. It is not otherwise usually grown as a houseplant. The common potato is a member of the Nightshade family, notorious for the toxicity of some of its species. The leaves of many Nightshades are poisonous, so it is perhaps not surprising that potato leaves and stems are hazardous. However, even the potatoes stored away in the potato bin can prove dangerous. The sprouts or "eyes" of potatoes and the green spots on potato skin that result from exposure to sunlight, as well as potato stems and leaves, all contain solanine, the glyco-alkaloid found throughout the Night-shade family. Solanine has a more pronounced effect on children than on adults and has resulted in fatal poisonings. On ingestion, nausea, abdominal pain, vomiting and diarrhea may develop. Nervous system effects may also be present, including drowsiness, weakness, paralysis, coma, and, in severe poisonings, death.

Recommendation   Remove all potato eyes and cut away sun-greened skin. Keep children out of the potato bin.

References   Bailey and Bailey, 1054-1056; Hardin and Arena, 141-145; Kingsbury (1964), 287-289, 293-294; Lampe and McCann, 157-160. See Bibliography for complete references.

Spathiphyllum wallisii

Common Name(s)   Spathe Flower, Peace Lily, Cleve-land Peace Lily, Snowflower, Mauna Loa, White Sails, White Anthurium
Family   Araceae (Arum)
Active Toxins   Raphides of calcium oxalate
Toxic Plant Parts   Entire plant

Plants of the *Spathiphyllum* genus are everywhere in commercial interiors because of their tolerance for low light and humidity and their unusual whitish or light greenish flower-like spathes. Typical of the genus is *Spathiphyllum wallisii*. It is a bushy, perennial herba-ceous plant that grows from a thickened underground stem called a rhizome. It produces oblong, lance-shaped leathery leaves. These grow on six-inch stems and may

Spathiphyllum wallisii

themselves reach six inches or more in length. Flowers appear in spring and summer from the center of the plant. These flowers grow on stalks that reach above the leaves and consist of a fleshy spike surrounded by a concave spathe. This shield-like spathe emerges white and then shades into green as it ages. Like other members of the Araceae (Arum) family such as *Arum, Alocasia* and *Colocasia,* the leaves of plants in the *Spathiphyllum* genus contain calcium oxalate raphides. If eaten by a child, these plants can cause pain, swelling and intense irritation of the mouth, lips and throat. They can also irritate the digestive tract, causing abdominal pain, nausea, vomiting and diarrhea. If a significant amount of plant material is ingested, there is danger of obstruction of the airways due to swelling of the throat. However, because of the immediate discomfort caused by eating these plants, it is unlikely a child will consume enough to cause such a severe reaction. In its 1988 annual report, the American Association of Poison Control Centers National Data Collection System reported that there were 1,057 exposures to *Spathiphyllum* species during the reporting period.

Recommendation Instruct children never to eat this or any nonfood plant. *Spathiphyllum* species should be kept out of the reach of small children.

References Bailey and Bailey, 1062; Lampe and McCann, 161-162; Litovitz, et al., 525; Plowman, 97-122. See Bibliography for complete references.

Strelitzia reginae

Common Name(s) Bird-of-Paradise
Family Strelitziaceae (Strelitzia)
Active Toxins See text
Toxic Plant Parts See text

Strelitzia reginae is a popular cut flower used widely by florists in modern flower arrangements. It is also kept as a houseplant. The leaves of this plant are large, reaching perhaps 16 inches long indoors, leathery and shaped in a pointed oval. The leaves grow on sturdy stalks 12 to 30 inches in length. Overall, the plant may reach three feet in height indoors. The truly distinctive feature of this plant, however, is its bird-like flower. The plant flowers from the age of five or six years. Flowers grow on a long stalk, which may grow to 30 inches indoors. Initially, the plant produces a nearly horizontal beak-shaped bract. From this, bright orange flowers with violet tongues grow vertically. The effect is that of a brilliantly-colored, crested bird. Some sources, including some poison control centers, treat this plant as nontoxic. However, there are reliable reports that the plant may cause gastrointestinal upset if ingested. Nausea,

Strelitzia reginae

vomiting and diarrhea may result. This plant should not be confused with *Caesalpinia gilliesii* (also sometimes sold as *Poinciana gilliesii*), which is also called Bird-of-Paradise. *Caesalpinia gilliesii* is a shrub not normally kept indoors. It also may cause gastric upset if the seeds are ingested.

Recommendation   Instruct children never to eat this or any nonfood plant. Display this plant out of the reach of small children.

References   Bailey and Bailey, 196, 1078-1079; Hardin and Arena, 86; Lampe and McCann, 40-43; Micromedix, Inc. 1989 *Poisindex* reference 2331406. See Bibliography for complete references.

Synadenium grantii

Common Name(s)   African Milk Bush
Family   Euphorbiaceae (Euphorbia or Spurge)
Active Toxins   Complex terpines
Toxic Plant Parts   Latex

Synadenium grantii

Synadenium grantii, a member of the spurge family, is a succulent shrub native to Africa that can reach twelve feet in height. It was domesticated in Britain in the mid-1800s and has been kept as a houseplant since. Its popularity has increased of late. Like many other Spurges, the African Milk Bush has a caustic latex—the milky fluid beneath the plant's skin. In Africa, the latex has been used as a poison. When it comes in contact with skin, it can cause pain, swelling and a severe rash. It can also cause intense eye irritation. When ingested, African Milk Bush can likewise cause intense digestive tract irritation, leading to nausea, vomiting, diarrhea. Death is possible, principally through dehydration brought on by vomiting and diarrhea. Some scientists have suggested that the plant may not produce immediate discomfort or bad taste on being eaten. Therefore, there is risk that a child may eat a large quantity.

Recommendation   Instruct children never to eat this or any nonfood plant. Do not keep this plant in households with young children.

References   Bailey and Bailey, 1088; Micromedix, Inc. 1989 *Poisindex* reference 2522939; Spoerke, et al. 283-284, and sources cited therein. See Bibliography for complete references.

Syngonium podophyllum

Common Name(s)   Arrowhead Vine, White-veined Arrowhead Vine
Family   Araceae (Arum)
Active Toxins   Raphides of calcium oxalate
Toxic Plant Parts   Leaves, perhaps other parts

Syngonium podophyllum

Syngonium podophyllum and its many varieties are popular for their vining habit and their attractive arrowhead or shield-shaped leaves. These plants are also sometimes sold as *Nephthytis tryphylla,* a name of no botanical significance. *Syngonium podophyllum* is a climbing species with leaves that vary greatly between juvenile and adult stages. Juvenile leaves are distinctly arrow-shaped and undivided or only slightly divided. Adult leaves are ovate and divided into five to 11 sections. This plant rarely reaches full adulthood in a household environment. *Syngonium* has not been the subject of a great deal of study, but tests on rats and mice conducted during the 1970s showed significant mortality when this plant was administered in high doses. The toxic principle at work in *Syngonium* is not clear, but it is probably raphides of calcium oxalate. This substance is found in other members of the Arum family, such as *Philodendron.* This warrants treating the plant with caution, because ingestion of calcium oxalate raphides can cause pain, swelling and intense irritation of the mouth, lips and throat. It can also irritate the digestive tract, causing abdominal pain, nausea, vomiting and diarrhea. Ingestion of a significant amount may lead to swelling of the tongue, back of the mouth and throat. Such swelling can cause dangerous obstruction of airways. However, because of the immediate discomfort caused by ingesting calcium oxalate raphides, it is unlikely a child will consume enough to cause such a severe reaction.

Recommendation   Instruct children never to eat this or any nonfood plant. This plant should be kept out of the reach of small children.

References   Bailey and Bailey, 1089; Der Marderosian and Roia, in Kinghorn, 107, 122. See Bibliography for complete references.

Syringa vulgaris

Syringa vulgaris

Common Name(s)   Lilac
Family   Oleaceae (Olive)
Active Toxins   Glycosides
Toxic Plant Parts   Leaves, perhaps other plant parts
Syringa vulgaris is the common Lilac found in yards and gardens everywhere. It is not ordinarily kept as a houseplant, however, its flowers are regularly used by florists in cut flower arrangements. Oils extracted from the flowers are also used in perfumes and cosmetics. The leaves of *Syringa vulgaris* are simple, opposite, ovate and may reach up to five inches in length. The flowers, which are small, may be white, lilac, pink, red or purple and are arranged in dense branching clusters characteristic of this species. The flowers are also highly

fragrant. There have been no reports of toxic ingestions of this plant by humans. However, studies have been conducted using mice and rats and these show that extracts of the leaves may cause a profound drop in blood pressure and may, in high doses, cause death. The lethal dose that caused death in half of the subjects tested was 2% of body weight. Glycosides have been identified in *Syringa vulgaris* and these appear to be the cause of the toxic reactions in mice. These glycosides may be present in flowers as well as leaves.

Recommendation Instruct children never to eat this or any nonfood plant. Display this plant out of the reach of small children.

References Bailey and Bailey, 1090-1092; Balinet, 215-221; Micromedix, Inc. 1989 *Poisindex* reference 2336710. See Bibliography for complete references.

Taxus species

Common Name(s) Yew, English Yew, Canada Yew, Japanese Yew
Family Taxaceae (Yew)
Active Toxins Alkaloids
Toxic Plant Parts Entire plant, except the red cup-shaped aril on the berry.

Taxus cuspidata

This is the common Yew popular as an outdoor landscape plant. The most common species are *Taxus baccata* (English Yew), *Taxus brevifolia* (Western Yew), *Taxus canadensis* (Canada Yew) and *Taxus cuspidata* (Japanese Yew). These are densely-branched, evergreen shrubs with needle-like leaves arranged in a spiral on the branches. They produce seeds that in a fleshy, scarlet berry-like aril. *Taxus* species are not usually kept as houseplants, but they are sometimes brought indoors in wreaths and holiday arrangements. Yews contain potent taxine alkaloids that can cause severe poisonings. Symptoms include dizziness, dry mouth, abdominal cramping, nausea and vomiting. A rash may appear on the skin and the face may become pale and the lips turn a blue tint. Weakness, low blood pressure, slowed heartbeat, heart rhythm disturbances and coma can follow in severe poisonings. Yews can cause fatal poisoning, generally as the result of heart or respiration failure. Where much plant material has been ingested, symptoms may appear and the victim's condition worsen very quickly. Cattle grazing on Yew foliage have dropped dead virtually in their tracks. *Any* ingestion of any part of the Yew should be considered a medical emergency and should be treated immediately by a physician. In its 1988 annual report, the American Association of Poison Control Centers National Data Collection System reported that there were 1,388 exposures to *Taxus* species during the reporting period. This high number of ingestions may be due, at least in part, to the fact that children are attracted to the fruits of *Taxus* species.

Recommendation   Instruct children never to eat this or any nonfood plant. Do not keep these plants in households with children, unless they can be displayed far out of the reach of small children. Supervise children closely when they are near Yews outdoors.

References   Bailey and Bailey, 1098-1099; Hardin and Arena, 42-43; Kingsbury (1964), 121-123; Lampe and McCann, 167-168; Levy and Primack, 74-75; Litovitz, et al., 525; Miller, 425-437; Woodward, 105. See Bibliography for complete references.

Tillandsia cyanea

Tillandsia cyanea

Common Name(s)   Tillandsia
Family   Bromeliaceae (Bromelia or Pineapple)
Active Toxins   See text
Toxic Plant Parts   See text

The *Tillandsia* genus contains nearly 400 species, many of which are epiphytic (that is, they grow on other plants without deriving nourishment from them). Many *Tillandsia* species are grown indoors or in greenhouses. One of the most common of these is *Tillandsia cyanea*. It has thin, pointed, curving leaves growing in a rosette. These may reach 16 inches long and up to one inch across. They are a grayish green color, with reddish bands on the underside. A flowering stalk and a stiff flower head grow from the center of the rosette. The flower head contains a number of rose or pink overlapping bracts, between which grow single blue or violet flowers. No reports of toxic reaction on ingestion of this plant could be found. The Bromeliad or Pineapple family as a whole is relatively innocuous. As a result, many poison control centers treat the entire family as non-toxic and it seems likely this plant is harmless as well. Note that many Bromeliads have coarse or spiny leaves. These may pierce or scratch the skin.

Recommendation   Instruct children never to eat this or any nonfood plant. Evaluate each Bromeliad plant for its potential to scratch or injure the skin. This may vary within a species or as a plant ages. Plants which do not pose undue risk of injury to children's skin are suitable for display in households with children.

References   Bailey and Bailey, 1114-1116; see Micromedix, Inc. 1989 *Poisindex* reference 3353078. See Bibliography for complete references.

Tolmiea menziesii

Common Name(s) Piggyback Plant, Youth-on-Age, Thousand Mothers
Family Saxifragaceae (Saxifrage)
Active Toxins See text
Toxic Plant Parts See text

Tolmiea menziesii is a perennial evergreen herbaceous plant that grows from a thickened underground stem called a rhizome. It is often seen in rock gardens outdoors, but is also regularly kept as a houseplant. Its leaves are rounded, hairy, slightly lobed and have toothed margins. Leaves may reach four inches across and grow on stalks that may reach eight inches in length. The plant takes its common names from its unusual method of reproduction. New small plants form at the base of the leaves. These weigh the plant stems down so that they appear to droop toward the ground. Small greenish-purple flowers are produced in early summer. Many poison control center publications report that the this plant is nontoxic. In light of the absence of any evidence of toxicity, that view appears correct.

Recommendation Instruct children never to eat this or any nonfood plant. This plant is probably suitable for display in households with children.

References Bailey and Bailey, 1117; Micromedix, Inc. 1989 *Poisindex* reference 2318924. See Bibliography for complete references.

Tradescantia fluminensis

Common Name(s) Wandering Jew, Variegated Wandering Jew
Family Commelinaceae (Spiderwort)
Active Toxins See text
Toxic Plant Parts See text

Tradescantia fluminensis

Tradescantia fluminensis is closely related to *Zebrina pendula,* which is also called Wandering Jew. *Tradescantia* species are from Brazil, *Zebrina* species generally from Mexico. They are herbaceous plants with a trailing growth habit. Leaves are ovate to lance-shaped and two to three inches in length. They are green above and pinkish purple below. Flowers are white. Wandering Jews are frequently kept in hanging baskets because of their trailing habit. Most poison control centers treat *Tradescantia* species as nontoxic. There has been a reported case of skin rash resulting from contact with this plant, but it may have been an allergic reaction. While ingestions of Wandering Jew are reported from time to time, there is no record of a toxic reaction. The plant's reputation as being harmless is therefore probably deserved.

Recommendation   Instruct children never to eat this or any nonfood plant. This plant is probably suitable for display in households with children.

References   Bailey and Bailey, 1119-1120; Lampe and McCann, 5; Micromedix, Inc. 1989 *Poisindex* reference 2725278. See Bibliography for complete references.

Tulipa hybrid

Tulipa gesnerana

Common Name(s)   Tulip, Common Garden Tulip, Late Tulip
Family   Liliaceae (Lily)
Active Toxins   Tulipalin
Toxic Plant Parts   Bulbs

Tulipa gesnerana is one of about 150 species of Tulip. Within *Tulipa gesnerana,* there are many varieties. In addition, a large number of hybrid tulips exist. More than a dozen different hybrids are available to florists, with far more available to gardeners. Tulips take many different forms, but in general, they grow from bulbs and produce cup-like flowers on long stalks. Flowers come in a wide range of colors. Leaves are generally linear or lance-shaped. Tulip leaves and flowers are generally regarded as non-toxic. Bulbs, however, contain a substance called tulipalin that has been reported to cause skin rashes, especially among those handling the bulbs frequently. Among Dutch flower workers, there is an affliction known as "tulip fingers," that results from repeated handling of tulip bulbs. Because the affliction is caused by an allergen, only sensitized individuals are affected. Frequent exposure is probably a prerequisite. Once sensitized, further exposure can cause rashes, deep skin fissures, splitting fingernails and pain. Tulip bulb dust can also cause reactions if inhaled by a sensitized individual. Ingestion of bulbs in substantial quantity may also cause nausea and vomiting.

Recommendation   Instruct children never to eat this or any nonfood plant. Tulip bulbs, as with any flower bulbs, should be stored out of the reach of small children. Cut tulips are suitable for display in households with children.

References   Bailey and Bailey, 1132-1134; Lampe and McCann, 191, 194; Micromedix, Inc. 1989 *Poisindex* reference 2279431; Mitchell and Rook, 445-447; Stoner and Rasmussen, 8-9. See Bibliography for complete references.

Vriesea species

Common Name(s)   Vriesea, Bromeliad, Flaming Sword, Vase Plant
Family   Bromeliaceae (Bromeliad or Pineapple)
Active Toxins   See text
Toxic Plant Parts   See text

Vrieseas are compact, usually colorful Bromeliads known for their spectacular flower spikes. These plants are often called Vase Plants because their leaves are arranged in rosettes that cup water at their center. Perhaps the most common species is *Vriesea splendens* (Flaming Sword). That plant has stiff, sword-shaped leaves to 18 inches long growing in an open rosette. At the center of the rosette, as with many Bromeliads, a cup is formed by the leaves and this cup may hold water. The leaves are dark green with greenish purple or greenish red transverse stripes. Adult plants produce a flower stalk from the center of the plant. This may reach three feet in length and carries a yellow flower surrounded by many crimson bracts. The name "Flaming Sword" is frequently given to other Bromeliads with red or orange flower spikes. The Bromeliad or Pineapple family as a whole is relatively innocuous and no evidence exists that *Vriesea* species are toxic. Note that many Bromeliads have coarse or spiny leaves or bracts, which may pierce or scratch the skin.

Recommendation Instruct children never to eat this or any nonfood plant. Evaluate each Bromeliad plant for its potential to scratch or injure the skin. This may vary within a species or as a plant ages. Plants which do not pose undue risk of injury to children's skin are suitable for display in households with children.

References Bailey and Bailey, 1163-1164; Micro-medix, Inc. 1989 *Poisindex* reference 2329715. See Bibliography for complete references.

Xanthosoma lindenii

Common Name(s) Xanthosoma, Indian Kale, Spoon Flower
Family Araceae (Arum)
Active Toxins Raphides of Calcium Oxalate
Toxic Plant Parts Entire plant

Xanthosoma lindenii

Xanthosoma is the New World counterpart of *Coloca-sia* and *Alocasia*. Perhaps 40 species are found in nature. Of those several species are kept as houseplants. *Xanthosoma lindenii* is probably the most common and is typical. It grows from a tuber and reaches up to 18 inches in height indoors. Its leaves are white-veined and arrow- or shield-shaped. These may reach up to eight inches in length. Other *Xanthosoma* species are culti-vated in tropical and subtropical regions of the Americas for their tuberous root, known as the cocoyam, tanier and yautia. This root yields a starchy, taro-like staple food. Like other members of the Arum family, *Xantho-soma* species contain calcium oxalate raphides, but the quantity of these needle-like crystals varies greatly with species. In some of the species used for food, the content is acceptable. Likewise, in testing of *Xanthosoma hoffmannii* during the 1970s, rats fed an extract of the plant showed no reaction. However, no reports of human ingestion of the species used as houseplants are available. Some species may contain calcium oxalate raphides in substantial quantity. Prudence dictates treating any *Xanthosoma* not known to be edible as though it has significant potential to irritate the mouth, throat and digestive tract.

Recommendation   Instruct children never to eat this or any nonfood plant. Unless known to be edible, *Xanthosoma* species should be kept out of the reach of small children.

References   Bailey and Bailey, 1175; Cuebas de Escabi and Cedeno-Maldonado, 169-176; Der Marderosian and Roia, in Kinghorn, at 107, 122. See Bibliography for complete references.

Yucca aloifolia

Yucca species

Common Name(s)   Yucca, Spanish Bayonet, Dagger Plant, Spineless Yucca
Family   Agavaceae (Agave)
Active Toxins   See text
Toxic Plant Parts   See text

About 40 species of Yucca are found in nature, principally in arid regions of North and Central America. Two species are commonly kept indoors: *Yucca aloifolia* and *Yucca elephantipes. Yucca aloifolia,* called the Spanish Bayonet or Dagger Plant, varies greatly in shape according to variety and how it is cultivated. Leaves are usually long, stiff, sharply pointed and finely toothed along the margin. Indoors they may reach two feet in length. Young plants may be stemless, but the plant is also available growing from a cane-like stem cutting. *Yucca elephantipes,* called Spineless Yucca, likewise has tufts of long, stiff, sharply pointed leaves with finely-toothed margins. These may reach three feet in length and are slightly less stiff than the leaves of *Yucca aloifolia. Yucca elephantipes* is usually sold with leaves growing from a trunk cutting. These trunks are rough and woody. Neither species of Yucca will usually flower indoors. No evidence exists that these *Yucca* species are toxic if ingested. However, the sharp, stiff leaves of *Yucca aloifolia* do pose some risk of injury to the skin.

Recommendation   Instruct children never to eat this or any nonfood plant. These plants are probably suitable for display in households with children.

References   Bailey and Bailey, 1178-1179; Micromedix, Inc. 1989 *Poisindex* reference 2329723. See Bibliography for complete references.

Zantedeschia aethiopica

Common Name(s)   Calla Lily, Arum Lily, White Calla, Pig Lily, Florist's Calla, Garden Calla, Trumpet Lily, Common Calla
Family   Araceae (Arum)
Active Toxins   Calcium oxalate raphides, possibly other toxins
Toxic Plant Parts   Leaves, possibly other parts.
The Calla Lily is grown both as a potted plant and commercially for use as a cut flower. *Zantedeschia aethiopica* is a stemless species that grows from a thickened underground stem called a rhizome. Leaves are arrow or shield shaped and may reach 20 inches in length and eight inches in width. Leaves are very dark green and may have stalks up to three feet long. The flowers are unusual and very showy. They consist of a golden fleshy flower spike, wrapped by a white spathe. Flowering usually takes place in late winter or early spring. Like other members of the Araceae (Arum) family such as *Arum, Alocasia,* and *Colocasia,* the leaves and possibly other parts of the Calla Lily contain calcium oxalate raphides. If eaten by a child, these plants can cause pain, swelling and intense irritation of the mouth, lips and throat. They can also irritate the digestive tract, causing abdominal pain, nausea, vomiting and diarrhea. Ingestion of a significant amount may lead to swelling of the tongue, back of the mouth and throat. Such swelling can cause dangerous obstruction of airways. However, because of the immediate discomfort caused by eating this plant, it is unlikely a child will consume enough to cause such a severe reaction. Contact with the plant may also irritate the skin.
Recommendation   Instruct children never to eat this or any nonfood plant. Calla Lilies should be displayed out of the reach of children.
References   Bailey and Bailey, 1181; Lampe and McCann, 178-179; Levy and Primack, 68; Plowman, 97-122. See Bibliography for complete references.

Zebrina pendula

Common Name(s)   Wandering Jew (Red and Green)
Family   Commelinaceae (Spiderwort)
Active Toxins   See text
Toxic Plant Parts   See text
Zebrina pendula is closely related to *Tradescantia fluminensis,* which is also called Wandering Jew. *Tradescantia* species are from Brazil, *Zebrina* species generally from Mexico. This is a fast-growing species with drooping stems that have ovate, pointed leaves. These leaves are green above and purple underneath. In

Zebrina pendula

some varieties, these leaves may be striped along their length with silver and green. In spring and summer, this species produces small purple-pink flowers with three petals. Wandering Jews are frequently kept in hanging baskets because of their trailing habit. Most poison control centers treat *Zebrina pendula* as nontoxic. There has been a reported case of skin rash resulting from contact with *Tradescantia fluminensis*. It may have been an allergic reaction, however. While ingestions of Wandering Jews are reported from time to time, there is no record of a toxic reaction. The plant's reputation as being harmless is therefore probably deserved.

Recommendation   Instruct children never to eat this or any nonfood plant. This plant is probably suitable for display in households with children.

References   Bailey and Bailey, 1182; Lampe and McCann, 5; Micromedix, Inc. 1989 *Poisindex* reference 2725302. See Bibliography for complete references.

Zinnia elegans

Zinnia elegans

Common Name(s)   Zinnia, Common Zinnia, Youth-and-Old-Age

Family   Compositae (Composite)

Active Toxins   See text

Toxic Plant Parts   See text

Zinnias are common garden flowers, but are also grown commercially for use by florists as cut flowers. They are not usually cultivated as house plants. *Zinnia elegans* is the species most often grown for use by florists. It is available in many cultivars and in every color but blue. Leaves are lance-shaped or oblong to five inches in length. Flower heads are quite large, reaching to six inches across, and consist of many rays arranged concentrically. No evidence exists that this plant is toxic.

Recommendation   Instruct children never to eat this or any nonfood plant. This plant is probably suitable for display in households with children.

References   Bailey and Bailey, 1184; Micromedix, Inc. 1989 *Poisindex* reference 2319469. See Bibliography for complete references.

Appendix

Regional Poison Control Centers

ALABAMA

Alabama Poison Center
809 University Blvd. East
Tuscaloosa, AL 35401
(205) 345-0600 (Admin.); (800) 462-0800 (Alabama only)

ARIZONA

Arizona Poison Control System
Arizona Health Sciences Center, Rm. 3204K
University of Arizona
Tucson, AZ 85724
(602) 626-7899 (Admin.); (602) 626-6016 (Tucson)
(602) 253-3334 (Phoenix); (800) 362-0101 (Arizona only)

CALIFORNIA

Los Angeles County Medical Association Regional Poison Control Center
1925 Wilshire Blvd.
Los Angeles, CA 90057
(213) 664-2121 (Admin.); (213) 484-5151

UCDMC Regional Poison Control Center
2315 Stockton Blvd.
Sacramento, CA 95817
(916) 453-3414 (Admin.); (916) 453-3692

San Diego Regional Poison Center
UCSD Medical Center
225 Dickson St.
San Diego, CA 92103
(610) 294-3666

San Francisco Bay Area Regional Poison Control Center
San Francisco General Hospital, Room 1E86
1001 Potrero Ave.
San Francisco, CA 94110
(415) 821-8324 (Admin.); (415) 476-6600

COLORADO

Rocky Mountain Poison Center
645 Bannock St.
Denver, CO 80204-4507
(303) 893-7774 (Admin.); (303) 629-1123
(800) 332-3073 (Colorado only)
(800) 525-5042 (Montana only)
(800) 442-2702 (Wyoming only)

FLORIDA

Tampa Bay Regional Poison Control Center
P.O. Box 18582
Tampa, FL 33679
(813) 251-6911 (Admin.); (813) 253-4444;
(800) 282-3171

GEORGIA

> Georgia Poison Control Center
> Box 26066, 80 Butler St., SE
> Atlanta, GA 30335
> (404) 589-4400

INDIANA

> Indiana Poison Center
> Wishard Memorial Hospital
> 1001 W. Tenth St.
> Indianapolis, IN 46202
> (317) 630-6382 (Admin.); (317) 630-7351;
> (800) 382-9097; (317) 630-6666 (TTY)

KENTUCKY

> Kentucky Regional Poison Control Center of Kosair Children's Hospital
> P.O. Box 35070
> Louisville, KY 40232-5070
> (502) 562-7264 (Admin.); (502) 589-8222;
> (800) 722-5725 (Kentucky only)

LOUISIANA

> Louisiana Regional Poison Control Center
> Louisiana State University School
> of Medicine in Shreveport
> P.O. Box 33932
> Shreveport, LA 71130-3932
> (318) 673-6364 (Admin.); (318) 425-1524;
> (800) 535-0525

MARYLAND

> Maryland Poison Center
> 23 N. Pine St.
> Baltimore, MD 21201
> (301) 528-7604 (Admin.); (301) 528-7701;
> (800) 492-2414 (Maryland only)

MASSACHUSETTS

> Massachusetts Poison Control System
> 300 Longwood Ave.
> Boston, MA 02115
> (617) 735-6607 (Admin.); (617) 232-2120; (800) 682-9211

MICHIGAN

> Blodgett Regional Poison Center
> 1840 Wealthy, SE
> Grand Rapids, MI 49506
> (616) 774-7854 (Admin.); (800)
> 442-4571 (AC 616 only);
> (800) 632-2727 (Michigan only)

> Poison Control Center
> Children's Hospital of Michigan
> 3901 Beaubien Blvd.
> Detroit, MI 48201
> (313) 745-5329 (Admin.); (313) 745-5711;
> (800) 462-6642 (Area code 313 only); (800) 572-1655

MINNESOTA

Hennepin Regional Poison Center
Hennepin County Medical Center
701 Park Ave.
Minneapolis, MN 55415
(612) 347-3144 (Admin.); (612) 347-3141; (612) 347-6219 (TTY)

Minnesota Regional Poison Center
St. Paul Ramsey Medical Center
640 Jackson St.
St. Paul, MN 55101
(612) 221-3096 (Admin.); (612) 221-2113; (800) 222-1222

MISSOURI

Cardinal Glennon Children's Hospital, Regional Poison Center
1465 S. Grand Blvd.
St. Louis, MO 63104
(314) 772-8300 (Admin.); (314) 772-5200;
(800) 392-9111 (MO only)

NEBRASKA

Mid Plains Poison Center
8301 Dodge St.
Omaha, NE 68114
(402) 390-5434 (Admin.); (402) 390-5400;
(800) 642-9999 (Nebraska only);
(800) 228-9515 (surrounding states)

NEW JERSEY

New Jersey Poison Information and Education System
201 Lyons Ave.
Newark, NJ 07112
(201) 926-7443 (Admin.); (201) 923-0764
(800) 962-1253 (New Jersey only)

NEW MEXICO

New Mexico Poison and Drug Information Center
University of New Mexico
Albuquerque, NM 87131
(505) 277-4261 (Admin.); (505) 843-2551;
(800) 432-6866 (New Mexico only)

NEW YORK

Long Island Regional Poison Control Center
Nassau County Medical Center
2201 Hempstead Turnpike
East Meadow, NY 11554
(516) 542-3707 (Admin.); (516) 542-2323

New York City Poison Control Center
455 1st Ave., Rm. 123
New York, NY 10016
(212) 340-4497 (Admin.); (212) 340-4494;
(800) 225-0658 (Outside New York only)

NORTH CAROLINA

Duke University Poison Control Center
Box 3007
Duke University Medical Center
Durham, NC 27710
(919) 684-4438 (Admin.); (919) 684-8111;
(800) 672-1697 (North Carolina only)

OHIO

Central Ohio Poison Center
Columbus Children's Hospital
700 Children's Drive
Columbus, OH 43205
(614) 461-2012 (Admin.); (614) 228-1323; (800) 682-7625

Southwest Regional Poison Control System
c/o Drug and Poison Information Center
231 Bethesda Ave. M.L. Number 144
Cincinnati, OH 45267-0144
(513) 872-5111; (800) 872-5111

PENNSYLVANIA

Pittsburgh Poison Center
3705 5th Ave. at DeSota St.
Pittsburgh, PA 15213
(412) 647-5600; (412) 681-6669

RHODE ISLAND

Rhode Island Poison Center
Rhode Island Hospital
593 Eddy St.
Providence, RI 02902
(401) 277-5906 (Admin.); (401) 277-5727; (401) 277-8062 (TTY)

TEXAS

North Central Texas Poison Center
P.O. Box 35926
Dallas, TX 75235
(214) 920-2586 (Admin.); (214) 920-2400;
(800) 441-0040 (Texas only)

Texas State Poison Center
University of Texas Medical Branch
Galveston, TX 77550-2780
(409) 761-3332 (Admin.); (409) 765-1420;
(713) 654-1701 (Houston)
(516) 478-4490 (Austin); (800) 392-8548 (TX only)

UTAH

Intermountain Regional Poison Control Center
50 N. Medical Dr., Bldg. 428
Salt Lake City, UT 84132
(801) 581-7504 (Admin.); (801) 581-2151;
(800) 662-0062 (Utah only)

WEST VIRGINIA

West Virginia Poison Center
West Virginia University School of Pharmacy
3110 McCorckle Ave., SE
Charleston, WV 25304
(304) 347-1212 (Admin.); (304) 348-4211;
(800) 642-3625 (West Virginia only)

WASHINGTON, D.C.

National Capital Poison Center
Georgetown University Hospital
3800 Reservoir Rd., NW
Washington, D.C. 20007
(202) 625-6073 (Admin.); (202) 625-3333

Bibliography

(Books marked with an * are useful in identifying plants.)

Agarwal, S. K. and P. R. Rastogi. 1971. "Triterpenoids of *Hibiscus rosa sinensis* Linn." 33 *Ind. J. Pharm.* 41-42.

Altmann, H. 1980. *Poisonous Plants and Animals.* Chatto and Windus, London.

Arditti, J. and E. Rodriguez. 1982. *"Dieffenbachia:* Uses, Abuses and Toxic Constituents: A Review." J. Ethnopharmacology 5:293-302.

Arena, J.M. 1979. *Poisoning: Toxicology, Symptoms, Treatment.* Charles C. Thomas, Springfield.

Arena, J.M. June 15, 1989. "Plants that Poison." 21 *Emergency Medicine* 20-35.

Arnold, H.L. 1968. *Poisonous Plants of Hawaii.* C.E. Tuttle, Rutland, Vermont.

Ayres, S. Jr. and S. Ayres III. 1958. "Philodendron as a cause of contact dermatitis." 78 *Arch. Dermatol.* 330-333.

* Bailey, L. H. and E. Z. Bailey. 1976. *Hortus Third.* Macmillan, New York.

* Bailey, L. H. 1971. *Manual of Cultivated Plants.* (rev. ed.) Macmillan, New York.

Balinet, G. A. February 1971. "Pharmacology of *Syringa vulgaris* leaf extract." 19 *Planta Medica* 215-221 (In German, with summary in English).

Balint, G. A. et al. 1974. "Ricin: The toxic protein of castor oil seeds." 2 *Toxicol.* 77-102.

Barnes, B. A. and L. E. Fox. 1955. "Poisoning with *Dieffenbachia."* 10 *J. Hist. Med. Allied Sci.* 173-181.

Baskin, E. 1967. *The Poppy and Other Deadly Plants.* Delacorte Press, New York.

Bruynzeel, D. P. February 1989. "Contact dermatitis due to Paeonia (Peony)." 20 *Contact Dermatitis* (Denmark) 152-3.

* Campbell, G. R. 1983. *An Illustrated Guide to Some Poisonous Plants and Animals of Florida.* Pineapple Press, Miami.

Casarett L. J. and J. Donel (eds.). 1975. *Toxicology, the Basic Science of Poisons.* Macmillan, New York.

Center for Disease Control. August 12, 1977. "Poisoning associated with herbal teas." 26 *Morb. Mortal. Wkly.* 257-259.

Chang, Chi-Ching and H. Beevers. 1968. "Biogenesis of oxalate in plant tissues." 43 Plant Physiol. 1821-1828.

Cheeke, P. R. and L. R. Shull. 1985. *Natural Toxicants in Feed and Poisonous Plants.* AVI Publishing, Westport, Connecticut.

Chestnut, V. K. 1976. *Thirty Poisonous Plants of North America.* Shorey, Seattle.

* Chiusoli A. and M. L. Boriani. 1986. *Simon and Schuster's Guide to House Plants.* Simon and Schuster, New York. This book has several hundred color photographs of common houseplants.

Creekmore, H. 1966. *Daffodils Are Dangerous: The Poisonous Plants in Your Garden.* Walker and Company, New York.

Crowder, J. I. and R. R. Sexton. 1964. "Keratoconjunctivitis resulting from the sap of candelabra cactus and pencil tree." 72 *Arch. Opthamol.* 476-484.

Cuebas de Escabi, D. and A. Cedeno-Maldonado. 1985. "Content and accumulation of oxalic acid in edible species of *Xanthosoma."* 69 J. Ag. of U. of Puerto Rico 169-176.

Dalvi, R. R. and W. C. Borvic. 1983. "Toxicity of solanine: an overview." 23 *Vet. Hum. Toxicol.* 13-15.

Davini, E., et al. 1986. "The quantitative isolation and antimicrobial activity of the aglycone of aucubin." 25 *Phytochem.* 2420-2422.

Der Marderosian, A. H. and F. C. Roia. "Literature review and clinical management of household ornamental plants potentially toxic to humans." In Kinghorn, A.D. ed. 1979. *Toxic Plants.* Columbia University Press, New York.

Der Marderosian, A. H., et al. 1976. *"Phytochemical and toxicological screening of household ornamental plants potentially toxic to humans."* 1 J. of Toxicol. and Env. Health 939-953.

Der Marderosian, A. H. 1966. "Poisonous plants in and around the home." 30 *Am. J. of Pharm. Ed.* 115-140.

* DeWolf, G. P. (ed.). *1987 Taylor's Guide to Houseplants.* Houghton Mifflin, New York. This guide has over 400 color photographs of houseplants, and is an excellent aid in identifying plants.

Dipalma, J. R. 1984. "Poisonous Plants." 29 *Am. Fam. Physician* 252-254.

Dominquez, X., et al. 1967. "Chemical study of the latex, stem, bracts, and flowers of 'Christmas Flower' (*Euphorbia pulcherrima* L.)' 56 J. Pharm. Sci. 1184-1185.

Dorsey, C. 1958. *"Philodendron dermatitis."* 88 Calif. Med. 329-330.

Dreisbach, R. H. 1971. *Handbook of Poisoning.* Lange Medical Publications, Los Altos, California.

Duncan, W. H. 1958. *Poisonous Plants in the Southeastern United States.* Duncan, Athens, Ga.

Dutta, S. K. and S. N. Dhar. November-December 1984. "New proteolytic enzyme from *Pedilanthus tithymaloids.*" 46 *Ind. J. Pharm. Sci.* 223-224.

Editors of Nutrition and the M.D. August 1979. "Toxic reactions to herbal teas." 5 *Nutrit. and the M.D. 4.*

Edwards, N. March 1983. "Local toxicity from a Poinsettia plant: A case report." 102 J. of Pediatrics 404-405.

Elsohly, M. A. et al. October 1974. "Euparone, a new benzofuran from *Ruscus aculeatus.*" 63 *J. Pharm. Sci.* 1623-1624.

Farlow, W. G. 1982. *Mushroom Hunters Guide and Common Poisonous Plants.* And Books, .

Fernald, M. L., et al. 1958. *Edible Wild Plants of Eastern North America.* (rev.) Harper and Row, New York.

Fiddes, F. 1958. "Poisoning by aconite." 2 *Br. Med. J.* 779-780.

Fischer, F. C., et al. May 1982. "Cyanogenesis in Passifloraceae." 45 *Planta Medica* 42-45.

French, G. 1958. "Aconite-induced cardiac arrhythmia." 20 *Br. Heart J.* 140-142.

* Frohne, D. and H. J. Pfänder. 1983. *A Colour Atlas of Poisonous Plants: A Handbook for Pharmacists, Physicians, Toxicologists and Biologists. Wolfe House, London.*

Gadd, L. 1980. *Deadly Beautiful: The World's Most Poisonous Animals and Plants.* Macmillan, New York.

Gehlbach, S. H., et al. 1975. "Nicotine absorption by workers harvesting green tobacco." 1 *Lancet* 478-480.

Gooneratne, B. 1966. "Massive generalized alopecia after poisoning by *Gloriosa* superba." 1 *Br. Med. J.* 1023-1024.

* Graf, A. B. 1985. *Exotica IV: A Pictorial Cyclopedia of Exotic Plants.* Roehrs Company, East Rutherford, N. J. This book is a standard reference for horticulturalists. It contains over 12,000 separate photographs of tropical and near-tropical plant species. The photographs range from extremely poor quality in some cases to excellent, highly descriptive photographs. More common plant species tend to have more and better photographs. This book is expensive, so it may best be consulted at the library.

* Graf, A. B. 1986. *Tropica: A Color Encyclopedia of Exotic Plants.* Roehrs Company, East Rutherford, New Jersey. *Tropica* is a standard reference text useful in identifying tropical houseplants. It contains thousands of color photographs which aid in identification. It is expensive, so it may best be consulted at the library.

Greenberg, R. S. and S. K. Osterhout. 1982. "Diurnal trends in reported poisonings." 19 *J. of Toxicol. and Clin. Toxicol.* 167-172.

Haddad, L. M. and J. F. Winchester (eds.). 1983. *Clinical Management of Poisoning and Drug Overdose.* W. B. Saunders, Philadelphia.

Harchelroad, F., et al. 1988. "Identification of common houseplants in the emergent care setting." 30 Vet. Hum. Toxicol. 161-163.

* Hardin, J. and J. M. Arena. 1974. *Human Poisoning from Native and Cultivated Plants.* Duke University Press, Durham.

Hart, R. C. 1961. "Toxicity of traditional Christmas greens." 30 *Indust. Med. Surg.* 522-525.

Hausen, B. M. and K. H. Schultz. 1977. "Occupational allergic contact dermatitis due to leatherleaf fern." 98 *Brit. J. of Dermatol.* 325-329.

Hausen, B. M. and A. Shoji. 1984. "Orchid Allergy." *Arch. Dermatology,* 1206-1208.

Horticultural Research Institute. 1980. *Proceedings: Poison Plant Symposium.* Am. Assoc. of Nurserymen, Chicago.

James, W. R. 1973. *Know Your Poisonous Plants: Poisonous Plants Found in Field and Garden.* Naturegraph, Happy Camp, California.

Jasperson-Schib, R. 1970. "Toxic Amaryllidaceae." 45 *Pharm. Acta. Helv.* 424-433 (German).

Jones, L. A. and W. G. Troutman. April 1988. "Patterns of public access to a regional poison control center: 1979 through 1986." 30 *Vet. Hum. Toxicol.* 122-125.

Keegan H. and L. MacFarlane (ed.). 1963. *Venomous and Poisonous Animals and Noxious Plants of the Pacific Region.* Pergamon Press, Oxford.

Keeler, R. F. 1979. "Toxins and teratogens of the Solanaceae and Liliaceae." In Kinghorn, A.D. ed. 1979. *Toxic Plants.* Columbia University Press, New York.

Kinghorn, A. D. (ed.). 1979. *Toxic Plants.* Columbia University Press, New York.

Kingsbury, J. M. 1965. *Deadly Harvest: A Guide to Common Poisonous Plants.* Holt, Rinehart and Winston, New York.

Kingsbury, J. M. 1964. *Poisonous Plants of the United States and Canada.* Prentice Hall, Englewood Cliffs.

Kopferschmidt, J. et al. 1983. "Acute voluntary intoxication by ricin." *2 Hum. Toxicol.* 239-242.

Kozma, J. J. 1969. *Killer Plants: A Poisonous Plant Guide.* Milestone Publishing Co., Jacksonville, Ill.

Kuballa, B., et al. 1981. "Study of *Dieffenbachia*-induced edema in mouse hindpaw: Respective role of oxalate needles and trypsin-like protease." 58 *Toxicol. Appl. Pharmacol.* 444-451.

Lampe, K. F. and R. Fagerstrom. 1968. *Plant Toxicity and Dermatitis: A Manual for Physicians.* Williams and Wilkins, Baltimore.

* Lampe, K. F. and M. A. McCann. 1985. *AMA Handbook of Poisonous and Injurious Plants.* American Medical Association, Chicago.

Leach, D. G. 1966. "History of rhododendron poisoning." 16 *Garden J.* 215-239; see also 1977 17 *Garden J.* 15-18, 33.

Leveau, A. M., M. Durand and R. R. Paris. 1979. "Sur la toxicite des fruits de L'*Aucuba japonica* (Cornacees)." 13 *Plantes Medicinales et Pytotherapie* 199-204.

* Levy, C. K. and R. B. Primack. 1984. *A Field Guide to Poisonous Plants and Mushrooms of North America.* Stephen Greene Press, Brattleboro.

Lewis, W.H. and M. Elvin-Lewis. 1977. *Medical Botany: Plants Affecting Man's Health.* John Wiley and Sons, New York.

Lim, T. K. and E. Soepadmo. December 1984. "Eye injury from sap of *Pedilanthus tithymaloides* Poit." 25 *Singapore Med. J.* 412.

Litovitz, T. L., et al. 1988. "1988 Annual Report of the American Association of Poison Control Centers National Data Collection System." 7 *Am. J. of Emerg. Med.* 495-544.

Manoguerra, A. S. and D. Freeman. 1983. "Acute poisoning from the ingestion of *Nicotiana glauca*." 19 *J. Toxicol., Clin. Toxicol.* 861-864.

Micromedix, Inc. 1989. *Poisondex*. Poisondex is a database compiled to provide health professionals with information on many household and industrial poisons. Many poison control centers use Poisondex as their principal resource on treatment of plant poisonings.

Miller, R. W. 1980. "Brief survey of *Taxus* alkaloids and other taxine derivatives." 43 *J. Nat. Prod.* 425-437.

Mitchell, J. and A. Rook. 1979. *Botanical Dermatology: Plants and Plant Products Injurious to the Skin*. Greengrass, Vancouver.

Mitchell, J. C. and A. J. Rook. 1976. "*Scindapsus* dermatitis." 2 *Contact Derm.* 125.

Morton, J. F. 1958. "Ornamental plants with poisonous properties." *Proceedings of the Florida State Horticultural Society,* 75:484-491.

Morton, J. F. 1971. *Plants Poisonous to People in Florida* and *Other Warm Areas*. Hurricane House, Miami.

Muenscher, W. C. 1939. *Poisonous Plants of the United States*. Macmillan, New York.

Murray, S. S., et al. 1983. "Acute toxicity after excessive ingestion of colchicine." 58 *Mayo Clin. Pro.* 528-532.

North, P. 1967. *Poisonous Plants and Fungi*. Blandford Press.

O'Leary, S. 1964. "Poisoning in Man from Eating Poisonous Plants." 9 Arch. Environ. Health 216-242.

Oberst, B. B. and R. A. McIntyre. 1953. "Acute nicotine poisoning." 11 *Pediatrics* 338-340.

Oga, S., et al. August 1984. "Pharmacological trials of crude extract of *Passiflora alata*." 50 Planta Medica 303-306.

Pakrashi, A., et al. 1986. "Flowers of *Hibiscus rosa-sinensis,* a potential source of contragestative agent." 34 Contraception 523-536.

Plowman, T. 1969. "Folk uses of New World aroids." 23 *Econ. Bot.* 97-122.

Pohl, R. W. 1964. "Poisoning with *Dieffenbachia*." 177 *J. Am. Med. Assoc.* 812-813.

Quam, V. C., et al. 1985. "Investigation for toxicity of a household plant—Australian umbrella tree (*Brassaia actinophylla*)." 43 North Dakota Agricultural Experiment Station Reports, 15-17.

Radford, D. J., et al. May 1986. "Naturally occurring cardiac glycosides." 144 *Med. J. Australia* 540-544.

Reitbrock, N. and B. G. Woodcock. July 1985. "Two hundred years of foxglove therapy: *Digitalis purpurea*." 6 *Trends Pharmacol. Sci.* 267-269.

Rhee, J. K., et al. 1981. "Screening of the wormicidal Chinese raw drugs on *Chlonorchis sinensis*." 9 *American J. of Chinese Medicine* 277-284.

Ricciuti, E. R. 1978 *The Devil's Garden: Fact and Folklore of Poisonous Plants*. Walker Publishing Co., New York.

Ross, S. A. and D. W. Bishay. 1984. "Diglucosides from the leaves of *Limonium sinuatum* grown in Egypt." 30 *Herba Pol.* 91-95.

Rost, L. and R. Bos. August 1979. "Biosystematic investigations with *Acorus calamus* and *Acorus gramineus*." 36 Planta Medica 350-361.

Rothe, A. 1986. "Hoya carnosa—Is it allergenic?" 14 *Contact Derm.* 250-252.

Sakai, W. S. and Hanson, M. 1974. "Mature raphid and raphid idioblast structure in plants of the edible Aroid genera *Colocasia, Alocasia* and *Xanthosoma*." 38 Ann. Bot. 739-748.

Sauder, P., et al. 1983. "Haemodynamic studies in eight cases of acute colchicine poisoning." 2 *Hum. Toxicol.* 169-173.

Schenk, G. 1955. *The Book of Poisons*. Rinehart: New York.

Schmutz, E.M. 1979. Plants that Poison: An Illustrative Guide for the American Southwest. Northland, Seattle.

Southon, S. et al. 1988. "The effect of *Gypsophila* saponins in the diet on mineral status and plasma cholesterol concentration in the rat." 59 Br. J. of Nutrition 49-55.

Speroni, E. and A. Minghetti. December 1988. "Neuropharmacological activity of extracts from *Passiflora incarnata.*" 54 Planta Medica 488-491.

Spoerke, D. G., et al. August 1985. "Pediatric exposure to the houseplant *Synadenium grantii.*" 28 Vet. Hum. Toxicol. 283-284.

Spoerke, D. G. and A. R. Temple. 1978. "One year's experience with potential plant poisonings reported to the Intermountain Regional Poison Control Center." 20 *Vet. Hum. Toxicol.* 85-89.

Srivastava, S. K. and P. S. Krishnan. 1962. "An oxalic acid oxodase in the leaves of *Bougainvillea spectabilis.*" 85 Biochem. J. 33-38.

Stal, S. N. and S. P. Sen. 1979. "The photosynthetic production of oxalic acid in *Oxalis corniculata.*" 11 Plant Cell Physiol. 119-128.

Stephens, H.A. 1980. *Poisonous Plants of the Central United States.* University of Kansas, Lawrence.

Stone, R. and Collins. 1971. *"Euphorbia pulcherrima:* Toxicity to rats." 9 *Toxicon* 301-302.

Stoner, J. G. and J. E. Rasmussen. 1983. "Plant Dermatitis." 9 J. Amer. Acad. of Dermatology 1-14.

Stowe, C., et al. 1975. "Schefflera toxicosis in a dog." 167 Am. Vet. Med. Assoc. J. 74.

Sunell, L. A. and P. L. Healy. 1979. "Distribution of calcium oxalate crystal idioblasts in corms of taro (Colocasia esculenta)." 66 *Am. J. Bot.* 1029-1032.

Swain, T. (ed.) 1972. *Plants in Development of Modern Medicine.* Harvard University Press, Cambridge.

Szabuniewicz, M., et al. 1971. "Treatment of experimentally induced Oleander poisoning." 189 Arch. Pharmacodyn. Ther. 12-21.

Tampion, J. 1977. *Dangerous Plants.* David and Charles, New York.

Tan, C. H. 1983. "Is *Hibiscus rosa sinensis* Linn. a potential source of antifertility agents for males?" 28 Int'l J. of Fertility 247-248.

Uehleke, H. and M. Brinkschulte-Freitas. 1979. "Oral toxicity of an essential oil from myrtle (*Myrtus communis*) and adaptive liver stimulation (Rats, mice)." 12 *Toxicol.* 335-342.

Van Etten, C. 1969. *Toxic Constituents of Plant Foodstuffs.* Academic Press, New York.

Wang, H., T. Zhao and C. Che. 1985. "Dendrobine and 3-Hydroxy-2- Oxodendrobine from *Dendrobium nobile.*" 48 J. of Natural Products, 796-801.

Watt, J. and M Breyer-Brandwijk. 1962. *The Medicinal and Poisonous Plants of Southern and Eastern Africa.* E. and S. Livingstone, London.

Williams, W. K. 1977. *A Handbook for Physicians and Mushroom Hunters.* Van Nostrand Reinhold Co., New York.

* Woodward, L. 1985. *Poisonous Plants: A Color Field Guide.* Hippocrene Books, New York.

Wyeth Laboratories. 1966. *The Sinister Garden: A Guide to the Most Common Poisonous Plants.* Wyeth Laboratories, New York.

Yamauchi, K. et al. August 1976. "Mechanism of purgative action of geniposide, an iridoid glucoside of the fruit of gardenia, in mice." 30 Planta Medica 39-47.

Yang, K. H. et al. 1983. "Protective effect of *Aucuba japonica* against carbon tetrachloride-induced liver damage in rats." 6 Drug and Chemical Toxicology 429-441.

Zaki, A. Y. et al. 1981. "Preliminary phytochemical and pharmacological screening of *Carissa carandas* L. and *Carissa grandiflora* DC. growing in Egypt." 22 Egypt. J. Pharm. Sci. 113-126.

Index